Psychiatry and Sexual Health

Psychiatry and Sexual Health

An Integrative Approach

Edited by Juan E. Mezzich and Ruben Hernandez-Serrano

on behalf of the WPA Educational
Program on Sexual Health

JASON ARONSON
Lanham • Boulder • New York • Toronto • Oxford

WORLD PSYCHIATRIC ASSOCIATION

Published in the United States of America
by Jason Aronson
An imprint of Rowman & Littlefield Publishers, Inc.

A wholly owned subsidiary of
The Rowman & Littlefield Publishing Group, Inc.
4501 Forbes Boulevard, Suite 200, Lanham, Maryland 20706
www.rowmanlittlefield.com

PO Box 317
Oxford
OX2 9RU, UK

British Library Cataloguing in Publication Information Available

Library of Congress Cataloging-in-Publication Data Available

Printed in the United States of America

♾™ The paper used in this publication meets the minimum requirements of American National Standard for Information Sciences—Permanence of Paper for Printed Library Materials, ANSI/NISO Z39.48-1992.

Contents

PART 2
COMPREHENSIVE DIAGNOSIS OF PERSONS WITH SEXUAL DISORDERS

PART 3
COMPREHENSIVE TREATMENT AND HEALTH PROMOTION OF PERSONS WITH SEXUAL DISORDERS

Introduction

Sexual health, a long-neglected field, is now increasingly recognized as a key component of overall health and quality of life. In response to this, the World Psychiatric Association (WPA) established in 1997 a new Scientific Section on Psychiatry and Human Sexuality. Shortly afterwards, WPA started the development of an Educational Program on Sexual Health. The present volume, *Psychiatry and Sexual Health: An Integrative Approach,* represents the knowledge base for this educational program.

The institutional source for this educational program is the WPA, since 1950 the home of organized psychiatry across the world. Currently, it comprises 130 national member societies, representing over 180,000 psychiatrists worldwide. The scientific structure of WPA is substantiated by its 64 Scientific Sections, whose domains cover the full range of our professional field. WPA continues to grow in membership, programs and institutional strength.

Education became a priority mission of WPA in the early 1990s. This was reflected in the development of a number of educational programs such as those on Depressive Disorders, ICD-10, Schizophrenia and Stigma, Core Curricula in Psychiatry for medical students and for the training of specialists, and the WPA International Guidelines for Diagnostic Assessment (IGDA). It also involved the establishment of a Secretary for Education in the WPA Executive Committee, an Operational Committee on Education, and an Education Coordination Center.

The WPA Program on Sexual Health builds on the pioneering work of Richard von Krafft-Ebing, Havelock Ellis, Sigmund Freud, Albert Moll, Herbert Marcuse, Iwan Bloch, Magnus Hirschfeld, Alfred Kinsey, William Masters, Virginia Johnson, Helen Singer Kaplan, John Money, and Herman Musaph, among many other scientists and clinicians. Also helpful have been the contributions made by the World Association for Sexology since 1978.

The field of human sexuality touches on all walks of human life; it expresses itself in plastic arts, music, poetry, literature, religion, economics, politics, and health. The latter is the framework we have used for the WPA Sexual Health Educational Program (SHEP), but keeping in mind the broadness of the field of sexuality. Psychiatrists are important contributors to the fields of sexual health, medical sexology, and sexual medicine. Psychiatrists' contributions are inscribed within an emerging double helix of science and humanism, in which both evidence-based research and clinical wisdom are of importance.

More specifically, our approach to clinical care and health promotion is based on a broad concept of health, from illnesses, dysfunctions, and conflicts to the positive aspects of health (adaptive functioning, social supports, and quality of life). It is also based on the need to engage actively all participants in clinical care: health professionals, the patient, the couple, the family, and society at large. This knowledge base has three main components:

- Part 1: Conceptual Basis of Sexual Health
- Part 2: Comprehensive Diagnosis of Persons with Sexual Disorders
- Part 3: Comprehensive Treatment and Health Promotion of Persons with Sexual Disorders

Drawing from its vast intellectual resources, the WPA established a multidisciplinary and international workgroup of distinguished scholars, clinicians, and researchers to develop the Educational Program on Sexual Health. They were assisted by a larger group of consultants working in the various areas of sexual health. The WPA Educational Committee conducted a review of the various phases of this program. We greatly appreciate this collaboration.

This volume represents an attempt to present the field of psychiatry and sexual health in a contextualized and integrative manner. It is integrative by approaching comprehensively what should be known about the health of a person or couple under evaluation, and also by promoting the coordination of needed health services. The volume focuses attention not only on the sexual disorders but also on the people who experience them, as well as on opportunities for enhancing their general health and quality of life. This work also represents a small contribution to clarify some of the myths and taboos that still survive in the world of human sexuality today. In the words of César Vallejo, *"Brothers, there is still much to be done."*

Contributors

Workgroup

Juan E. Mezzich (USA) (Program Director)
Ruben J. Hernandez-Serrano (Venezuela) (Scientific Director)
Said Abdel Azim (Egypt)
Barbara Bartlik (USA)
Carlos E. Berganza (Guatemala)
Giovanni Caracci (USA)
Dona Davis (USA)
Rafael Garcia (Dominican Republic)
Michael Metz (USA)
Antonio Pacheco-Palha (Portugal)
Raul Schiavi (France)
Robert Taylor Segraves (USA)
Chiara Simonelli (Italy)
Donna Stewart (Canada)
Gorm Wagner (Denmark)

Advisors

Fernando Bianco (Venezuela)
Alcira Camilucci (Argentina)
Nora Cavagna (Argentina)
Ricardo Cavalcanti (Brazil)
Mary Ann Cohen (USA)
Otto Dörr-Zeegers (Chile)
Marc Ganem (France)
Tarek Gawad (Egypt)
Leon R. Gindin (Argentina)
Janice Irvine (USA)
Reidar Kjaer (Norway)
Maria L. Lerer (Argentina)
Vicente Molina (México)

Juan Carlos Nuñez ((Argentina)
Tarek Okasha (Egypt)
Angel Otero (Cuba)
Aminta Parra (Venezuela)
Jiri Raboch (Czech Republic)
Vivian Ravelo (Cuba)
Diana Resnicoff (Argentina)
Rodolfo Rodriguez (Ecuador)
Sharna Striar (USA)
Adrian Sapetti (Argentina)
Carmen Secades (Argentina)
Carlos Seguin (Argentina)
Gerard Valles (France)
Celestino Vasallo (Cuba)
Olga Vásquez (Uruguay)
Virginia Martínez Verdier (Argentina)

Reviewers from the WPA Educational Committee (2002–2005)

Roger Montenegro (Argentina) (Chair)
Parameshvara Deva (Malaysia)
Pier Maria Furlan (Italy) (Consultant))
Miguel Jorge (Brazil)
Srinivasa Murthy (India) (Consultant)
Allan Tasman (USA)

Staff

Ana Cordero (USA)
Albert Cruz (USA)
Ruben E. Hernandez Perez (Venezuela)
Boris Livshits (Belarus)
Sonia Martinez (Dominican Republic)
Habibur Rachman (Bangladesh)
Patrick Sue (Myanmar)
Ekaterina Sukhanova (USA)
Snehamala Veeravalli (India)
Erica von Nardroff (USA)
Luz Yanayaco (Peru)
NiNi Zaw (Myanmar)

Acknowledgments

This program was supported by an unrestricted educational grant from Pfizer, Inc., and by various components of the World Psychiatric Association.

PART 1

CONCEPTUAL BASES OF SEXUAL HEALTH

Comprehensive Definition of Sexual Health

As an internationally based medical and educational organization, the World Psychiatric Association (WPA) advocates an integrative bio-psycho-socio-cultural approach to issues of sexual health and illness. This integrative approach goes beyond the recognition that sex has physiological, psychological, social, and cultural components and incorporates the view that these must be seen in a dynamic and complex, changing and interactive context. Physical aspects of sexuality such as anatomy and biochemistry cannot be treated in isolation from psychological factors such as development, personality, identity, thoughts and feelings or from social factors such as gender roles, interpersonal relationships, and structures of inequality. Cultural considerations are also of importance since definitions, expressions, regulations, and meanings associated with human sexuality are culturally based and informed. It should be noted that, even at this point in time in contemporary medicine, special practices or beliefs in one society may not be acceptable to all societies.

Given the increasingly global arena for the discussion of health concepts, the framework for any such discussion should be widely international. What follows is the definition of sexual health proposed for this Educational Program of the WPA. An attempt has been made to make it simple, comprehensive, open-ended, and flexible.

1.1.1. Summary Definition

Sexual health may be defined as a dynamic and harmonious state involving erotic and reproductive experiences and fulfillment, within a broader physical, emotional, interpersonal, social, and spiritual sense of well-being, in a culturally informed, freely and responsibly chosen, and ethical framework; not merely the absence of sexual disorders.

A brief analysis of the key elements considered in the construction of this definition of sexual health follows:

- It focuses the concept of sexual health around *erotic and reproductive experiences and fulfillment* that may include notions of romantic love and intimacy.

- It places such sexual experiences and fulfillment within a multidimensional (physical, social, emotional) characterization of well-being, which is constitutive of World Health Organization's (WHO, 1948) definition of health in general, and enriches it with an *interpersonal dimension* (based on its particular relevance to human sexuality) and a *spiritual dimension* (reflecting discussions at WHO's Executive Board [1999] when revising the definition of health).
- It qualifies further such a state of well-being as *dynamic* (amendment of the definition of health [WHO, 1999]) and *harmonious* (reflecting the importance of a sense of balance prevalent in many conceptualizations of health in general and mental health in particular).
- It contextualizes the above-mentioned sexual experiences and fulfillment and their associated general sense of well-being within a framework that is: *culturally informed*, which any worldwide educational program dealing with cultural diversity within and among different ethnic, national and social groups must pay attention to; *freely and responsibly chosen*, implying noncoercive behaviors that respect the rights of each individual and balance a sense of freedom and autonomy with a sense of responsibility; and *ethical*, noting that considerations of this type are becoming an important element of WHO's concept of health, as recently discussed by its Director General [Brundtland, 1999] and are a constitutional objective of WPA.
- It further points out that sexual health *does not merely imply an absence of sexual disorders*. This is consistent with the WHO's basic definition of general health.

Such a comprehensive definition of sexual health must be drawn from an integrated series of wide-ranging perspectives. This definition incorporates historical, physiological, psychological, interpersonal, sociocultural, and ethical views, including attention to human rights issues. This integrated approach is stressed throughout the sections of this book and is consistent with a recent WHO (2002) Statement on Sexual Health.

1.1.2. Historical Perspectives

Throughout human history, sex as a means for pleasure and reproduction has captured the human imagination. In Southern Asia, the Far East, and the Middle East, ancient manuals described secrets of intercourse, offered suggestions on how to enhance erotic pleasure and response, and enumerated varieties of coital positions. These include the Kama Sutra (The Precepts of Pleasure), a manual from AD 200 to 400 in India; the Fang-ching-shu (Art of the Bed Chamber), a series of manuals from China from 206 BC to AD 220; and the Perfumed Garden from the sixteenth-century Islamic world (Bullough, 1976). The Chinese have used vaginal muscle training to treat women's sexual dysfunctions for at least 1,000 years (Ng, 1992). Aphrodisiacs are described in early Egyptian texts. Evidence of the practice of love magic, the production of potions and charms, and the use of mechanical devices to heighten or prevent sexual pleasure may be found across the ages. Healers and special advisors have been sought to treat or cure sexual dysfunctions probably since time immemorial (Ford and Beach, 1951).

The Greek philosopher Aristotle laid the foundations for Western sexology with his theories on the mechanisms of reproductions and the origins of sex in the fourth century BC. His writings were a mixture of masterful insight and popular superstition (Bullough, 1976; Gregersen, 1994). Aristotle's ideas dominated European thought at the time the fourteenth-century Florentine painter Leonardo da Vinci was producing his anatomical drawings. The social historian Thomas Laqueur (1990) in his book *Making Sex* documents the dynamic nature of Western medical conceptualizations of human sexuality as they reflect changing constructions of gender from the Greeks to Freud.

The modern or scientific study of human sexuality is generally regarded to have begun in twentieth-century Europe. The first generation of European sexologists from England, the Netherlands, Austria, and Germany combined biological, anthropological, and historical data with psychological case studies. Early sexologists shared the belief that sexuality was not merely specific acts or behaviors but had importance for all aspects of an individual's life as well as for the society as a whole (Bland and Doan, 1998). The founders of modern sexology—including von Krafft-Ebing, Ellis, Hirschfeld, Bloch, Moll, and Marcuse—produced exhaustive classifications of multiple aspects of sexuality that included fantasies, fetishes, bodily pleasures, and pathologies. Each was very much a man of his society, social class, and times, but despite the depiction of the Victorian age as sex negative, these were diverse times. While von Krafft-Ebing in his work on sexual pathologies stressed that sexual excess weakened the body and regarded nonprocreative sexual acts as signs of illness, Ellis advocated rights to sexual pleasure and tolerance of variation. At the same time Burton (showing that colonialism works both ways) and others were translating the erotic manuals from India and Arabia with the aim of improving the erotic skills of the European men, and Hirschfeld worked to normalize male homosexuality in the legal view (Bullough, 1976; Gregersen, 1994). Women's sexuality was usually explored from a male perspective apart from a few brave women physicians and nurses who worked in contraception and sexuality. Sex manuals were written at the turn of the century that served as popular sex education guides for generations that followed (Van de Velde, 1930; Vachet, 1932; Jeffreys, 1985).

It was, however, Freud and his theoretical model of psychoanalysis and universal phases of sexual development and maturation that came to dominate medical paradigms and clinical approaches to sexual problems from the early to mid-twentieth century. Freud held that sexual and gender identity disorders were expressions of underlying unconscious psychological conflicts that required resolution by means of psychoanalytical exploration and treatment (Schiavi, 2000). After World War II, psychoanalysis expanded far beyond the scopes of psychiatry and social sciences, spreading into literature and art and beginning to influence ordinary people's thinking. Sex, in the popular imagination, started to be viewed and accepted as the prime mover of human life.

Later in the century, the discovery of penicillin moderated the threat of syphilis, gonorrhea, and other STIs. In 1956, the oral contraceptive pill became available. Although Freud's theories have led to a popular recognition of the importance of sexuality, little was known about the actual sexual practices of Euro-American populations (or, for that matter, people elsewhere). In the 1940s and 1950s, Alfred Kinsey and his collaborators, by means of long and carefully structured surveys, set the agenda for the modern scientific sex survey. They collected and statistically analyzed data on sexual behavior from large samples of American men and women. The Kinsey studies generated a great deal of controversy because they showed that in the United States of the 1940s and 1950s traditional morality was increasingly at variance with actual behavior (Irvine, 1990).

The 1960s ushered in what was to be called the "free love" generation and the globalization of popular media. Readily available, convenient, and effective means of birth control played a role in clarifying the separation between the reproductive and hedonistic components of sexuality. In North America the intellectual underpinnings of these developments can be traced to the Human Potential movements of the 1960s. Sexual liberation, self-awareness, self-actualization, and individual expansions were key themes of these movements (Irvine, 1990). Simultaneous orgasm, erotic pleasure, and partner communication and equality were seen as goals for sexual fulfillment. William Masters and Virginia Johnson's (1966) laboratory studies of sexual physiology and the human sexual response cycle were an integral part of this movement. The research of Masters and Johnson (1970) revolutionized therapeutic views about sexual dysfunctions, opened a new field of sex therapy, and influenced the American psychiatric nosology on sexual dysfunctions. Helen Kaplan (1974) also played an important role in the development of sex therapies that combined behavioral techniques with a psychodynamic approach (Schiavi, 2000). Today, the World Association for Sexology (WAS) (now the World Association for Sexual Health), the Sexual Information and Education Council of the United States (SIECUS), the World Health Organization (WHO), and the World Psychiatric Association (WPA) play an important role in defining and researching a wide variety of sexual health issues.

Clearly a brief review of the various versions of the WHO's *International Classification of Diseases* (ICD) and the American Psychiatric Association's *Diagnostic and Statistical Manual of Mental Disorders* (DSM) shows that the nomenclature on sexual disorders has changed over the last two quarters of the twentieth century. ICD-5, ICD-6, and ICD-7 do not mention sexual problems. The category Sexual Deviation first appeared in ICD-8 (WHO, 1967), which included a comprehensive classification of mental disorders. In ICD-9 (WHO, 1977, 1978) the categories expanded to include Sexual Deviations and Disorders. The disorders included frigidity, impotence, and psychogenic dyspareunia. ICD-10 (WHO, 1992) expanded even further with Disorders of Sexual Preference, Sexual Difficulties not Caused by Organic Disorders, Gender Identity Disorders, and Psychological and Behavioral Disorders Associated with Sexual Development and Orientation. Similarly, in DSM-I (APA, 1952) there was not a separate listing for sexual dysfunctions and sexual difficulties, as they were considered to be symptoms of disorders and not disorders themselves. DSM-II (APA, 1968) mentions only two sexual problems (impotence and dyspareunia) in a subcategory of Psychophysiologic Genito-urinary Disorders, linking them with disturbances in menstruation and micturition. By the time DSM-III (1980) and DSM-III-R (1987) were published, the Sexual Dysfunctions, largely grounded in work of Masters and Johnson, had been expanded (Tiefer, 1995).

The AIDS/HIV pandemic has had a profound impact on sexual health, sexual behavior, and communication about sexuality. AIDS prevention stresses the importance of communication and safe sexual practices, as well as the importance of understanding how sociocultural and behavioral factors can play a major role in shaping sexual experience among different populations.

1.1.3. Physiological Perspectives

First and foremost, sexual health must be viewed in terms of overall physical well-being; this includes adequate nourishment, freedom from diseases, and a safe and secure environment. More specifically, knowledge about the anatomical and physiological bases of sexual health as well as the normal physiological sequences of male and female sexual response is necessary for an informed understanding of sexual function and dysfunction. This knowledge is rooted in Masters and Johnson's (1966) early model of the human sexual response cycle described in the following four stages: excitement, plateau, orgasm, and resolution. These stages were modified by Kaplan (1974) and further adapted in ICD-10 (1992) and DSM-IV (1994).

According to the Masters and Johnson's model, which is not without its critics and revisionists (Schiavi and Segraves, 1995), men's and women's sexual responses to physiological stimulation are marked by the same four-stage sequence (see figure 1.1.1). Central to Masters and Johnson's paradigm are the concepts of increasing vasocongestion and myotonia or muscle tone and their release. The four stages of the human sexual response cycle (Kaplan, 1974) in male and female have been described as follows:

- Desire: Distinct from any response identified solely through physiology and reflecting the patient's motivation, drives and personality; characterized by sexual fantasies and desire to have sex.
- Excitement: Subjective sense of sexual pleasure and accompanying physiological changes; all physiological responses noted in Masters and Johnson's excitement and plateau phases are combined in this phase.
- Orgasm: Peaking of sexual pleasure, with release of sexual tension and rhythmic contractions of the perineal muscles and pelvic reproductive organs.
- Resolution: A sense of general distension, well-being, and muscle relaxation; men are refractory to orgasms for a period of time that increases with age, whereas women can have multiple orgasms without a refractory period.

Now it is increasingly important to discuss and research the plateau phase and the sexual satisfaction, with a circular reinforcing model. Innervation of the sexual organs is primarily mediated through the autonomic nervous system. The sympathetic nervous supply is carried in the hypogastric nerve, which arises at levels T11-L3 of the spinal cord and is responsible for ejaculation. In women, vaginal sexual arousal is a vasocongestive and neuromuscular event controlled by facilitatory parasympathetic and inhibitory sympathetic inputs (Giuliano, Rampin, and Allard, 2002). The sympathetic system is responsible for the smooth muscle contractions of the vagina, urethra, and uterus that occur during orgasm. Parasympathetic activity is dominant during erection, clitoral engorgement, and vaginal lubrication. This nerve activity is under control of the brain. Erection in men can occur as a spinal reflex when higher control has been lost (due to spinal cord injury and bladder repletion, among other causes).

Whipple and Komisaruk (1998) have proposed another potential excitatory effect on female genital sexual arousal through vagus nerve stimulation. Nevertheless, at this time, there are no data on the pharmacology of the central neural pathways controlling

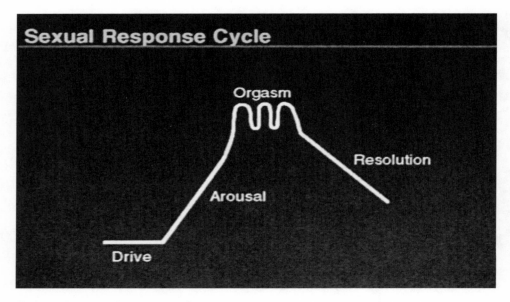

Figure 1.1.1. Sexual response cycle.

the sexual genital response. Although there is likelihood that the central nervous system control of the genital sexual response might be identical in males and females, assumptions should be backed up by experimental data (Giuliano, 2002).

Hormonal Correlates of Sexual Response

The principal sex hormones in the male are testosterone, dihydrotestosterone, and androstenedione, which are produced in a pulsating fashion in the testes under the control of luteinizing hormone (LH). Testosterone seems to be connected to libido in both men and women. In men, testosterone can maintain sexual interest and the capacity for ejaculation and may have some role in the maintenance of erectile response. In women, the most relevant hormones are estrogen and progesterone, both produced by the ovaries under the control of gonadotrophins and follicle stimulating hormone (FSH). The adrenal cortex and the ovaries produce androgens. There are marked variations in the circulating levels of these hormones during the menstrual cycle. Estrogens maintain the vaginal mucosa in its normal and premenopausal state and allow vaginal response to sexual stimulation (engorgement and lubrication). Androgens as well as prolactin are important determinants of sexual interest and desire in both sexes. In males, elevated levels of prolactin may interfere with the sexual response.

1.1.4. Psychological Perspectives

Components of psychological sexual health can include a healthy body image, self-esteem, sexual knowledge, capacity to experience pleasure, relaxation, and erotic inspiration.

Bancroft (1989) proposes that removing psychological problems such as guilt, tension, or anxiety will improve sexual functioning. He also stated that lack of knowledge and education about elementary anatomy and physiology of sex may underlie significant sexual problems. Jardin, Wagner, Khoury, Giuliano, Padma-Nathan, and Rosen (2000) included other factors, such as relationship issues, partner conflict, sexual misinformation, limited sexual practices, and depression into their psychological definition of sexual health.

It has long been recognized that there is a relation between anxiety and sexual performance. Masters and Johnson's (1970) treatment for sexual disorders focused on anxiety reduction. Contemporary clinicians also hypothesize anxiety as a primary mechanism interfering with sexual arousal and performance (LoPiccolo and LoPiccolo, 1978; Obler, 1973; Althof, 2000). The relationship between anxiety and sexual performance, however, has also been criticized as overly simplistic. For example, Schnarch (2000), in a discussion of introducing sexual novelty to partners in long-term relationships, emphasizes the importance of anxiety tolerance rather than anxiety per se. Barlow (1986) hypothesized (based on laboratory studies) that the physiological concomitants of anxiety may be less important than cognitive distractions such as dysfunctional sexual beliefs and attitudes (e.g., relationship between performance and the male gender ideology). Discussing the female orgasmic disorders, Heiman (2000), stresses the importance of identifying and distinguishing among different types of anxiety. All these investigators found that the influence of anxiety on sexual performance is different for a sexually functioning or nonfunctioning individual.

1.1.5. Interpersonal Perspectives

Healthy interpersonal relationships for couples include mutual support for each other's autonomy and independence as well as interdependence; the ability to experience and share intimacy; and the resources to develop skills for interpersonal cooperation and conflict resolution.

Interpersonal communication plays a central role in a couple's everyday life. Through this communication, positive and negative emotions and affects are shared. On the positive side, there is friendship, love, and intimacy; on the negative side hostility, hate, and distrust, among other emotions. Negative emotions can impair a healthy sexual life.

On the other hand, patterns of deficient communication lead to the same result. So it is imperative before approaching the sex life of a couple to assess their feelings and emotions for each other and the patterns of communication they use. Conflicts can seriously disrupt the sex life of the couple. Struggle for power is common in the first few years of a relationship and may be responsible for some conflicts. It is important for a couple to be able to resolve in a healthy manner the inevitable conflicts that will arise.

Children can change the life of a couple. Affective overinvestment in the children can lead to poor investment in the partner by assuming the role of mother or father and forgetting the role of sexual partner. Children can also alter the space in the house, especially in smaller apartments or shared rooms, influencing in this manner the expression of intimacy.

1.1.6. Social, Cultural, and Spiritual Perspectives

In conceptualizing sexual health, it is erroneous to assume that everybody makes the same assumptions about meanings and behaviors that contemporary medical sexology does. This is particularly important when considering the sexual dysfunctions, gender identity disorders, and paraphilias. Sexual health is culturally shaped, explained, and dealt with in terms of established cultural conventions and meanings. Even what is considered to be sex or sexual is culturally constructed. Culture can be described as everything that people have, think, and do as members of a society (Ferraro, 2000). Culture is a system of shared meanings that stem from a collectivity of people who share a common history. Any culturally informed analysis of sexuality must also include political, structural, and economic forces that shape, enable, constrain, and prohibit sexual expressions.

Anthropologists, transcultural psychiatrists, and historians have documented extensive variations of human sexual behavior, erotic meanings, and norms over time and across cultures (Bhugra and de Silva, 1995; Davis and Whitten, 1987; Gregersen, 1994; Herdt, 1999; Katz, 1995). Anthropologists in particular have shown how cultures do not necessarily categorize sexual practices or code sexual conduct as Western influenced biomedicine does (Herdt, 1999) and how the very act of informant participation in Western-based sex research projects can lead to changes in native beliefs and practices (Farquhar, 2002).

Health professionals are beginning to realize the need for more sophisticated knowledge about ethnicity, culture, gender, and class. Current DSM and ICD texts on the Sexual Disorders have started to make reference to the fact that religious, cultural, and ethnic considerations can be important (Davis, 1998; Davis and Herdt, 1996; Mezzich, Kleinman, Fabrega, and Parron, 1996). Exotic, well-defined, culture-bound syndromes such as D'hat (a severe anxiety and hypochondriacal concern about loss of semen in some Asian males) and Koro (a sudden intense anxiety in some Pacific Rim cultures that the genitalia will recede into the body, causing death) accord well with what many psychiatrists see as the cross-cultural domain. It would be shortsighted, however, to reduce cultural variation to a few culture-bound exotic syndromes since this focus on the exotic other can obscure the fact that the major Western diagnostic systems can be just as culture-bound as the traditional Chinese or Indian ones are. Contemporary approaches to human sexuality must incorporate a multicultural, multiethnic perspective that reflects the diversity of sexual experience both within and among the nations and societies of the world, as well as a respect for people who hold various different beliefs and attitudes. Unlike the culture-bound syndromes that are so amenable to medical models, this is not an easy endeavor (Davis, 1998; Desjarlais et al., 1995; Parker, 1997).

Clearly biomedicine's definitions of sexual well-being, based in the Human Potential movements of the 1960s in North America (Irvine, 1990; Tiefer, 1995), that stress mutual orgasm and pleasure along with partner relationship issues like communication, assertiveness, and equality (e.g., Zilbergeld, 1992) are not acceptable in all cultures. Bolin and Whelehan (1999) call Western notions of good and bad sex "erotocentric."

A useful term for conceptualizing diversity in sexual health is "sexual culture." The term "sexual culture" refers to a group's consensual model of cultural ideals about sexual behavior. Yet it is also imperative to note that ideal culture does not necessarily predict actual sexual behavior in a society; an individual's cultural identity does not always correlate with cultural norms. These norms change over time and the range of variation in sexual behaviors increases with globalization (Herdt, 1997), the latter having important implications. When it comes to sexuality, all societies, however, are full of contradictions. For example the United States, which presents itself as a model of sexual liberation and choice, continues to have both gender-based double standards for sexual behavior and discrimination toward gays and lesbians.

One major factor that influences sexual behaviors, their contexts, and meanings is ethnicity. Ethnicity refers to cultural groups or named social groups that are formed based on perceptions of shared ancestry, cultural tradition, and common history that distinguish the group from other groups. In contemporary social science, ethnicity takes on importance as it refers to being different or separate in the view of outside observers, and thus involves issues of power, privilege, and marginalization, not just culture traits. It is important to recognize that in today's world system, ethnic identities may overlap each other, in addition to class, regional and religious identities, to construct a maze of identities within a single person. Another component of collective identity comes from people who view themselves as members of sexual cultures. These cultures include gender or transgender groups, based on shared sexual identity, sexual orientation, practices, or disabilities (Bolin and Whelehan, 1999).

Assessing cultural and ethnic issues in sexual expression, particularly within a single ethnically heterogeneous nation state, is a complex undertaking. Issues of age, education, religion, gender, and class (and overall health status) may further confound assessment. Definitions of ethnicity are extremely problematic. They can be stereotypical and often overlook the situated and multiple aspects of ethnic identities (Davis, 1998). However, recent studies drawing on data from a random probability sample, such as that by the Laumann consortium (Laumann et al., 1994), do suggest that, at least in the United States, there may be differences in reports of sexual dysfunction among populations characterized as White, Black, Hispanic, and Asian/Pacific Islander. These differences are reflected in types of sexual practices and reports of sexual dysfunctions.

Gender also constitutes a major source of diversity within a culture, ethnic group, religious group, and social class. What is good for men is not always viewed as good for women in a particular setting. For example, in the United States some women take issue with the Sexual Dysfunction sections of DSM-IV for its male gender bias. Categories of Sexual Disorders in DSM-IV are criticized for their mechanistic and genital focus, emphasis on performance and timing, and forms of arousal women cannot assess in their own bodies. They disparage the notion that the sex that matters is the sex that can be measured (Davis, 1998; Irvine, 1990; Tiefer, 1995). Women's health advocates also claim that women's sexual priorities have been suppressed or neglected and that identical performance standards for men and women mask real-world differences in power and constructions of gender.

When speaking of traditional sexual behavior or philosophies in a cultural context of contemporary processes of globalization, it is important to recognize two factors. The first is that traditional sexual philosophies or practices such as those found, for example, in Taoism, Tantrism, and Confucianism have been radically modified by Western contact and colonialism as well as by internal political changes. For example, methods of birth control used throughout the world reflect both Western technology and views of sexuality (Whelehan, 2000). The second points to the fact that colonialism can work both ways. For example, sex life in India had considerable effect on British attitudes (Bullough, 1976).

Three major theoretical approaches mark the work of scholars interested in culture and human sexuality. These are the biological perspective, the social construction perspective (Irvine, 1995), and the biocultural perspective (Bolin and Whelehan, 1999; Frayser, 1999). The biological perspective posits that there is a universal internal sex drive or instinct—that sexuality is universally expressed throughout different cultures and different historical times. Examples of a predominant biological approach would certainly describe the biomedical sciences; most of the work of Masters and Johnson on the human sexual response cycle as well as DSM-IV sections on the Sexual Dysfunctions (see Davis, 1998, Davis and Herdt, 1996). The social or cultural constructionist approach posits that sexuality is not universal through history or across cultures; that the existence of an internal, essential sex drive or force is unlikely; that biology plays a small role if any in determining sexuality; and that sexuality is deeply influenced and constructed by social, political, economic, and cultural factors. The constructionist arguments reflect intellectual trends in postmodern gay, lesbian, and feminist studies and are well developed in anthropological and historical texts (Irvine, 1990; Laqueur, 1990; Tiefer, 1995; Parker, 2000). These two perspectives are often treated as opposing camps, although there is considerable leeway for a middle ground or biocultural approach.

1.1.7. Ethical Perspectives

Ethics is defined in *Webster's* dictionary as the study of standards of conduct and moral judgment or philosophy. The word "moral" here refers to matters that relate to, deal with, or determine the capacity to make distinctions between right and wrong in conduct.

Morals generally refer to those values a society accepts as universal principles, as contrasted with the principles that are relative to a particular context or era. General moral principles govern the behavior of all citizens and are deemed both universal and immutable.

The term "ethics" is usually reserved for the moral principles particularly applied to certain groups, such as those in a specific profession. Role-bound morality can consist of internal and external standards of ethical conduct (Sadock and Sadock, 2000). Ethical principles in medicine originate in the Hippocratic teachings. Ethics are basic for most professional organizations and, in addition, many business groups have codes of ethics reflecting a consensus about general standards of appropriate professional conduct.

The doctor-patient relationship is guided by the following ethical principles: patient autonomy, nonmaleficence, beneficence, and justice. The principle of patient autonomy is of central importance and, conceptually, is in many ways coextensive with the legal concept of competence. A patient makes an autonomous choice by giving informed consent when that choice is (1) intentional, (2) free of undue outside influence, and (3) made with rational understanding. Nonmaleficence is the duty of the physician to avoid inflicting physical and emotional harm on the patient. That principle is captured by *primum non nocere,* "first, do no harm." Beneficence deals with prevention of harm and promotion of well-being and has been the primary driving principle of medical and psychiatric practice throughout history. The principle of justice in psychiatry does not operate in a vacuum but is responsive to the ever-changing social, political, religious, and legal mores of the moment (Sadock and Sadock, 2000).

From a practical point of view, according to Sadock and Sadock (2000) the transgressions that psychiatrists most frequently commit fall into a few categories, and certain activities may fit in more than one category. These are sexual boundary violations, nonsexual boundary violations, violations of confidentiality, mistreatment of the patient (incompetence, unethical alliances), and illegal activities (e.g., improper billing, insider stock trading).

1.1.8. An Integrative Approach

An integrative, bio-psycho-socio-cultural approach is imperative for any consideration of human sexuality. One of the problems of studies that attempt to bridge the gap between culture and biology is that they tend to view biology (and perhaps to some extent psychology) as constituting a substratum (Vance, 1991:879), a kind of universal clay that culture shapes, molds, and operates upon.

Yet two recent studies raise some very interesting questions about the interactive effects of culture (sexual desire) and biology (reproductive hormones). The first study recorded different effects of oral steroidal contraceptives on the sexual well-being of samples of women from Scotland and the Philippines (Bancroft, 1999), where oral contraceptive use had a significant negative effect on sexual interest among the women in Scotland but no negative effect on the Filipino women. Researchers offer cultural explanations for the variable effects of the hormones among the Scot and Filipino samples. This study, as does the following one, begs for a more interactive and informed investigation of manifestations of a direct biological effect in different cultural contexts.

The second study concerns male reproductive hormones (Worthman, 1999). In U.S. and European populations, testicular hormone testosterone (T) and adrenal androgen dihydroepiandrosterone (DHEA) show a natural linear decline beginning at about age forty. These declines are associated with declines in sexual functioning, for example, coital frequency, angle of erection, and ejaculatory propulsion. Yet mounting data from non-Western populations suggest that the T and DHEA patterns of Western males are unusual. For example, Aymara men in Bolivia who are over twenty-five years old do not display the same strong declines in T, and among Tibetan men T on the average increased with age up to age sixty. DHEA showed similar differentiating patterns. Studies of the same male hormones in two New Guinea samples showed hormone level to be associated with health, nutrition, and acculturative stress. According to Worthman (1999), these studies suggest that the U.S./European biology of sexuality and aging may be one of many and that such biology may vary across a range of human social and physical ecologies.

Clearly these two studies illustrate the inherent limitations in a sexology that assumes a universal biology of sexuality that is independent of cultural variables. It also points to the problem of assuming that research limited to U.S. and European populations (even though there is great variation among their constituent peoples) can provide any kind of normative data. Giving biology its due, it is also imperative that lessons in the more constructionist vein not be overlooked.

Life Cycle and Sexual Health

S exual health throughout the life cycle is determined by a complexity of bio-psycho-social factors that play a remarkable and multidimensional role in individuals from infancy to old age (Seidman and Rieder, 1994; Gagnon, 1989). Child, adolescent, adult, and geriatric psychiatrists can provide care for individuals throughout the life cycle.

Sexual health has relevance for psychiatrists as it reflects emotional development over the life span and may result in or be a symptom of psychiatric disorders. Psychiatrists have a unique opportunity to play a role in sex education and reproductive choice, promoting healthy sexuality, risk reduction, and prevention of HIV and other STIs, as well as prevention of violence. Psychiatrists could be helpful educators on the basis of their bio-psycho-social training and their long-term, ongoing relationships with patients.

Bancroft (1989) has proposed an eclectic interactional model of sexual development that includes three strands and six stages. These strands are sexual differentiation into male or female and the development of gender identity, sexual responsiveness, and the capacity for close dyadic relationships. Stages are termed prenatal, childhood, adolescence and early adulthood, marriage (or the establishment of a stable sexual relationship), parenthood, and mid-life.

1.2.1. Children

The basis for sexual health is established in early infancy and is built on the bonding experience between infant and parental figures. When parents provide a nurturing, holding, and unconditionally loving environment, they form the bonds for future healthy intimate relationships. It is unconditional love that provides the baby with a sense of the value of its body and the worth of the self to another person. When it functions well, this bond enables the child to become a secure, fulfilled, healthy adult.

Gender identity is defined through childhood and adolescence. Genetic and biological factors are implied, as well as social and psychological factors, such as identification models and social pressure. Sexual preferences, orientation, and gender roles may also be defined during this period.

Although most parents want to provide their children with such a nurturing environment, their own early experiences of parental neglect, deprivation, or trauma may interfere with their parenting capacities. Even if parenting skills are adequate, current life situations, domestic violence, losses, civil wars, and torture can be barriers to adequate parenting.

Early childhood trauma, both physical and sexual, is a risk factor for future problems. These include vulnerability to violence, depression, anxiety, and posttraumatic stress disorder (Alexander and Lupfer, 1987; Briere and Runtz, 1987); aggressive and reckless behaviors (Valois, Kammermann, and Wanzer Drane, 1997); gang involvement (Resnick and Blum, 1994); running away from home (Stiffman, 1989); drug and alcohol use (Rohsenow, Corbett, and Devine, 1988; Walker, Katon, Hansom, et al., 1992); sexually transmitted infections (Allers, Banjack, White, and Rousey, 1993; Zierler, Feingold, Laufer, et al., 1991; Allers and Benjack, 1991; Thompson, Potter, Sanderson, and Maibach, 1997; Goodman and Fallot 1998); an increased likelihood of engaging in commercial sex work; and forced as well as sex and sex-for-drugs exchanges (Paone, Chavkin, Willets, Friedman, and DesJarlais, 1992).

Also, high academic achievement and living with both parents was significantly correlated with virginity and appeared to be protective for boys and girls (Raine, Jenkins, Aarons, Woodward, Fairfax, El-Khoratzaty, and Herman, 1999). Nonetheless, Stanton, Romer, Ricardo, Black, Feigelman, and Galbraith (1993) found that early initiation of sex was not associated with school truancy, illicit drug use, and drug trafficking among African-American adolescents. Healthy psychosexual development begins in infancy, with the capacity for sexual response and erotic feelings. Childhood sexuality begins with sex play in infancy, with masturbation in both sexes, erectile function in boys and clitoral sensation and later vaginal lubrication in girls. In early childhood, there may be sexual exploration often motivated by pleasurable sensations, curiosity, and a quest for development of a sexual identity along with gradual recognition of sexual differences (Ehhardt and Wasserheit, 1991).

While exploratory sexual play among children is more or less acceptable in Western society, sexual contact between children and adults is considered unacceptable and traumatic. In addition to the tragic consequences of incest, sexual contact between adults and children may lead to serious psychopathology including substance-related disorders, posttraumatic stress disorder, multiple personality disorder, major depressive disorder as well as other psychiatric disorders. In Kenya, Zambia, and other countries, children under the age of sixteen are being infected with AIDS by older men who use them for forced sex and commercial sex work because young girls are considered less likely to be infected than adult women. As a result, 20% of girls in the region are HIV positive by the age of sixteen (Piot and O'Rourke, 2000). In some areas of the world, having intercourse with a virginal girl is seen as a cure for AIDS.

The prevalence of childhood sexual abuse in women entering a substance abuse treatment program was close to 75%. The consequences of early childhood trauma extend throughout the life cycle but are especially profound in adolescence.

1.2.2. Adolescents

Adolescence is frequently a time of turmoil in the life of an individual. It is a time of major bio-psycho-social transitions. Children have sudden growth spurts, burgeoning secondary sexual characteristics, major hormonal changes, and enormous changes in physiological, psychosexual, and emotional functioning. Developmental issues involve separation-individuation, separation from parents, establishment of an adult sexual identity, and the capacity for intimacy. In the United States, puberty begins at any point between 10 and 15 years of age, with the average age of menarche at about 12.8 and of increasing testicular size at about the same time or earlier (Ehhardt and Wasserheit, 1991). By about 15, boys are fertile. Breast development in girls usually begins between 10 and 11 (8.5–13 age range) and fertility begins around 13 years. Many teenagers experience mood swings and worries and have difficulties adjusting to the rapidity of the changes in appearance, size, and new hormonal surges. There is a gradual transition from a focus on parents to a shift to peers.

In healthy adolescents, close friendships form with same-sex peers in early adolescence and may include sexual experimentation. Eventually (Paone, Chavkin, Willets, Friedman, and DesJarlais, 1992; Freud, 1974; Ehhardt and Wasserheit, 1991; Piot and O'Rourke, 2000) adult size is attained and struggles with autonomy and dependence abound. Needs for peer-group approval may lead to risk-taking behavior, including sexual risk-taking.

Childhood sexual trauma is a risk factor for many adolescent problems including promiscuity, teenage pregnancy, running away (Stiffman, 1989), substance-related disorders (Rohsenow, Corbett, and Devine, 1988; Walker, Katon, Hanson, et al., 1992), STI and AIDS (Allers, Banjack, White, and Rousey, 1993; Zierler, Feingold, Laufer, et al., 1991; Allers and Benjack, 1991; Thompson, Potter, Sanderson, and Maibach, 1997; Goodman and Fallot 1998), depression, and eating disorders. It has been suggested that the child whose body was not adequately protected may be unable to provide adequate self-protection as an adolescent.

In the United States, adolescents have a dramatic increase in sexual activity. The majority expresses this through masturbation, although the rate of masturbation may vary along different cultures and social groups. In a re-analysis of Kinsey data, it was concluded that 94% of men and 40% of women had masturbated to orgasm. They began to have sexual intercourse at middle or late adolescence. More recent studies indicate that sexual activities start at earlier ages.

The majority of boys have had intercourse by age 16–17 and girls by age 17–18. By age 19, more than 80% have had sexual intercourse (Brookman, 1990; Seidman and Rieder, 1994), but the sexual experience rate is associated with gender, age, ethnicity, and household composition (McKnight et al., 1994). African-American adolescents report significantly younger age at first intercourse. Gender differences in sexual behavior were also found more frequently among African-American students than among Caucasian or Hispanic students (Warren, Santelli, Everett, et al., 1998). These authors assert that the proportion of U.S. high school students who reported being sexually experienced remained at 53–54% from 1990 to 1995 (recent studies suggest that the percentage may be much higher today) while the percentage of sexually active students who used condoms at last sexual intercourse rose from 46% to 54% between 1991 and 1995.

Nonetheless, adolescents do not consistently use condoms, and in the United States, unprotected sexual encounters result in one million teenage pregnancies annually. The majority of young adults aged 18–24 have multiple, serial sex partners (Seidman and Rieder, 1994). Wellings, MacDowall, Catchpole, et al. (1999) found that trends in several measures (births, abortions, STIs, and condom sales figures) point consistently to an increase in sexual activity and unsafe sex occurring at or around the Christmas and other holiday periods, with a longer but less pronounced subsidiary period coinciding with the summer vacation. Of the cumulative total of AIDS cases in the United States (702,748), approximately 30,000 occurred in 13 to 24 year olds. It is estimated that of the 33.6 million persons living with HIV throughout the world, 50% were infected between age 15 and 24 years (Piot and O'Rourke, 2000).

Early intervention is needed to help adolescents learn how to use condoms if they are sexually active and to empower them to make responsible choices regarding sexual partners and activities. Use of peer counselors and groups may help teenagers to gain control over sexual intimacy and contraception and to reduce risky behavior. College students may be knowledgeable about HIV/AIDS prevention measures, yet they may underestimate the risk in unprotected sexual behavior.

1.2.3. Adults

Mature adult sexuality is characterized by expressions of love, romance, and sexuality in deeply committed relationships. A sexual behavior survey (De Buono, Zinner, Daamen, et al., 1990) was conducted in 1975, 1986, and 1989 on 779 North American women college students with a mean age of 22 years who attended a gynecological student health clinic. Although condom use increased from 11% in 1975 to 21% in 1986 and to 40% in 1989, there were no changes in the numbers of partners despite the high level of education attained. Approximately 80% of college students surveyed (Kotloff, Tacket, Wasserman, et al., 1991; MacDonald, Wells, Fisher, et al., 1990) are sexually active but only about 13%–15% of those participating in national surveys reported consistent condom use (Kotloff, Tacket, Wasserman, et al., 1991; MacDonald, Wells, Fisher, et al., 1990) despite multiple partners.

In later adulthood, from ages 25 to 59, there is a gradual decrease in the number of sexual partners as individuals begin to enter more stable long-term relationships. Although there is a gradual trend toward monogamy, there has been a decrease in the proportion of persons in committed relationships because of the trend toward postponing marriage and the increase in separation and divorce. It is estimated that 90% of men ages 25 to 59 are heterosexually active. It appears that during their lifetime 20% of men have one sexual partner, 55% have 2–19 partners, and 25% have 20 or more partners. Approximately 25% of adults have had anal intercourse (Seidman and Rieder, 1994). The majority of women from 25 to 59 are monogamous. About 25% of unmarried heterosexually active women had two or more partners in the preceding year. The frequency of intercourse generally decreases with age.

Up to 20% of adult men report they have had a homosexual experience; 1%–6% reports such an experience during the preceding year (Seidman and Rieder, 1994). According to the National Survey of American Men, 2.3% of men ages 20 to 39 reported "same gender sexual activity" during the preceding 10 years (Billy, Tanfer, Grady and

Kleppinger, 1993). It is estimated that of adult men under 60, 3% identify themselves as gay or bisexual. It is estimated that about 2% of women are gay or bisexual. Although patterns are changing, there has been a gradual decrease in numbers of partners and an increase in monogamous gay relationships. It is crucial to emphasize the importance for adults of all ages to continue to use condoms and to be aware of risky sexual behaviors, including adults in the older age group.

1.2.4. Older Adults

Beginning at approximately age 50, there appears to be a gradual continuous decline in sexual interest and activity (Bortz, Wallace, and Wiley, 1999; Feldman, Goldstein, Hatzichristou, et al., 1994). Some of this decline in sexual activity appears to be a function of normal aging (Panser, Rhodes, Girman, et al., 1995; Segraves and Segraves, 1995). Sarrel (2001) considers that change in estrogen production at menopause has been associated with anatomical and physiological changes which impair sexual function. Similar findings (Berman et al., 2001) suggest that androgen may play a role in regulating vaginal smooth muscle relaxation and blood flow. Diminished androgen receptor expression in vaginal subepithelium of women on estrogen replacement therapy may result from estrogenic stimulation, leading to less free testosterone and less production of androgen receptors. Persistent symptoms of vaginal atrophy and dryness in menopausal women receiving estrogen replacement therapy may in part be related to decreased androgen receptors. Nevertheless, perceptions of elderly male sexual function and its impact on health-related quality of life may differ among races, sites, and countries (Duffy, 1998; Laumann, Paik, and Rosen, 1999; Masumori, Tsukamoto, Kumamoto, et al., 1999). Some decline is clearly associated with age-related disease processes and their treatment (Jensen, Lendorf, Stimpel, et al., 1999; Read, King, and Watson, 1997). Health status, positive attitudes toward sexual function, and perceived partner's responsiveness are prominent moderators of the age effect (Bortz, Wallace, and Wiley, 1999). Holzapfel (1994) argues that sexual expression among the elderly is a predictor of general health, while Davey-Smith, Frankel, and Yarnell (1997) suggest that sexual activity seems to have a protective effect on men's health. In one way or the other, a minority of individuals remain sexually active on a once a week to once a month basis into their 80s and 90s (Segraves and Segraves, 1995). At this moment there is little data about sexual function in women over age 60, as most studies of sexual function have drawn the line at age 59 and are usually limited to ages 18 to 59. Interestingly, women ages 50 to 59 showed a higher level of sexual desire and a lower level of sexual difficulties compared with the younger women, with only 27% showing a lack of interest in sex versus 30%–32% in the younger age cohorts (Sarrel, 2001). Trudel (2002) found that the majority of subjects age 60 or over expressed an interest in sexuality.

Nevertheless, as adults live longer, healthier lives, it is important to recognize that sexuality and romance can continue throughout the life cycle. Older persons may have strong sexual needs despite the societal stereotypes of older persons as "sick and sexless" (Kennedy, Haque, and Zarankow, 1997). Both men and women continue to experience sexual interest regardless of their sexual preference (Kennedy, Haque, and Zarankow, 1997; Bretschneider and McCoy, 1988).

With advancing age, women outnumber men. By age 80, there are four women for every man. Most women over 65 are widowed; most men are married (Butler and Lewis, 1990). Partner availability is a problem. Gender differences in sexual response become less pronounced in the older age range. There is an enhanced psychological component, more congruent expectations, a decline in the biological component, and higher level of complementarity in relationships.

Problems arise when one partner loses interest in sex or is incapacitated. Sexual abstinence may lead to both genital and libidinal atrophy (Kennedy, Haque and Zarankow, 1997). Problems such as presence of other caregivers in the home or having to care for a partner with dementia or physical disability may later alter perceptions of sexuality and romance.

Age-related changes in women include a decrease in estrogen and progesterone and an increase in follicle stimulating and luteinizing hormones after menopause. The size of the cervix, uterus, and ovaries decreases. Vaginal thickness, elasticity, vasocongestion, and lubrication diminish, and fertility ceases. In men, testosterone levels decrease along with testicular size and nocturnal penile tumescence. Although there is less spermatogenesis, fertility is maintained in men even past 90 years of age. The prevalence of erectile dysfunction increases from 25% at age 65 to 50% at 75 (Rousseau, 1986). Figures from the Male Aging Study of Massachusetts (Feldman, Goldstein, Hatzichristou, et al. 1994), are much higher than those reported by Rousseau. The DENSA study reported 43% of men with ED in several grades at 50 years of age.

Factors that contribute to sexual dysfunction in the older adult are medications, diabetes, stroke, neuropathy, Parkinson's disease, chronic obstructive pulmonary disease, angina, end-stage renal disease, vascular disease, and surgical interventions. Although dementia may contribute to sexual dysfunction, hypersexuality may also occur with frequent and unwanted demands for sex as a result of perseveration or frontal lobe-related disinhibition. These reactions can be disturbing to caregivers as well as partners. They can be treated with redirection, or other activities, and may require antipsychotics or mood stabilizers. Education of family and staff can be helpful to encourage nonjudgmental and nonpunitive attitudes. Sexuality may be expressed in many ways other than intercourse in this population.

Older adults are sexually active and as a result of the misconception that AIDS is not a disease of older persons, AIDS prevalence is increasing in this population. Women and men over 50 need to be aware of the risk of AIDS and use condoms. At age 50, 10% of Americans engage in risky behaviors for HIV infection, resulting in a growing prevalence rate in this population (Patterson, Nagel, and Adler, 1995). Psychiatrists can be helpful to older adults by providing couple therapy, treating sexual dysfunction, and educating patients, families, and caregivers.

Sexual health has been explored from infancy to older adulthood. The importance of competent parenting and prevention of early childhood, sexual, and physical abuse can improve physical, mental, and sexual health and prevent the burgeoning of the AIDS pandemic.

Policy and Human Rights Considerations

Human sexual rights involve ethical and legal concepts. It connotes social justice and equitable rights and holds as a basic principle that every individual is entitled to a certain standard of well-being. Clearly political and economic instability and poverty have a major impact on sexual and reproductive health of individuals. Moreover, the establishment of provisions for human rights provides a political basis upon which governments and global legal institutions can act. There has been some international movement toward the assertion of specific sexual and reproductive rights, including contraceptive choice.

According to Freedman and Isaacs (1993), any discussion of ethical issues in today's global world can raise a host of questions and challenges due to tensions between demographic priorities and reproductive choice, and between international standards and local custom and religion. Understanding sexual standards, values, practices, and world views from a culturally informed or relativist perspective should not imply acceptance.

1.3.1. Challenges and Issues

A few examples demonstrate the importance of human rights issues. The global burden of disease associated with inadequate addressing of reproductive and sexual needs is calculated to be between 4% and 15%, with sexually transmitted infections, maternal mortality and morbidity, and cancers of the reproductive tract accounting for 20% of the total years of healthy life lost (WHO, 1999). There are approximately 330 million cases of sexually transmitted infections. Over 30 million men women and children are infected with AIDS as this continues to ravage the world, notably in the developing world with 5.2 million newly infected people every year. Unsafe abortions are calculated to be 20 million a year, with close to 70,000 women dying as a result (U.N. Development Program, 1999). Estimates assess the number of unwanted pregnancies at 120 million a year. It is estimated that more than 585,000 women die each year from complications of pregnancy and maternity (U.N. Population Fund [UNFPA], 1997). There is still a huge gap between maternal mortality in developed and developing countries, with 26 women dying per 100,000 live births in the former versus 700 per 100,000 live births in the latter (U.N.

20

Document, 1994). Genital mutilation affects about 120 million women in total and 2 million girls per year. In addition, it is estimated that 2 million girls between the age of 5 and 15 are introduced to commercial prostitution every year (WHO, 1999).

In a recent report to the U.N. Commission on Human Rights (Coomaraswamy, 2002), any violation of women's reproductive rights is regarded as violence against women. Coomaraswamy (2002) reports that inadequate levels of knowledge about human sexuality, inadequate or inappropriate reproductive health information and services, culturally embedded discrimination against women and girls, and limits on women's control over their sexual and reproductive lives contribute to violations of women's reproductive health. More specifically, the listing of cultural practices identified as violations impinging on women's sexuality in this report include female genital mutilations, honor killings, forced marriage, forced abortion, pledging girls (as temple prostitutes), rape and abuse of lower class or caste women, son preference, maternal depletion from frequent pregnancy and birth, neglect of reproductive health services, lack of trained birth attendants, incest, and fear and regulation of female sexuality.

In any discussion of human sexual rights, the right to education concerning sexual health issues is of utmost importance. This includes sexual trauma awareness and prevention and improvements in treatment and rehabilitation. Education can help to empower women and children to assert control over their own bodies and to value the body and the self, which leads to self-efficacy and care. Programs of education about safe sex, including use of male and female condoms, dental dams, rubber gloves, increasing their knowledge of STI, and encouragement of monogamous long-term relationships, are some examples. Education to prevent child abuse and improve parenting skills would be a major primary preventive measure to preserve sexual and reproductive rights. Sexual trauma awareness and prevention, including skill-building for women at risk, heightened awareness and prevention of domestic violence, substance abuse prevention and treatment, and research and services for violence against women, would improve the sexual environment for women. Improvement in drug use prevention and rehabilitation would include viability of antiretroviral drugs for victims of sexual assault and prevention of perinatal HIV transmission worldwide. In addition to education, local women's organizations, the mass media, and enforcement of existing laws and development of new ones can make significant strides in advancing the sexual and reproductive rights of women and children (Coomaraswamy, 2002).

1.3.2. International Agencies

Although a few international agencies have gender-related programs that address sexual and reproductive health, none of them has the scope and reach of the United Nations. The United Nations Population Fund (UNFPA) plays a central role. Its main purpose is assisting countries in dealing with sexual and reproductive health and setting up family planning programs to promote realistic and sustainable development. UNFPA has many programs, helping 160 countries every year in the developing world. It attempts to enhance sexual and reproductive health from all the main perspectives, including the prevention of sexually transmitted infections and HIV/AIDS, contraceptive programs (1989

Global Initiative on Contraceptive Requirements and Logistic Management Needs in Developing Countries), and adolescents' reproductive health needs. Approximately 20% of the budget is earmarked for education and increased awareness of sexual and reproductive issues.

Another important agency is the United Nations Children Fund (UNICEF), which is very active in the sexual and reproductive health of children, fighting against sexual exploitation, pornography, abuse, and discrimination. In addition, UNICEF works with governments and nongovernmental organizations (NGOs) on supporting AIDS prevention programs and reproductive rights.

In the UN system, the Commission on the Status of Women is the entity that specifically addresses the sexual and reproductive needs of women. As a branch of the Economic and Social Council (ECOSOC), the Commission examines gender inequalities and attempts to advance women's rights agenda in a variety of areas including social, economic, and political domains. The United Nations held a landmark Fourth World Conference on Women in Beijing in 1995, where gender discrimination and violence against women, inter alia, were examined in detail and specific recommendations were offered.

Additionally, the Committee on the Elimination of Discrimination against Women (under the Division for Advancement of Women) monitors the implementation of the UN Convention on the Elimination on All Forms of Discriminations against Women (CEDAW) and has been fundamental in fostering our understanding of sexual and reproductive and legal issues. The United Nations Development Fund for Women (UNIFEM), a voluntary fund working on the empowerment of women in developing countries, works directly with governments on the administration of justice in a number of countries, monitoring sexual health, human rights, and the reporting and rectification of violations. An example of interaction among these agencies, underscoring the intimate link between the child and maternal health, UNICEF, UNESCO and UNFPA have joined forces in advancing sexual and reproductive rights. Moreover, WHO has started a number of programs dealing with sexual health, family planning, adolescent sexuality, contraception, and maternal health (U.N., 1999), many of which are carried out in collaboration with other U.N. agencies. They work closely with nongovernmental organizations to monitor the implementation of legal and human rights recommendations, often depending on local NGOs for the success of their programs.

The legal significance of these activities within the United Nations is profound and potentially far reaching, since the implementation of the resolutions and plans of action produced are binding upon the countries ratifying U.N. conventions. Countries' commitments include periodic national reports and demonstration of evidence of compliance with U.N. commissions' directives. The system therefore goes beyond ceremonial discussing of the issues and has a built-in evaluation mechanism.

1.3.3. Significant Documents and Official Declarations

Among the many documents which address human rights and its relationship with sexual health, a few stand out for their significance for their tone and legal implications. The Committee on the Elimination of Discrimination against Women's Ninth Session led to the document "Avoidance of Discrimination against Women in National Strategies for the Prevention and Control of Acquired Immunodeficiency Syndrome (AIDS)" (UN (1994a), which recommends an intensification of states' efforts to raise the awareness of the effects of AIDS on women and children, with particular attention devoted to their rights and the understanding of factors related to reproductive role of women in our society. Participation of women in primary health care is particularly emphasized.

The Committee on the Elimination of Discrimination against Women also issued a document called "Female Circumcision" (UN, 1994b), in which it recommends various measures to eradicate this practice, including widespread dissemination of information at various levels in organizations, involvement of political, religious, and community leaders to address the issue, often replacing this rite of passage into adulthood with another ceremony of significance, and introducing training and educational programs based on evidence gathered on the deleterious consequences of female circumcision.

Another important document resulted from a landmark population conference in Cairo in 1994. The document, Program for Action of the United Nations International Conference on Population and Development, is called "Reproductive Rights and Reproductive Health" (UN, 1994b). This is a comprehensive document divided into five parts: Reproductive Rights and Reproductive Health; Family Planning; Sexually Transmitted Disease and Prevention of HIV Infection; Human Sexuality and Gender Relations; and Adolescents. The overall call for action of this document aims at making reproductive care, including family planning, universally available by 2015. Of particular interest is the repeated focus on involvement of men, adult and adolescent, in programs enhancing education on sexual and reproductive matters, especially concerning the responsibility of family planning, child-rearing practices, and the dangers of sexually transmitted infections. The language is strong and direct. For example, when discussing the need to protect women, youth, and children from any abuse, the text reads: "Governments should set the necessary conditions and procedures to encourage victims to report violations of their rights. Laws addressing those concerns should be enacted where they do not exist, made explicit, strengthened and enforced, and appropriate rehabilitation services provided."

The Beijing Declaration and Platform for Action is the result of the Fourth World Conference on Women held in 1995 (UN, 1995). Acknowledging that much remains to be accomplished in the promotion and preservation of sexual and reproductive health, the document proposes several strategic objectives. The first objective is to increase women's access throughout the life cycle to appropriate, affordable, and quality health care, information, and related services. The second objective is to strengthen preventive programs that promote women's health. The third objective is to undertake gender-sensitive initiatives that address sexually transmitted infections, HIV/AIDS, and sexual and reproductive health issues. The fourth strategic objective is to promote research and disseminate information on women's health, and the last objective is to increase resources and monitor follow up for women's health.

Professional associations of sexologists have also actively issued a series of sexual rights statements. The Pan American Health Organization in collaboration with WHO and the World Association for Sexology (Valencia Declaration 1997) asserts the principle that sexual health is a basic and fundamental human right. These basic rights include (1) the right to sexual freedom; (2) the right to sexual autonomy, sexual integrity, and safety of the sexual body; (3) the right to sexual privacy; (4) the right to sexual equity; (5) the right to sexual pleasure; (6) the right to emotional sexual expression; (7) the right to sexually associate freely; (8) the right to make free and responsible reproductive choices; (9) the right to sexual information based on scientific inquiry; (10) the right to comprehensive sexuality education; and (11) the right to sexual health care (this important document is reproduced in appendix 2).

Of course, the issuing of declarations of rights does not necessarily guarantee either governmental or public opinion compliance or agreement with them. A recent study carried out in a Caribbean country (José, Ferreira, Pérez, et al., 1999) showed that a public opinion debate on sexual education contents, as well as sexologists' discussions of this debate, failed to acknowledge the rights to free association, free and responsible reproductive decision, and sexual equality and equity. Worldwide events suggest that the debate will probably continue throughout decades, but an increasing geographical extension of the debate will surely promote more open local discussion.

1.3.4. Future Directions

What emerges from the current landscape is how much has been accomplished by resourceful and legally accepted agencies, yet how much still needs to be done. The constant background theme of this discourse is education. It seems to be vital in nearly all the fields of human sexuality and reproduction, which include, among many others, infectious diseases, contraception, maternity care, abortion, adolescent sexuality, free will in sexual and reproductive choices, freedom from sexual coercion, intimidation, and discrimination, and access to appropriate sexual and reproductive health care and options: in sum overall control of one's sexual and reproductive functions and rights.

Sexual and reproductive rights as well as legal aspects remain at the forefront of the agenda for policy makers and international organizations. The tremendous progress that has been made due to advocacy, advancement in communications and information techniques, global collaborations, and human rights efforts continue to be challenged by newer and evolving threats such as trafficking of women, armed conflicts, and polarization of social and economic conditions caused by globalization and sexually transmitted infections.

Perhaps the main remaining obstacle for the fulfillment of women's sexual rights is old and culturally rooted views of women as subordinate, powerless, and bound to specific, patriarchically dictated roles. The agencies and documents outlined in this review attempt to solve this problem by advocating and monitoring the empowerment of women to the right to responsible sexuality and adequate reproductive health care, even in adverse circumstances.

Communication and Sexual Health

Communication between a patient and therapist is vital for the diagnosis and treatment of sexual problems. Many sexual dysfunctions arise from relationship and communication difficulties. Treatment failure is usually attributed to lack of communication, extramarital sex, longstanding anger or resentment over unfulfilled sexual or nonsexual needs, power struggles in the relationship, and a loss of physical or emotional intimacy (Leiblum and Rosen, 2000). Professionals involved in the treatment of patients or couples with sexual or relationship difficulties should have good interview and communication skills. Special attention should be given to cultural aspects of sexuality, particularly in those regions and countries where discussing sexual issues can have great moral, religious, and social connotations.

1.4.1. Doctor-Patient Relationship

The physician-patient relationship is a critical element for communication in sexual health. The clinician must establish thoughtful and empathetic rapport with the patient. A culturally sensitive manner must be adopted when discussing key sexual issues. Patients should be allowed to express their concerns and wishes.

Taking a sexual history should be approached as part of a routine evaluation. A bio-psycho-social framework for sexual history-taking takes into account medical, psychological, intrapsychic, interpersonal, social, cultural, and ethnic variables (Cohen and Alfonso, 1997). Healthcare providers (physicians, nurses, midwives) in every area from primary care, internal medicine, gynecology, oncology, urology, pediatrics, psychiatry, neurology, nephrology, and surgery need to integrate sexual history-taking into routine assessments. This is also relevant for psychologists, social workers, and other mental health clinicians.

Sexual history-taking is vital for diagnostic, therapeutic, and preventive reasons. It can lead to diagnosis and treatment of sexual dysfunctions. Distress over sexual functioning can cause stress, anxiety, and depression to both the patient and the partner. It can lead to treatment non-adherence. This can be the case with antihypertensive, antipsychotic, and antidepressant medications. Appropriate communication can be therapeutic when patients are distressed, ashamed, or embarrassed to talk about sexual matters. Being able to discuss the problem in a nonjudgmental environment can bring significant relief to many patients. Once a sexual disorder is recognized, it can be treated through clarification, education, psychotherapy, couple therapy, or treatment of underlying physical problems.

Clinicians may feel uncomfortable talking about sexual issues. Barriers stemming from gender, culture, age, religion, sexual orientation, and ethnic background can inhibit discussion of sexual issues. If clinicians are uncomfortable about sexuality, patients are even more so. Yet it is imperative that physicians be comfortable talking about sexual problems because these problems are common in physical and psychiatric illness. They are also prevalent in cancer, end-stage renal disease, diabetes, vascular disorders and neurological disorders and are side effects of many medications.

A nonjudgmental tone and warm, nurturing, accepting approach facilitates open dialogue. Comfort discussing sexual as well as relational issues is important. A bio-psycho-social framework is important to provide a multifactorial approach.

1.4.2. Couple and Family

General theoretical models of relationship adjustment versus dysfunction (e.g., Wylie, 1993) focus on a number of features, such as how couples establish and maintain intimacy and mutual support, how partners provide for each other's autonomy needs, and how they solve life's problems together. Identification of how couples respond to inevitable areas of conflict in their needs and preferences is frequently viewed as a metaphorical "window" through which one can observe how close relationships function. Unresolved relationship conflict can be defined as "the dissatisfying impasse partners reach in unsuccessful attempts to resolve differences." In contrast, successful resolution of conflicts can contribute to a couple's positive expectation that they will be able to resolve other differences in the future, a positive cognitive set associated with relationship satisfaction.

Relationship conflict has long been thought to cause, maintain, and influence the therapeutic outcome of sexual problems in the absence of a physical cause. The results of conflict can influence partners' relationship satisfaction, and relationship satisfaction can influence sexual satisfaction. Recent research by Trudel (2002) determines that sexual communication is an important factor in the relationship between sexuality and marital functioning. With respect to findings among men and women under 60, the presence of a satisfactory orgasm also proved a key variable in predicting marital satisfaction. Sexual satisfaction among all subjects under 60 and among men 60 or over appeared to be an important variable in marital functioning. These various sexual variables and others that emerged as significant in this study contribute to our ability to predict positive marital functioning and could be prime targets of intervention for the marital and sexual therapist (Trudel, 2002). General relationship deficiencies, such as unresolved conflict, undermine the mutual acceptance that is important to healthy sexual functioning. Conflicts are inevitable among couples, and how these conflicts are handled can have a major impact on satisfaction in relationships. A number of variables influence the course of these conflicts, such as the attributions that partners make about each other's intentions and the ways that partners interact. Clinical reports suggest a bidirectional causal link between unresolved or escalating relationship conflict (regarding nonsexual as well as sexual areas) and the development of sexual dysfunction. On the one hand, distressing relationship conflict can interfere with sexual desire, arousal, and intimate behavior. On the other hand, sexual dysfunction may give rise to increased conflict and distress in a couple's overall relationship. Dysfunctional conflict resolution may be a cause or result of some sexual problems, whereas constructive interaction concerning conflict can add to emotional and sexual intimacy in a couple's relationship. These patterns warrant systematic attention in assessment and intervention in sex therapy.

1.4.3. Work Place

The importance of employees and employers becoming aware of sexual harassment has become clearer in the past decade. The right of employees to work free of sexual comments, unwanted stares, or touching has become law in a number of countries. However, some employees may remain unaware of their rights or fearful of retaliation if they report such sexual harassment, and some employers may be unaware of their duties. Strong support from management, educational efforts, and training seminars are important to prevent workplace sexual harassment.

1.4.4. Mass Media

Mass media can have a pervasive effect on people's conceptions of sexuality, their attitudes, values, and behaviors. Bearing this in mind, health professionals must engage the media to take responsible actions regarding sexual matters. Newspapers and magazines have an important role. Radio and television, particularly the latter, have special importance because values and attitudes are transmitted not only in documentaries and debates but also in TV movies, soap operas, news programs, advertising, and so on (Geada, 1987; Toro-Fernandez, 1995).

Media should have a place in their programming to accurately discuss a range of sexual matters, correcting possible misinformation from other sources (Habach, 1995). Schools for journalism and mass media professionals should be provided with and encouraged to convey complete, objective information on human sexuality including biological, psychological, social, and ethical dimensions.

The Internet is influencing all facets of daily life, particularly sexual practices and behavior. The lure of cyberspace for both the undersexed and oversexed, paraphilic and nonparaphilic alike, is considerable. In both positive and negative ways, Websites, chat rooms, and virtual marketplaces have stimulated sexual appetites and, in some cases, reinforced preexisting sexual deviations or compulsions (Cooper, Scherer, Boies, and Gordon, 1999; Leiblum, 1998). Use of the Internet continues to expand exponentially with current worldwide estimates at 407 million users (NUA, 2000, cited by Cooper, 2002). Cooper et al. found that between 20% and 33% of Internet users engage in some form of online sexual activity. This includes recreation, entertainment, exploration, information about sexual problems and concerns, education, purchasing of sexual materials, the search for sexual partners, sexual arousal, downloading and sharing of erotica, sexually explicit discussions, and so on (Egan, cited by Cooper, 2002). Egan reports that sexual activities on the Internet are available at any time, cost little or nothing, and allow users to maintain anonymity, providing them safety and the ability to obscure or misrepresent their online identities. This technology is redefining multiple facets of sexual expression and allowing new ways of relating romantically and sexually. It also provides instant, anonymous access to sexual information, sexually explicit materials, and interaction with other like-minded individuals. The Internet also offers a massive virtual library of sexual information that is often free and available instantaneously, continuously, and anonymously.

Cooper et al. report that distraction is the most common reason people reported for engaging in online sexual activity: "to distract myself/take a break" (78%); "to educate myself" (35%) was another major reason. Most people reported that it has not had a negative impact on their lives.

There is no doubt that the Internet has become a significant element in the current sexual landscape, and therapists cannot afford to remain ignorant about what is available in cyberspace. There is a need for sites that convey clear and responsible information based in scientific facts directed to the needs of Web surfers. As a response to these needs, Kingsberg, Althof, and Leiblum (2002) published a list of books helpful to patients where they included a list of 34 Internet sites valuable for patients and therapists.

Educational Considerations

As previously stated in the section on human sexual rights, all human beings should have a guaranteed right to a comprehensive sexual education and to sexual information based on scientific inquiry. A comprehensive sexuality education program developed by SIECUS includes six key components: human development, relationships, personal skills, sexual behavior, sexual health, and society and culture. These topics are described in further detail in part 3 and figure 3.7.1. While educational considerations include the training of health care professionals as well as sex education in primary and secondary schools and youth organizations, clubs, or centers, it is important to recognize that sexual education is a life-long issue.

1.5.1. Professional Training

Lack of sexual information among health professionals is evident; not many medical schools provide education or training in human sexuality. In reality, the search for advice about sexual difficulties is frequent among clients of primary care units and specialists, particularly in general practice, psychiatry, urology, and obstetrics and gynecology (Mira, et al., 1992). Physicians should be able to talk about sex with their patients.

General practitioners and primary care nurses are sometimes asked by patients to provide sexual education and discuss problems in the patient's sexual life. In general patients do not volunteer to talk about sex, but if asked by a professional, they are willing to talk. Specialists are also sought for sexual help within their scope of practice. A complete case history in any medical or nursing clinical case must include a group of items on sexual history. Psychologists are also frequently asked about problems in the sexuality of their clients.

Medical and nursing undergraduate courses should include human sexuality in psychiatry, psychology, gynecology, family medicine and urology. The topics should include sexual anatomy and physiology, normal and abnormal sexual responses, sexual dysfunctions, and sexual identity and orientation. Students must be able to collect a complete sexual history, identify the principal difficulties brought by the patient, and counsel them, giving information and some specific suggestions to the individual or the couple. Clinical psychologists and social workers should also be trained in clinical care regarding human sexuality. Graduate short courses should be available in order to address specific questions such as therapy for sexual dysfunctions, paraphilias and other problems (Machado Vaz, 1987).

1.5.2. Primary and Secondary School Education

Although sex is apparently no longer a taboo in many societies, there is a great deal of misinformation that creates all sorts of problems, including, among young people, unwanted pregnancy, sexual dysfunctions, difficulties accepting other sexual choices, and the risk of contracting sexually transmitted infections including AIDS (Nuno Miguel, 1987; Júlio Gonçalves, 1987; Osio, 1995).

Parents should be encouraged to participate in the sexual education of their children—not waiting for teachers, books or other media to do so. Parent meetings with teachers and sexual counselors in schools might be helpful to discuss fears and doubts about sexuality (Albornoz, 1995).

School should be the second most important educator in this area, but to achieve this goal teachers must be prepared and willing to meet their students' needs and requests for information (SIECUS, 1995; Valle Salazar, 1995).

Youth centers located in schools, campus, or in town centers (especially for young people who drop out of school or are working) where young people can find information and discuss sexual issues with a health professional can be instrumental in sexual education.

Sexuality and Sexual Education in Special Situations

Sexuality in special situations, particularly among handicapped people, has traditionally been ignored. Sexual evaluation and sexual education programs addressed to the mentally and physically handicapped contribute to a more fulfilled and healthy life. Specialized texts are necessary for specificity.

1.5.3. Family and Community Education

In many parts of the world, parents are considered the primary teachers of their children in sexual matters. It is also common that parents specifically or implicitly delegate sexual education to respected individuals or groups in the community such as teachers, religious leaders, doctors, schools, or various cultural "rites of passage" that may evolve imparting of sexual values or experience.

It is also common that in many communities around the globe little or no specific sexual education is offered. For example, in some surveys of sex education, no more than half of U.S. parents reported that they had ever directly talked with their children about sexuality. There also appeared to be several levels of information sharing, progressing from basic biological and reproductive information (e.g., menarche) to imparting parental values and beliefs about sexuality (e.g., encouraging children to "wait until marriage" to have sexual intercourse). Interestingly, even among parents and institutions that teach children about the anatomy of sex, it is not apparently common for parents to teach children about sexual physiology, that is, details of what the body experiences during sexual arousal. If this impression is accurate, it may help explain why the rate of sexual dysfunction is as frequent as it is. In addition, there are studies that suggest that such sexual ignorance is correlated with youthful sexual promiscuity. The more youth are instructed with honest sexual information within the values of the community, the more likely they are to behave responsibly sexually.

Scientific Research

Advancement in the field of sexual health will require conducting active biological, psychological and social investigations and giving thoughtful attention to the results of such research at the clinical and public health levels. Psychiatry must recognize the need for more sophisticated knowledge of ethnicity, culture, gender, and class if psychiatrists are to extend health care beyond the reach of the Euro-American middle classes. Physicians should also learn about the basic principles of qualitative research methodology so that they can have a better understanding of the nuances of sensitive issues such as sexual behavior and concerns.

1.6.1. Methods of Sex Research

Scientific sex researchers have employed a wide variety of methods in their research. Before research begins, however, a number of decisions must be made about the scope and nature of the study at hand. Research questions should be formulated clearly, so that the methods are used to adequately respond to those questions. Subjects of the study must be identified and sampling procedures established. Variables of interest and assessment instruments must be determined. Data must be collected and then analyzed through appropriate statistical techniques. Finally, conclusions must be drawn by comparing the findings obtained with relevant literature.

Research methods relevant to psychiatry and sexual health include laboratory investigations and longitudinal and cross-sectional studies. These can use interviews, surveys, questionnaires, and participant observation methods. Within each methodological approach one can find a great range in the quality of individual studies. Each method has its assets, limitations, and ethical challenges in different settings.

1.6.2. Ethics of Sex Research

Sexual research projects often involve sensitive ethical issues. The Council for International Organizations of Medical Sciences (CIOMS) lists four ethical principles that should govern all research with human subjects. These are (1) respect for the autonomy and self-determination of persons; (2) beneficence or the obligation to maximize benefits and minimize harms; (3) nonmaleficence, meaning do no harm; and (4) justice, which

31

requires equal treatment of all subjects of the study and requires that the study is designed so that the subjects of the study are among its beneficiaries.

1.6.3. Future Research

In front of us we find a number of challenging developments, such as emerging genetic findings, interactions between genetics and the environment, and the complexity of the human mind and body and its social and cultural context. A new era has begun in the last twenty years, producing many insights, including better understanding of penile function and dysfunction and the introduction of effective oral medication to relieve erectile dysfunction. Advances in pharmacological effects may offer new explanations of ejaculatory dysfunction. Despite recent advances in the understanding of sexual physiology, some consider that today's challenge comprises searching for central brain and spinal nuclei, neurotransmitters, receptors, and second messengers involved in the control of penile erection. These researchers state the need to understand whether one or several peripheral pathways exist between the brain and the penis and believe that the anatomical interrelationships and interactions among the different brain nuclei that modulate erectile capacity and sexual function should be further explored. In addition, behavioral assessment should be further pursued.

Concerning female sexuality, the situation seems to be more difficult and complex. Nevertheless the past years have seen significant advances in the knowledge of female sexuality. Learned societies dealing with women's sexuality, such as the International Society for the Study of Women's Sexual Health, are being established and becoming increasingly active. They are sponsoring the presentation and publication of physiological and psychosocial factors concerning female sexuality and female sexual pathology.

Recent findings suggest a role for testosterone in maintaining sexual function and response in women (Lazarus et al., 2001), another area that requires further study. Another area worth mentioning is the use of vasodilators in the treatment of women's sexual dysfunctions. Studies of oral and topical medications are being investigated for the treatment of female sexual disorders, especially Arousal Disorders (Neal et al., 2001).

It is hoped that the desire and arousal mechanisms in women will also be better understood. One insight may come through molecular biology, where technologies may be used for genetic analysis and therapy; such genetic analysis is already in its early infancy regarding erectile dysfunction.

Epidemiology and Public Health Considerations

Epidemiology has been defined as the study of the distribution and determinants of health-related states or events in specified populations, and the application of this study to control of health problems (Last, 1988, cited in Beaglehole, Bonita, and Kjelltröm, 1993). Epidemiology is concerned not only with death, illness, and disability, but also with more positive health states and the means to improve health (Beaglehole, Bonita, and Kjelltröm, 1993).

1.7.1. General Considerations

Studies have for several decades suggested that men and women in various countries and cultures commonly experience sexual concerns and sexual problems. Surveys of different populations generally report that virtually every individual has concerns about sexuality (concerns about whether they are "normal" or "healthy" in their thoughts, feelings, and behavior) at some point in their lives.

One of the tasks of epidemiological research is to establish statistically what is normative behavior in any specified population.

1.7.2. Epidemiology of Sexual Disorders

Generally there has been an acute dearth of valid or reliable statistical data on the epidemiology of sexual disorders. This is particularly true when it comes to non-Western settings. The close of the twentieth century saw, however, a small number of large-scale sex surveys being administered in a variety of Western national settings, including the United States, Britain, Sweden, and France (Laumann et al., 1999; McConaghy, 1993) as well as China. Along with data on sexual attitudes, beliefs and practices these surveys collected data on the prevalence of sexual dysfunction.

Sexual Dysfunction

It has been difficult to establish the prevalence and correlates of most sexual dysfunctions (erectile dysfunction being an exception), since very little systematic epidemiological research has been conducted in the field (American Psychiatric Association, 1994; Bortz, Wallace, and Wiley, 1999; Laumann, Paik, and Rosen, 1999; Panser, Rhodes, Girman, et al, 1995). Multiple studies report that approximately 30%–50% of the population experiences sexual dysfunction at any given point of time (Laumann, Park, and Rosen, 1999; Dunn, Croft, and Hackett, 1999). While prevalence studies consistently report frequent sexual dysfunction among U.S. couples (50% of couples at any given time), an even greater percent (78%–95%) complain of sexual difficulties (Laumann et al., 1994; Metz and Seifert, 1993).

It is most important to note, however, that this body of research also has substantive methodological limits. For example, major and minor complaints are conflated, diagnostic categories overlap, study populations are not representative, and data come from self-reports. Moreover, some epidemiological studies indicate that although informants report experiencing a sexual difficulty, they do not consider it to be a serious or debilitating disorder. For example, in a Swedish study among sexually active Swedish men who had at least experienced erectile failure "quite often" during the preceding year, only 69% stated that this was a significant problem.

Kaplan, Sadock, and Grebb (1994) report that in the U.S. general population 20% have sexual desire disorders, 10%–20% of men have erectile dysfunction, and 30% of women have orgasmic dysfunction. From 30% to 40% of men treated for sexual dysfunction have premature ejaculation. There is no doubt that figures concerning sexual dysfunctions vary from one place to another. An extensive review of the literature on epidemiological data of sexual dysfunction revealed that Scandinavians have lower rates of sexual dysfunction, Japanese higher rates, with Americans and British falling somewhere in between.

In their survey of the U.S. general population, Laumann, Paik, and Rosen (1999) found that sexual dysfunction is more prevalent in women (43%) than men (31%) and was associated with various sociodemographic characteristics, including age and educational attainment. Women of different racial groups demonstrate different patterns of sexual dysfunction. Experience of sexual dysfunction is more likely among women and men with poor physical and emotional health.

According to Watson and Davis (1997), about 10% of patients attending general practice have some kind of current sexual or relationship difficulty. Nonetheless, sexual problems were recorded in only 2% of general practitioners' notes (Read, King, and Watson, 1997), and only one in ten of those who said they would like to receive professional help had received such help (Dunn, Croft, and Hackett, 1998).

Feldman, Goldstein, Hatzichristou, et al. (1994) report a prevalence of 52% of impotence in a Massachusetts male aging study. In this study the prevalence of complete impotence tripled from 5% to 15% between ages 40 and 70. After adjustment for age, a higher probability of impotence was directly correlated with heart disease, hypertension, diabetes, associated medications, and indexes of anxiety and depression. Cigarette smoking was associated with a greater probability of complete impotence in men with heart disease and hypertension. In the Olmsted County study of urinary symptoms and health status among men, Panser, Rhodes, Girman, et al. (1995) found that sexual dissatisfaction was significantly associated with erectile dysfunction, decreased libido, and their interaction, but not with age.

In England, Dunn, Croft, and Hackett (1998) assert that a third of men (34%) and two-fifths of women (41%) reported having a current sexual problem. The most common problems were erectile dysfunction and premature ejaculation in men; in women the most widely reported problems were lack of desire, vaginal dryness, and infrequent orgasm. In men, the proportion of respondents reporting sexual problems increased with age, but there was no similar trend in women.

In London, Read, King, and Watson (1997) found very similar prevalence rates. About 35% of men reported some form of specific sexual dysfunction, including premature ejaculation (31%) and erectile dysfunction (17%). The prevalence of sexual dysfunction in women was 42%; vaginismus was reported by 30% of them, and anorgasmia by 23%.

Population studies have been conducted in samples of U.S., Swedish and English women. Variable rates of sexual disorders have been noted, which may be related to methodological differences among studies. In older American women, the prevalence of orgasmic dysfunction showed no clear relationship to age, with trouble lubricating low at ages 18 to 45, after which it showed a moderate increase and remained stable from ages 45 to 59. Swedish and American studies show prevalence of sexual disorders among women to be over 45% (Laumann et al., 1999).

McConaghy (1993) cites an important series of studies (among white middle-class/advantaged subjects) that point to a distinction between sexual dysfunctions as problems of performance and "sexual difficulties" or "sexual problems." The latter are related to the tone of emotional relations (e.g., partner choosing inconvenient time and not using appropriate foreplay). Sexual "problems" are not only more prevalent but are more significantly related to lack of sexual satisfaction than are dysfunctions. In a similar vein, in community studies it appears that sexual dysfunctions are much less important (for men and for women, for young and for old) than emotional aspects of relationships in determining sexual satisfaction of couples. For example, community studies in Sweden and the U.K. (cited in McConaghy, 1993) found no association between presence of erectile dysfunction or PE in men and their sexual satisfaction and the sexual satisfaction of their partners. Couples' satisfaction was related to their emotional relationship.

Premature ejaculation was predominantly associated with anxiety. In women, the predominant association with arousal, orgasmic, and enjoyment problems was marital difficulties. Vaginal dryness was found to increase with age after menopause. Sexual problems cluster with self-reported physical problems in men, and with psychological and social problems in women. In a Danish study (Jensen, Lendorf, Stimpel, et al., 1999), 27% of hypertensive men had impotence. The main cause of erectile dysfunction was arterial dysfunction (89%), with intermittent claudication and ischemic heart disease as the best determinants.

Paraphilias

The real prevalence of paraphiliac behavior is unknown, although these disorders are more common in men than in women and seem to be more prevalent in Western developed countries than in the developing world. The United States has the highest rate of coercive paraphilias in the world. Exhibitionism is most commonly reported in the United States, England, Germany, and Canada but is also commonly reported among

Chinese in Hong Kong. Yet exhibitionism is quite rare in South America and in most Middle Eastern, African, and Asian countries. Paraphilias, both in fantasies and urges, may begin in childhood or in early adolescence and, once they are established, may lead a chronic course. In some individuals, they may diminish with advancing age.

Gender Identity Disorders

Before going into the difficulties encountered by people uncomfortable with their gender, let us clarify and briefly define gender and their related concepts. The term "sex" (Bolin and Whelehan, 1999) refers to morphological, chromosomal, and hormonal or biological aspects of being male or female (these, however, are also viewed through a cultural lens). "Gender" refers to the meanings and social aspects of sex that a particular society gives to the physical or biological traits that differentiate males from females. It is these meanings that provide a member of a society with ideas about how to act, what to believe, and how to make sense of their experiences (Marcia-Lees and Black, 2000). Gender is one of the central organizing principles around which social life revolves.

There are no recent epidemiological studies that provide data on prevalence of gender identity disorders. Data from smaller countries in Europe with access to total population and referrals indicate that roughly one in every 30,000 men and one in every 100,000 females seek gender reassignment. There are two components of gender identity disorders. There must be evidence of a strong and persistent cross-gender identification. And there also must be evidence of a persistent discomfort about one's assigned sex or a sense of inappropriateness in the gender role of that sex. It is important to note that not all societies share Western Judeo-Christian notions of gender, and some societies are more open to notions of multiple or changeable gender identities (Nanda, 2000). A more extensive consideration of the disorder is outlined in part 2 of this book.

1.7.3. Epidemiology of Comorbid Psychiatric Conditions

The discussion of comorbidities of sexual disorders requires a discussion of two major forms of comorbidities: psychiatric comorbidities and general medical comorbidities. This section deals with psychiatric comorbidities.

Depression and Anxiety Disorders

The psychiatric comorbidities of sexual disorders have been addressed in a number of population studies. Lindal and Stefansson (1993) reported the results of a population study of citizens of Iceland ages 55–57. Of Icelanders with a lifetime prevalence of a sexual disorder, 53% also had received another psychiatric diagnosis. Subjects with a sexual diagnosis were more likely to also report difficulties with alcohol abuse, depression, and anxiety disorders. A recent cross-sectional study (Johannes et al., 2000) of a representative sample of men ages 40 to 70 living in the Boston suburbs found that the presence of total erectile failure increased from 5% to 15% from ages 40 to 70. A major risk factor for erectile dysfunction was the presence of depression. This same population was then reexamined 8 years later (Arujo et al, 1998). Questionnaire measures of a passive personality style at baseline predicted the subsequent development of erectile dysfunction 8 years later. Population studies of female sexuality (Dunn, 1998, 2000) have found significant relationships between the presence of sexual disorders and self-reports of marital difficulties, anxiety, and depression. Interestingly, population studies of both sexes over age 60 have found significant relationships between loss of libido and depression in both sexes.

Another anxiety-related condition is posttraumatic stress disorders (PTSD). Reactions may occur shortly after the exposure to a traumatic experience or be delayed in time and subject to recurrence. In both cases, individuals experience associated symptoms of detachment and loss of emotional responsivity. Patients may feel depersonalized and unable to recall specific aspects of the trauma, though typically it is reexperienced through intrusion in thought, dreams, or flashbacks, particularly when cues of the original event are present. These aspects are particularly important for the sexual health of patients who had experienced a traumatic event and are initiating or continuing their sexual life with a partner. Regehr and Marziali (1999) studying women who were victims of rape postulated that the degree of response was associated with the severity of the stressor. Together with preexisting personality tendencies, these may be the primary contributors to the development of chronic PTSD symptomatology.

Posttraumatic stress disorders are very common conditions. Hidalgo and Davidson (2000) postulated that most people will experience a traumatic event at some point in their life, and up to 25% of them will develop the disorder. Lifetime prevalence of the disorder ranged between 10.4 and 12.3 per 100 women and 5.0 to 6.0 per 100 men (Sadock and Sadock, 2000). This commonly co-occurs with other psychiatric disorders. Data from epidemiological surveys indicate that the vast majority of individuals with PTSD meets criteria for at least one other psychiatric disorder, and a substantial percentage have three or more other psychiatric diagnoses (Brady, Killeen, Brewerton, and Lucerini, 2000). Acierno, Resnick, Kilpatrick, Saunders, and Best (1999), in a sample of 3,006 adult women, reported that past victimization, young age, and a diagnosis of active PTSD increased women's risk of being raped. By contrast, past victimization, minority ethnic status, active depression, and drug use were associated with increased risk of being physically assaulted. Gleaves, Eberenz, and May (1998), in a sample of 294 women diagnosed as suffering either from anorexia nervosa or bulimia, found that 52% reported current symptomatology consistent with PTSD.

Substance-Related Disorders

The prevalence of drug abuse is a great public health problem. Substance abuse may be a cover up and may also be used to enhance, extend, abbreviate, replace, or otherwise modify sexual behavior (Lowinson, Ruiz, Millman and Langrod, 1992). Numerous medications for medical conditions as well as drugs of abuse can affect sexual desire and performance (Sadock and Sadock, 2000). Different cultures show different patterns of abuse, and in many countries drug abuse correlates with a high incidence of risky behaviors and HIV infections. Garofalo, Wolf, Wissow, Woods, and Goodman (1999) found that drug use was an independent predictor of suicide attempt among gay, lesbian, bisexual, or not-sure youth. Lehmann, Lehmann, and Kelly (1998) report that lesbian sexuality was associated with alcohol or drug problems (39%), suicide attempts (27%), depression (49%), and physical or verbal abuse at school (34%). Frequency of use, dose, user expectations, chronicity, and circumstances of use are important in the effect of a drug on sexuality. A depressant might facilitate a sexual response at a low dose and inhibit at a high dose (Lowinson, Ruiz, Millman, and Langrod, 1992). A therapist must assess the impact of psychotropic medications on sexual response. These medications can impair orgasmic function as well as sexual functioning (Pohl, 1983; Segraves, 1985). Lowinson, Ruiz, Millman, and Langrod (1992) state that both men and women alcoholics appear to believe that alcohol improves sexual experience, and the general public regards a moderate amount as an aphrodisiac and as a useful substance for seduction.

Eating Disorders

Traditionally, eating disorders were considered a problem only in the developed countries; nevertheless the prevalence of this disorder is growing in the Third World. The eating disorders anorexia nervosa and bulimia have been identified over the past 15 centuries. Both conditions have increased since the late 1960s and are commonly encountered in clinical practice, not just in developed countries but also in the developing world. Weight preoccupation is a primary symptom in both anorexia and bulimia nervosa, but many patients demonstrate both behaviors. They usually exercise for hours and may demonstrate bizarre food preferences, social isolation, and diminished sexual interest and behavior. Prepubertal patients may have arrested sexual maturation (APA Guidelines for Eating Disorders, 1993).

Anorexia nervosa is characterized by willful and purposeful behavior directed toward losing weight, weight loss, preoccupation with body weight and food, peculiar pattern of handling food, intense fear of gaining weight, disturbance of body image, and amenorrhea. Bulimia means binge eating, which is defined as eating more food than most people in similar circumstances and in a similar period of time. There is a strong sense of losing control (Sadock and Sadock, 2000). Patients with anorexia nervosa are at high risk of developing a comorbid psychiatric illness. They have a high rate of major depression, anxiety disorders, obsessive-compulsive disorders, and social phobias. Gleaves, Eberenz, and May (1998), in a sample of 294 women diagnosed as suffering either from anorexia nervosa or bulimia, found that 52% reported current symptomatology consistent with PTSD and that the severity of PTSD symptomatology was unrelated to either type or eating disorder or severity of either anorexia or bulimia.

Patients with bulimia nervosa frequently suffer from major depression, substance abuse disorders, and personality disorders (Sadock and Sadock, 2000). Hypoactive sexual desire and sexual difficulties have also been identified in these populations (APA Guideline 1993). Physicians should be aware of and consider sexual dysfunction as a comorbidity in these patients; unless the basic cause is adequately treated, every effort to treat the dysfunction will be a waste of time.

Sexual behavior may be altered by physical conditions affecting the individual, and likewise general medical conditions can be affected by sexual behavior. Among the physical complaints more commonly encountered are high blood pressure, diabetes, cardiovascular disorders, neurological illness, and chronic pelvic pain among others.

Special attention should be paid to a very common condition in women known as chronic pelvic pain. Complaints may focus on the reproductive organ, urological, musculoskeletal-neurological, gastrointestinal, or myofascial. A psychological component is a factor, whether as an antecedent event or presenting as depression as result of the pain (Carter, 1998). Pelvic pain can also be secondary to psychogenic causes, but the pain should not be attributed to psychological causes unless a thorough evaluation has excluded organic causes (Sadock and Sadock, 2000). Chronic pelvic pain may have a deleterious effect over the sexual life of the patient and her partner; therefore, in addition to the physical treatment, patients should receive sufficient psychological support to overcome the effects of the condition and to assist them with underlying psychological disorders, including depression (Carter, 1998, Reiter 1998).

Risky Behaviors Associated with STIs and AIDS

Peter Piot, in his introductory report on the global AIDS epidemic, noted that the 1991 estimates for the decade were for 9 million people infected and 5 million dead in Sub-Saharan Africa. These estimates were a three-fold underestimation. AIDS is a development crisis and in some parts of the world is rapidly becoming a security crisis as well. There is now compelling evidence that the trend in HIV infection will have a profound impact on future rates of infant, child, and maternal mortality, life expectancy, and economic growth. Piot called the attention to the need to support community participation and targeting interventions to those who are most vulnerable, including young people before they become sexually active. The situation described by Piot is not unique to underdeveloped countries; similar trends are being described in the developed world.

Hoffman, Klein, Eber, and Crosby (2000) said that recent trends in the progression of the AIDS epidemic in the United States indicate that women's rates of acquiring HIV are escalating more rapidly than are men's. In recent years, strong suggestive evidence has arisen to suggest that women who use crack cocaine are at an elevated risk for acquiring HIV, probably as a result of their involvement in high-risk sexual behaviors. The data revealed that the women who used crack with the greatest frequency and the greatest intensity were the most heavily involved in risky sexual behaviors. However, some mention also needs to be made that a woman may not have complete control of her sexual activities and may not be able to insist on condom use in heterosexual contacts.

However, Hines, Snowden, and Graves (1998) said that African-American women when highly acculturated were more likely to engage in risky sexual behavior, including having multiple partners and not using a condom consistently. Alcohol use proved related to risky sexual behavior when considered in conjunction with respondents' level of acculturation.

Simon, Thometz, Bunch, et al. (1999) studied the prevalence of unprotected sex among men with AIDS in Los Angeles County. Of 617 men interviewed, 29% reported unprotected sex in the past year. The prevalence of unprotected sex was highest among men under 30 years of age (43%) and those who had first learned of their HIV-positive status less than 12 months prior to interview (44%). Of these, 22% reported unprotected insertive anal sex and 27% unprotected receptive anal sex. Of these, 53% reported unprotected vaginal sex and 18% unprotected anal sex.

The predictors of the intention to use condoms with new sexual partners have been examined with a sample of heterosexual adult females and males ($n = 711$) recruited through various channels. A substantial part of the sample had engaged in risky sexual behavior. Predictors were based on various theoretical models. Compared with men, women were in general more aware of the risks of AIDS and perceived fewer barriers to using condoms; but they also perceived less support for condom use among potential new partners.

Ventura-Filipe and Newman (1998) found that a lower proportion of HIV-positive respondents engaged in sexual contact with regular female partners ($p < .01$) and in vaginal intercourse with this type of partner ($p < .01$). A lower proportion of HIV-positive respondents engaged in overall sexual activity ($p < .001$) and reported lower frequency of penetrative sexual practices ($p < .05$). A high level of condom use with female and male partners was identified, with no significant differences being found between the two serostatus groups. Some risky sexual behavior was identified, however, especially with regular partners, suggesting that some men were continuing to practice unsafe sex.

Fishbein (1998) asserts that there is a growing body of evidence that theory-based behavioral interventions can effectively reduce risky behaviors that can lead to the acquisition and transmission of STI/HIV.

Health educators should be aware of factors such as alcohol and drug consumption, education, serostatus and condom use that increase the likelihood of getting infected. Progress has been made modifying certain behaviors, but there is still a long way to go before the progression of STIs and AIDS comes to an end.

1.7.4. Social Problems and Sexual Health

Across all cultures there is an increase in the number of reported cases of sexual abuse, violence against women and children, abortion, prostitution, and other form of trade involving these groups. Sexual abuse refers to sexual behavior between a child and an adult or between two children when one of then is significantly older or uses coercion. The perpetrator or the victim may be of the same or opposite sex. The sexual behavior may include touching the breasts, buttock, and genitals and may also include exhibitionism, fellatio, cunnilingus, and penetration of the vagina or anus with sexual organs or objects. Sexual abuse may also refer to sexual exploitation of children—for instance, conduct or activities related to pornography depicting minors and promoting or trafficking in prostitution of minors (Sadock and Sadock, 2000).

Belsey (1993) estimated that the rate of presumed international child abuse and neglect of children under 5 years of age should be between 13 and 20 per 100,000 live births. On a more empirical basis, Normann, Tambs, and Magnus (1992) state that reported prevalence of sexual abuse in children in international publications varied from 4% to 67%.

In the USA, Hall, Sachs, Rayens, et al. (1993) studied low-income single mothers and found a prevalence of sexual abuse of 22%. In a community sample in Australia, Fleming (1997) found that 20% of women had experienced child sexual abuse. Virtually all perpetrators were male and usually knew the child; 41% were relatives. The median age difference from that of the abused individual was 24 years. In France, Choquet, Darves-Bornoz, Ledoux, et al. (1997) found a rate for rape of only 0.9% among girls and 0.6% among boys. Bisset and Hunter (1992) report that general practitioners in Scotland saw approximately 2.5 victims of child abuse per 1,000 per year for girls younger than 16 years old.

In spite of the different rates of child sexual abuse found in different locations, there is much consistency on the relationship between rape and health risks. Current sleep disturbances, depressive symptoms, mania, somatic complaints, neurovegetative features, tobacco consumption, other substance abuse, and behavior problems (running away, attempted suicide, stealing, and school absenteeism) significantly correlate with child abuse (Choquet et al., 1997; Hall, Sachs, Rayens, et al., 1993; Jarvis and Copelman, 1997; Levitan, Parikh, Lesage, et al., 1998; Young and Katz, 1998).

1.7.5. Violence

Violence is often related to many factors, including civil strife and conflict. Institutionalized forms (planned state policies) of sexualized violence may include war rapes, sexual torture, and genital cutting. Other forms of sexual violence or abuse include coercion to engage in unwanted sexual behaviors. This includes involuntary prostitution and sexual slavery. Methods of coercion may be emotional, financial, physical, or sociocultural. Rape and beatings of women by male relatives are common and considered to be unremarkable in many areas of the world. Involuntary abortions, forced sterilizations, and circumcision can also be viewed as forms of reproductive violence.

Throughout history, rape has been a part of war and civil strife. Systematic, repeated rapes of civilian and refugee women has occurred recently in Mozambique, Bosnia, Somalia, South Africa, and El Salvador. The United Nations' investigations of crimes against Vietnamese boat people showed that 39% of women had been abducted or raped by pirates while at sea. Sharp increases in rates of rape have been reported for Bangladesh, India, Malaysia, and South Africa. Estimates for South Africa placed the incidence of rape at 34 per 1000 women. Agger and Mimica (1996) found that 2%–6% of the women they interviewed in Bosnia-Herzegovina and Croatia reported rape and sexualized violence. The personal sequelae of rape can include physical and emotional trauma, depression, pregnancy, sexually transmitted infections, and death. The consequence of rape in societies where a young women's worth is equated with her virginity is ruinous; this is especially true where the victim rather than the perpetrator is held responsible for their virginity (Desjarlais, et al., 1995).

The goal of torture, as currently practiced in over a third of the world's nations, is the creation of fear and destruction of the basic humanity of the individual. Torture results in devastating psychological dysfunctions (Desjarlais et al., 1995). The prevalence of sexual torture is unknown; both physical and psychological torture can involve sexual assault. In a survey of 135 torture victims, Lunde (1981) found that 53% had been subjected to sexual torture. Forms of sexual torture include touching, stripping, rape, threats to rape or attempted rape, and injury or damage of the genitals (blows, electrical currents, cutting). The purpose of sexual torture is to destroy the survivor's sexuality. In sexualized torture it is characteristic for the torturers to attack sexual identity and reproductive abilities. Sequelae of sexual torture include physical damage to the genitals, feelings of asexuality, sexual problems, flashbacks, and a host of psychosomatic symptoms.

A few studies on the relationship of sex and violence have been recently conducted in several countries. Asencio (1999) describes how low-income, predominantly second-generation, mainland Puerto Rican male adolescents, through the use of gender-based social constructs such as "machos" and "sluts," justify violence by linking it to beliefs about gender roles, sexuality, and biology and thus perpetuate gender-role conformity, particularly heterosexual male dominance. In a similar vein, Wood, Maforah, and Jewkes (1998) found that adolescent women in South Africa had to submit to conditions and timing of sex defined by their male partners through the use of violence associated to constructions of love, intercourse, and entitlement. The legitimacy of coercive sexual experiences was reinforced by female peers who indicated that silence and submission was the appropriate response. Being beaten was such a common experience that some peers were said to perceive it to be an expression of love. Informants indicated that they did not terminate the relationships for several reasons, beyond peer pressure and the probability of being subjected to added abuse for trying to end a relationship. Teenagers said that they perceived that their partners loved them because they gave them gifts of clothing and money.

In Ethiopia, Mulugeta, Kassaye, and Berhane (1998) studied the prevalence and outcomes of sexual violence among female high school students. The prevalence of completed rape and attempted rape was 5% and 10%, respectively. A total of 85% of the rape victims were under 18 years of age. Sexual harassment was reported in 74% of female students. Among the girls who reported to be raped, 24% had vaginal discharge and 17% became pregnant. Social isolation, fear and phobia, hopelessness, and suicide attempts were reported in 33%, 19%, 22%, and 6% of rape victims, respectively. In Brazil as well, despite a growing interest in gender violence and reproductive health, institutional violence has received little attention. They report that 20.5% of women in their study had never talked about their sexual life with their partners; and 38.3% have had sexual intercourse against their will, including situations ranging from sexual harassment to rape, referred to by 12.3% of the women.

Frank, Bauer, Arican, Fincanci, and Iacopino (1999) found that although the Turkish Medical Association has deemed "virginity examinations" a form of gender-based violence, forensic physicians for both legal and social reasons often subject women in Turkey to such examinations. Some 45% of them had conducted such examinations for "social reasons," and more than half reported that at least 50% of patients undergo examinations against their will.

D'Augelli, Hershberger, and Pilkington (1998) found in Pennsylvania that three quarters of lesbian, gay, and bisexual youngsters, ages 14–21 had told at least one parent about their sexual orientation, more often the mother than the father. Those who had disclosed their preference reported verbal and physical abuse by family members and acknowledged more suicidality than those who had not come out to their families.

In addition, Garofalo, Wolf, Wissow, Woods, and Goodman (1999) in Massachusetts report that gender, age, race/ethnicity, sexual orientation, and a host of health-risk behaviors were associated with suicide attempts among high school students self-identified as gay, lesbian, bisexual, or not sure of their sexual orientation. Gay, lesbian, bisexual, or not-sure youth were 3.41 times more likely to report a suicide attempt. Sexual orientation has an independent association with suicide attempts for males, while for females the association of sexual orientation with suicidality may be mediated by drug use and violence/victimization behaviors.

1.7.6. Poverty

In addition to well-established cultural factors, there is little doubt that the powerful link between poverty and abuse of sexual/reproductive rights determines the course of life of countless women worldwide. The WHO estimates that over 60% of women in developing countries are undernourished and anemic. In developing economies, structural adjustment programs designed for development often have a disproportionately negative effect on women (Desjarlais, et al., 1995). And although poverty disrupts the very fabric of human essence and dignity for everyone it affects, it impacts on women and children most with long-lasting and irreparable psychophysiological effects. The concerted efforts by international agencies and governments to improve the living conditions of people living in poverty sheds rays of hope that not only legal and human rights, but also the lost human dignity, at least for some, will be one day restored.

1.7.7. Abortion

In all societies, through all time, abortion has been practiced. Although today 90% of the countries of the world allow legal abortions when the life of a woman is in danger, a great percentage of abortions are still practiced illegally or unsafely with dire consequences for maternal morbidity and mortality. Abortion is an important (and sometimes controversial) public health issue worldwide. A woman's right to abortion varies dramatically across national borders and can have significant albeit diverse religious connotations. "One child" national population control policies (state involuntary or forced abortions), forced sterilization, and sex-selective abortions (of female fetuses, as in China and India) can all be viewed as forms of violence against women but also against men.

Two recent studies identified the main causes of abortion in Brazil as being single, the absence of emotional support from a partner, being a working woman, failure of the contraceptive method employed, and experience of previous pregnancies, children, and abortions (de Souza, Cecatt, Ferreira, and Santos, 1999). The majority of pregnancies among adolescents are unwanted, with medical, psychological, and mainly social repercussions. The main immediate consequences of an unwanted pregnancy are induced abortion, lack of prenatal care, personal and family disruption, adoption, and abandonment (Pinto e Silva, 1998).

Abortions are largely underreported in surveys. In a recent study in the United States (Smith, Adler, and Tschann, 1999), adolescents were less willing to report abortion than some behaviors such as cigarette smoking, but they were more willing to report abortion than family income, oral sex, or anal sex. Major and Gramzow (1999) found that women who felt stigmatized by abortion were more likely to feel a need to keep it a secret from family and friends. Secrecy was related positively to suppressing thoughts of the abortion and negatively to disclosing abortion-related emotions to others. Greater thought suppression was associated with experiencing more intrusive thoughts of the abortion. However, most women report feelings of relief after an abortion, and descriptions of increased psychological and psychiatric disturbances after abortion are politically, rather than scientifically, based.

PART 2

COMPREHENSIVE DIAGNOSIS OF PERSONS WITH SEXUAL DISORDERS

General Considerations

2.1.1. Introduction

The first part of the knowledge base for the WPA Educational Program on Sexual Health has dealt with the conceptual bases of this field. As part of that, a multidimensional definition of sexual health has been proposed. This has been followed by other important general considerations, such as the importance of communication at multiple levels in sexual health and the cultural framework that supports the understanding and experience of life and health in general and sexual health in particular. Consequently, the planning, organization, and utilization of diagnostic assessment of persons experiencing sexual disorders, which is the subject of this part 2, must be informed by the broad conceptual framework articulated in part 1. The main objective of diagnosis is to plan treatment, which is presented and discussed in part 3.

Virginia Sadock (2000) has pointed out that "sexuality is determined by anatomy, physiology, psychology, the culture in which one lives, one's relationships with others, and developmental experiences throughout the life cycle. It includes the perception of being male or female and all those thoughts, feelings, and behaviors connected with sexual gratification and reproduction, including the attraction of one person to another" (p. 1577). Sexual disorders, like most psychiatric disorders, are multifactorial in their origin, since developmental, cultural, individual psychological, interactional, and biological forces operate in their causality; therefore, the assessment of the patient with a sexual disorder must be comprehensive in order to ensure a valid understanding of the factors operating in the clinical condition and consequently a competent approach to treatment.

The need for comprehensiveness is relevant not only to understanding sexual disorders but to the whole task of diagnosis in medicine in general and psychiatry in particular. Diagnosis is more than identifying a disorder (nosological diagnosis) or distinguishing one disorder from the other (differential diagnosis); diagnosis is the thorough understanding of what is going on in the mind and the body of the person who presents for care.

Consistent with these considerations, a set of principles for diagnostic evaluation and schemas for the diagnostic classification of persons experiencing sexual disorders are presented next. The procedures for assessment and diagnostic formulations, presented in this part, are consistent with current standard diagnostic systems, such as ICD-10 (WHO, 1992) and DSM-IV (American Psychiatric Association, 1994), as well as recent developments such as the WPA International Guidelines for Comprehensive Diagnostic Assessment (World Psychiatric Association, 2001; Mezzich, Berganza, et al., 2003).

2.1.2. Interviewing and Information Sources

The overall diagnostic process of the patient experiencing sexual disorders—as with any other psychiatric condition—has as its main purpose the gathering and proper recording of clinical data that informs an effective comprehensive treatment plan. Data gathering in psychiatry rests upon three main sources of clinical information, which complement each other, namely: (1) the direct interview of the patient; (2) additional or extended sources of information (live and documentary); and (3) supplemental psychological, biological, and social procedures (e.g., psychometric testing, penile echo doppler, and Rigiscan). Recently, a panel of experts from different parts of the world (World Psychiatric Association, 2001) reviewed the comprehensive assessment of the psychiatric patient and proposed a series of guidelines applicable in different clinical settings. These guidelines constitute the bases for the review that follows, concerning the assessment of the sexually disordered patient.

The assessment of human sexual behavior involves the clinician stepping into very critical and sensitive issues for the patient, such as social taboos, stigma, shame, and denial, frequently in fragile equilibrium. Therefore, the clinical encounter with the patient presenting with a sexual concern needs to be handled in a very thoughtful, respectful, and sensitive way. Clinicians assessing these patients must follow the basic principles of diagnostic interviewing and the highest ethical standards in the field. These include creating an appropriate atmosphere of trust and comfort for patients to feel at ease with the discussion of their problems. It also implies the empathic attunement of the clinician to the patient, in order to go beyond the mere uncovering of relevant information. The clinician must communicate to the patient a sense of respect and true understanding of his or her suffering because of the clinical condition and must take into account the cultural background upon which the patient complaints are presented. Additionally, whenever possible, the patient's partner should be included in the assessment process in a culturally informed manner.

The above-mentioned considerations have implications for education and training in psychiatry, sexology, and medicine in general. As a general rule, and based on empirical evidence concerning regular clinical handling of sexual disorders, it is recommended that educational and professional institutions and health care professionals and trainees do the following

1. Be comfortable enough with their understanding of human sexuality as to provide a supportive, nurturing, and nonjudgmental environment for relevant discussion of sexual issues with their patients (Cohen and Alfonso, 1997).
2. Always explore patient's sexuality and sexual disorders and allow the patient the opportunity to discuss his or her sexual concerns in a flexible and comfortable way (Parra and Hernandez, 1995).
3. Evaluate the sexually disordered patient using a biopsychosocial framework, since most sexual problems are generally affected by biological, psychological, intrapsy-

chic, interpersonal, social, cultural, and ethnic variables (Cohen and Alfonso, 1997).

4. Always explore comorbidities, including the presence of various sexual disorders, other mental disorders, other general medical disorders, and the consequences of medical interventions in order to ensure a competent handling of the clinical condition of the patient.

Patient Interview

It should be pointed out at the outset that in many cases in the field of sexual health (e.g., infertility, sexual dysfunctions, unconsummated marriages, and some cases of compulsive sexual behavior), it is not an individual but a couple who presents for care. In these cases, it is the couple, not the single individual, that must be interviewed at the very beginning of the assessment process. While patterns of clinical assessment of these conditions are likely to vary across the world (Lavee, 1991), the participation of the sexual partner and, when appropriate, the family should be encouraged.

Through the patient interview, the clinician records the clinical history, including the chief sexual complaint as well as any comorbid psychiatric or general medical existing condition the patient may present. Additionally, important information can be recorded concerning family, developmental, social, and general medical background. Through systematic anamnestic techniques, detailed accounts of the history and of the current status of symptoms are carried out, and a mental status examination of the patient is conducted.

The basic elements of a productive and smooth interviewing process include engaging the patient in a process that ought to proceed gracefully and harmoniously, in order to provide the appropriate conditions for an effective gathering of relevant information (see Shea, 1998). The skillful clinician, by listening attentively (Anderson and Lynch, 1996), helps the patient to feel at ease and creates a good rapport for trust and openness to prevail. Once the rapport is developed, the clinician must help the patient express his or her concerns and main needs from the health services in such a way that the patient feels truly understood. This implies using preferentially open-ended questions that allow the patient to elaborate on the issues that are of his or her primary concern.

The systematic and thorough review and collection of data concerning different areas of psychobiosocial functioning, of relevance for the main clinical concerns of the patient, must follow. In addition, this part of the interview allows the clinician to obtain a complete assessment of the patient's mental status and clinical manifestations at the time of the observation period. Although different formats can be followed to assess and record this critical aspect of the patient's functioning, the one proposed by Skodol, Shaffer, and Gurland (1997) seems comprehensive and clinically sound. The goal here is to reach a good description of the clinical condition, the main problems and assets of the patient, and the level of priority that each problem has in order to plan interventions accordingly. All this information should allow the clinician, the patient, and, as appropriate, the partner to agree on a consistent plan for further diagnostic or therapeutic procedures. Here, more focused and leading questions may be necessary during the interview of the patient, and the use of structured complementary assessment procedures may be advisable.

Toward the end of the interview, the clinician must engender a sense of hope and positive expectations. The objective is to make sure that the patient has felt understood in his or her needs and worries and that he or she is now prepared to proceed along the continuing clinical process. At the same time, the presentation of a formulation that respects and considers the perspectives of the patient, building upon cultural opportunities—as language barriers are overcome—becomes critical at this point. It is important to establish the necessary therapeutic tone for the treatment plan to be agreeable for both the patient and the clinician.

Discussion of sensitive topics such as sexual imagery and masturbation, if the patient does not bring them up directly and spontaneously, should only be initiated when an appropriate rapport has been developed. The appropriate evaluation of such topics may take more than a single session.

Extended Sources of Information

Other sources of clinical information include the review of past records and information provided by the family, the couple, the referring sources, and consultants that may evaluate on request different aspects of the clinical condition of the patient. In the field of sexual disorders, it seems obvious that the main additional source of information is the sexual partner. It seems common knowledge that sexual problems in one member of the sexual couple are likely to cause sexual or other psychiatric problems in the other (Cohen and Alfonso, 1997). These conditions are referred to as "relational sexual disorders" (see section 2.2.1.5).

These extended sources may corroborate, complement, or correct information provided by the patient. They are a critical source of data, especially in circumstances in which the patient may be hesitant to provide detailed or straightforward information because of shame, fear of disapproval by the therapist, or cultural constraints. The clinician must discuss with the patient the need to consult these sources and obtain his or her consent. Special attention must be paid to issues of confidentiality, especially in cultural settings in which requesting information may create the conditions for a damaging breach of privacy and confidentiality.

Finally, the clinician ought to remember that the perspective of these additional sources of information is precisely that: a perspective, and not the "real truth." Therefore, the clinician must treat this information with the same degree of thoughtfulness and critical attitude with which he or she has treated the data provided by the patient.

2.1.3. Supplementary Assessment Procedures

Supplementary assessment procedures are frequently used as ways of confirming diagnostic hypotheses raised by the interview and the extended sources of information during the initial contact with the patient. They may include psychopathological assessment instruments, biological tests and procedures, and neuropsychological tests. They may also involve the use of various self and observer-rating scales, diagnostic checklists, and semistructured and fully structured diagnostic interviews (Skodol and Bender, 2000), as well as consultations with other specialists for a comprehensive or specific diagnostic assessment of suspected general medical conditions. Additional areas that need to be assessed through such supplementary procedures are those indicating the level of psychosocial functioning of the individual patient, as well as the social context in which the clinical condition takes place and is to be treated. Finally, and in line with developments in the area of psychiatric assessment, the patient's own perception of the quality of his or her life and the impact of the clinical problems upon such quality of life, must be carefully assessed.

Critical aspects concerning the use of supplementary assessment procedures, especially when assessing the sexually disordered person, include the need to be comprehensive and to ensure bio-psycho-social coverage of the clinical condition. On the other hand, well-trained evaluators must apply tests and procedures, and the psychometric properties of the tests employed must be clearly known (for a review, see Blacker and Endicott, 2000). This should guarantee that the results are reliable and useful for the clinical purposes intended. Finally, as in many other aspects of the assessment process, the cultural validation of these procedures must be carefully assessed (Rubio-Stipec, Hicks, and Tsuang, 2000), so that normative behaviors or conditions influenced by culture are not registered as pathology.

In summary, the evaluation of the person experiencing sexual disorders, as in the case of any other conditions presented for clinical care, must be performed under the highest professional standards and must be comprehensive. Given the nature of most of the sexual problems, their association with other comorbid conditions, and their impact upon the general functioning of the individual, the assessment process must include a full description of bio-psycho-social factors and perspectives critical to the understanding of the clinical condition and its treatment.

The diagnosis of a sexual disorder is primarily based on a clinical interview. However, in many cases it can be useful to add quantitative and qualitative assessment instruments and procedures. This provides additional systematic and supporting data to the diagnostic enterprise and contributes to strengthening the link between clinical work, and research, advancing the theoretical development of the field.

In recent years, researchers have made great efforts, all over the world, to investigate human sexuality and enhance the scientific bases of the field. This has led to the development of a good number of assessment instruments. Some of these new instruments are brief and self-administered and can be used in clinical settings, in research, and in epidemiological studies. Without pretending to be exhaustive, a listing of the most illustrative instruments and the areas they are concerned with follows.

Questionnaires and Scales for Sexual Dysfunctions

The International Index of Erectile Function (IIEF) (Rosen et al., 1997) and the Female Sexual Function Index (FSFI) (Rosen et al., 2000) can be easily used by health professionals to complement diagnosis and to detect treatment-related changes, although their employment is primarily for clinical research. Both IIEF and FSFI, as screening instruments, focus on current sexual functioning.

The IIEF has had a linguistic validation in several languages. In this fifteen-item questionnaire, five factors or response domains were identified: (1) erectile function, (2) orgasmic function, (3) sexual desire, (4) intercourse satisfaction, and (5) overall satisfaction.

Construct validity, test reliability, and detection of treatment outcome are adequate. Limitations of the instrument are the focus on current sexual functioning, the superficial assessment of nonerectile components of sexual response, and the limited assessment of couple relationship. Moreover, as the authors indicate, "Although the IIEF provides a broad measure of sexual function across five domains, it should be viewed as an adjunct to, rather than a substitute for, a detailed sexual history" (Rosen et al., 1997, p. 828).

The FSFI recognizes the need for a subjective criterion in defining sexual dysfunction and determines, through the nineteen-item answers, five separate domains: (1) desire / arousal, (2) lubrication, (3) orgasm, (4) satisfaction and (5) pain. The first domain can be valued independently as two measurable dimensions: peripheral response (arousal) and central, subjective response (desire) to sexual stimulation. Arousal and desire have a considerable overlap, consistent with clinical observation and contrasting with findings in studies of sexual dysfunction in men.

The assessment of sexual dysfunction in heterosexual couples or heterosexual individuals may be attempted through instruments such as the Golombok Rust Inventory for Sexual Satisfaction (GRISS) (Rust and Golombok, 1986a, 1986b). Two separate forms, one for women and the other for men, include twenty-eight items. The female subscales include (1) infrequency, (2) noncommunication, (3) female dissatisfaction, (4) female avoidance, (5) female non-sensuality, (6) vaginismus, and (7) anorgasmia. The male subscales include (1) impotence, (2) premature ejaculation, (3) male nonsensuality, (4) male avoidance, (5) male dissatisfaction, (6) infrequency, and (7) noncommunication. Overall scores, for women and men separately, provide a profile of quality of sexual functioning within a relationship. This brief and easy instrument normally takes between four and ten minutes to complete. It can be used to identify the areas of a couple's sexual relationship that need to be improved, assess improvement because of therapy, and compare the efficacy of different treatment methods. For larger studies the procedure can be computerized, using the score instructions in the handbook (Rust and Golombok, 1986a).

Another questionnaire widely used is the Sexual History Form (SHF) (Nowinski and LoPiccolo, 1979). This instrument, through twenty-eight items, evaluates the frequency of sexual activity, desire, arousal, orgasm, pain, and overall sexual satisfaction for women and men. It has been used for determining outcome and for the longitudinal assessments of the impact of chronic illness on sexuality (Schover et al., 1990, 1995). SHF is also available in French (Formulaire d'Histoire Sexuelle). A limitation of the SHF for research has been the lack of reliable and valid global scores that could measure differences in overall sexual function between groups and across time. To enhance the utility of SHF, Creti et al. (1987, 1998) developed a new form of the same instrument with forty-six items with a new scoring system that generates a single summary score: global sexual functioning. This new form seems to have good temporal stability, reliability, and validity and is responsive to changes secondary to therapeutic interventions.

Examples of other interesting approaches to sexual history taking are those offered by Cohen and Alfonso (1997) and Hernandez-Serrano, Parra, and Flores (2005).

There are many other instruments to investigate sexual satisfaction in individuals and couples, and some of them can be found in the *Handbook of Sexuality-Related Measures*

(Davis et al., 1998). In this handbook, organized in alphabetical order from abortion to victimization, more than 200 instruments useful to measuring sexuality-related constructs are discussed. Some of them are described only briefly or include only a sampling of items because the instrument is restricted by copyright regulations or sold commercially. References and addresses to obtain the materials are given.

Biological Procedures

For the comprehensive assessment of patients with psychosexual disorders, physical evaluation may be considered. In addition to the routine physical exam and the basic laboratory tests, there are specialized procedures that may be necessary in order to complement the evaluation of the biological aspects relevant to sexual disorders. For instance, patients complaining of erectile dysfunctions may be suffering from undisclosed diabetes and its complications, which require specific assessment. It is common practice in this field to start with the least invasive and least expensive procedures and resort to more complex ones when really needed. These procedures should be used when history, physical examination, and laboratory tests suggest the need for further procedures. Some of these laboratory and hormonal assessment procedures are listed below:

FOR MEN:
Dihydrotestosterone
Prolactin

FOR WOMEN:
Estrogen-progesterone-oxytocin
Prolactin
Luteinizing Hormone (LH) and (FSH)

FOR BOTH:
Free testosterone
Blood sugar
Liver enzymes
Kidney function
Thyroid function

OTHER SPECIALIZED PROCEDURES:
Echo Doppler and Duplex
Measure of vibratory sensations
Cavernosometry and cavernosography
Arteriography
Rigiscan
Measure of penile and vaginal responses under exposure to erotic stimuli
Neurological and prostatic studies
Electromyography

2.1.4. Comprehensive Diagnostic Formulation

The need for a comprehensive approach to evaluation and diagnosis is, of course, not restricted to the case of sexual disorders. Such need has been articulated, in fact, for a number of disorders and even for the whole of psychopathology and human disease (Engel, 1977). The first comprehensive diagnostic models were termed multidimensional or multiaxial and were applied to general medicine (College of American Pathologists, 1977) and psychiatry (for a review see Mezzich, 1979). They attempted to encourage the clinician to pay systematic attention to key informational domains by organizing the evaluation and diagnostic formulation along axes such as syndromes, etiology, adaptive functioning, stress, and supports. Eventually, with various degrees of visibility, multiaxial models have been incorporated within contemporary classification systems such as the International Classification for Oncology (Percy, van Holten and Muir, 1990), the mental health component of ICD-10 (World Health Organization, 1992; Janca et al, 1996a), the American Psychiatric Association's DSM-IV (American Psychiatric Association, 1994), and the Cuban Glossary of Psychiatry (Otero, 1999).

More recently, a comprehensive diagnostic model has been designed at the core of the World Psychiatric Association's *International Guidelines for Diagnostic Assessment (IGDA)* (Mezzich, Berganza, von Cranach, et al., for the World Psychiatric Association, 2003). This diagnostic model encompasses a Standardized Multiaxial Formulation (I. Illness; II. Disabilities; III. Contextual Factors; and IV. Quality of Life) and an Idiographic or Personalized Formulation.

Towards a Comprehensive Diagnostic Approach for Sexual Health

As part of the development of a World Psychiatric Association (WPA) Educational Program on Sexual Health, an International Survey on Human Sexuality (Mezzich and Hernandez-Serrano, 1999; see appendix 5) was conducted in 1999, with the participation of 187 qualified psychiatrists and 51 qualified sexologists from 75 different countries. Among its most prominent findings was the need for more professional training as well as patient and public education. Also mentioned as key factors for dealing with sexual health were the comorbidity of sexual disorders, relationship issues, cultural, social, and environmental factors, and ethical concerns.

From the findings of this survey and the informed judgment of expert panels meeting in New York and Buenos Aires in 1999 and 2000, the need emerged for a comprehensive diagnostic approach to the evaluation of individuals experiencing sexual disorders. The components of such a comprehensive diagnostic model follow:

FIRST COMPONENT: STANDARDIZED MULTIAXIAL FORMULATION
I. Clinical Disorders: (A) Sexual Disorders (Sexual Dysfunctions, Paraphilias, and Gender Identity Disorders) and (B) Other Mental and General Medical Disorders
II. Disabilities (social functioning)
III. Contextual Factors
IV. Quality of Life

SECOND COMPONENT: IDIOGRAPHIC OR PERSONALIZED FORMULATION (this includes what is unique and meaningful as jointly perceived and formulated by the clinician, the patient, the couple, and the family):

I.   Contextualized Clinical Problems
II. Patient's Positive Factors
III. Expectations for Restoration and Promotion of Health

A comprehensive diagnostic model for sexual health that covers sexual disorders, their mental and general medical comorbidities, relationship and contextual factors, quality of life, and a complementary idiographic or personalized formulation is presented in the following chapters. It is hoped that it will enhance scientific accuracy, therapeutic effectiveness, and ethical aspirations in this crucial area of human health.

Multiaxial Diagnostic Formulation

2.2.1. Axis I.A: Diagnostic Classification of Sexual Disorders

2.2.1.1. Introduction

As stated earlier, phenomenology of disorders currently permeates the way most noso-logical systems organize the classification of psychiatric disorders in general and sexual disorders in particular. However, the fundamental paradigm of this organization is syn-dromic and, to a lesser extent, etiological. Consequently, some degree of flexibility in efforts to reach consensus about issues of validity and reliability becomes necessary.

In the more specific field of the classification of the sexual dysfunctions, a some-what more agreeable paradigm has been in use since Masters and Johnson (1966) pro-posed it and the modifications by Kaplan (1974) and the work group of DSM-III were incorporated. More recently, concerns about the suitability of the classification for mul-ticultural populations are emerging (Davis, 1998).

Since sexual practices vary so much across sociocultural groups, defining sexual nor-mative behavior is a very complex task. Thus, it becomes unclear when and upon what organizing principle one can start classifying sexual "perversions," "deviations," or "dis-orders," the evolving terminology under which these clinical conditions have been known through the times. It is even less clear how the criteria for defining a specific sex-ual behavior as "perverted," "deviant," or "disordered" came about. In explaining their rationale to make recommendations to the "Options Book" for DSM-IV, the Work Group on Sexual Disorders "found limited published data supporting the current diagnoses and criteria sets" (Schmidt et al, 1996, p. 1082). This lack of consistent empirical evidence made it difficult for the Work Group to propose "data-based" recommendations for changes to the DSM-III-R schema. It is interesting, however, that several recommenda-tions proposed by the Work Group were intended to enhance DSM-IV's compatibility with ICD-10.

DSM-IV classifies sexual and gender identity disorders along three main categories: (1) sexual dysfunctions, (2) paraphilias, and (3) gender identity disorders, leaving a fourth residual category, Sexual Disorder Not Otherwise Specified, for coding sexual disturbances that do not meet the criteria of the three above-mentioned conditions. Concerning the sexual dysfunctions, DSM-IV lists, besides the residual category of Sexual Dysfunction Not Otherwise Specified, six different types, namely, (1) sexual desire disorders, (2) sexual arousal disorders, (3) orgasmic disorders, (4) sexual pain disorders, (5) sexual dysfunction due to a general medical condition, and (6) substance-induced sexual dysfunction. In the area of paraphilias, DSM-IV offers criteria for eight specific conditions and a residual one. Finally, it provides criteria for two categories of gender identity disorder, one for children and one for adolescents or adults, as well as for a residual one.

In ICD-10, the equivalent of the DSM-IV Sexual Disorders section is distributed along a different structure. First, a three-digit category, F52 Sexual dysfunction not caused by organic disorder or disease, is one of the seven that constitute the two-digit section F5 Behavioral syndromes associated with physiological disturbances and physical factors. The other two categories concerning sexual function and identity, F64 Gender identity disorder, and F65 Disorders of sexual preference (the term employed for the paraphilias), are incorporated into the two-digit section F6 Disorders of adult personality and behavior. Additionally, ICD-10 includes the category F66, Psychological and behavioral disorders associated with sexual development and orientation, which includes the four-digit category F66.1, Egodystonic sexual orientation. The above comparison reflects some degree of agreement concerning definitions and organization of sexual disorders between ICD-10 and DSM-IV systems, but also some remaining important differences.

In this knowledge base, four main categories of sexual disorders are described: (1) sexual dysfunctions, (2) paraphilias, (3) gender identity disorders, and (4) categories requiring further study. The description of the first three categories follows the criteria proposed by the most visible international classification systems. The fourth group of disorders refers to conditions that are important in daily clinical work but that have not been included as part of official nosological systems. Table 2.2.1 summarizes some of the similarities and differences across classification systems of sexual disorders in different parts of the world.

2.2.1.2. Sexual Dysfunctions

According to ICD-10, "sexual dysfunction covers the various ways in which an individual is unable to participate in a sexual relationship as he or she would wish. Sexual response is a psychosomatic process and both psychological and somatic processes are usually involved in the causation of sexual dysfunctions" (p. 355). Although it does not make it explicit, the ICD-10 definition of sexual dysfunctions is in line with the sexual response cycle that Masters and Johnson originally proposed (1966, 1980). Masters, Johnson, and Kolodny (1986) indicate that "Human sexual response is multidimensional, with input from feelings and thoughts, learning and language, personal and cultural values, and many other sources combining with our biological reflexes to create a total experience" (pp. 55–56).

In addition to its clinical diagnostic guidelines, ICD-10 provides strict research diagnostic criteria for the whole section of the sexual dysfunctions (World Health Organization, 1993). According to this system, four general conditions must be fulfilled for a sexual dysfunction to be diagnosed:

Table 2.2.1 ORGANIZATION OF THE SEXUAL DISORDERS ACCORDING TO CURRENT NOSOLOGICAL SYSTEMS

Variable	Nosological System			
	DSM-IV	ICD-10	Third Cuban Glossary (GC-III)	CCMD-3 Chinese classification
Number of main categories	3	4	4	4
Title for the entire group of disorders	Sexual and gender identity disorders	No unitary term due to way in which the disorders are organized	No unitary term due to way in which the disorders are organized	
Main categories for sexual disorders	1. Sexual dysfunctions 2. Paraphilias 3. Gender identity disorder 4. Sexual disorders not otherwise specified	1. Sexual dysfunction not caused by organic disorder or disease 2. Disorders of sexual preference 3. Gender identity disorders 4. Psychological and behavioral disorders associated with sexual development and orientation	1. Sexual dysfunction of nonorganic origin 2. Disorders of sexual inclination 3. Sexual identity disorders 4. Psychological and behavioral disorders of sexual development and orientation	1. Sexual dysfunction, not caused by organic disorder or disease 2. Disorders of sexual preference 3. Gender identity disorders 4. Psychological and behavioral disorders associated with sexual development and orientation
Total number of conditions	31	29	29	?

G1. The subject is unable to participate in a sexual relationship, as he or she would wish.

G2. The dysfunction occurs frequently, but may be absent on some occasions.

G3. The dysfunction has been present for at least 6 months.

G4. The dysfunction is not entirely attributable to any of the other mental and behavioral disorders in ICD-10, physical disorders (such as endocrine disorders) or drug treatment.

Vroege, Gijs, and Hengeveld (1998) reviewed the changes in the classification of sexual dysfunctions from DSM-III to DSM-IV and ICD-10 and proposed a schema to be considered for ICD-11 and DSM-V. These authors (p. 334) base their analysis of the schemas proposed by the taxonomic systems on two principles: "The extent to which: (1) in the diagnostic criteria due weight is given to the physiological and psychological aspects, and to the different phases of the sexual response cycle; and (2) these disorders apply to people of different sexes and sexual orientations, and to problems arising while using different sexual techniques."

Several concepts underlying classificatory efforts of the sexual dysfunctions become evident to the authors' analysis of the various diagnostic systems. First, they mention the issue of psychogenic versus organic (biogenic) causality, which seems to fluctuate through the years. In this respect, DSM-IV and ICD-10 differ considerably. While DSM-IV introduced two categories to address the organic component: "sexual dysfunction due to a general medical condition" and "substance-induced sexual dysfunction", ICD-10 maintains a single category of "sexual dysfunctions not caused by organic disorder or disease." This difference is of great nosological importance since there is no section in the complete taxonomic schema of the "family of classifications" of ICD-10 in which the specific impact of organic pathology upon the sexual functioning of the individual, or the couple, becomes explicit. Modifications to the taxonomic organization of this section have been proposed in order to make explicit the effect of organic variables upon the sexual functioning of the individual and the couple.

A second important concept is the issue of distress, as an inclusion criterion. DSM-IV requires that "the disturbance causes marked distress or interpersonal difficulty" (criterion B) to make a diagnosis of sexual dysfunction. ICD-10, on the other hand, not only does not make it explicit that the individual must suffer marked distress to receive a diagnosis of a sexual dysfunction but does not include interpersonal difficulty as a requirement for diagnosis. ICD-10's definition states simply that "sexual dysfunction covers the various ways in which an individual is unable to participate in a sexual relationship as he or she would wish" (WHO, 1992a, p. 355).

A third important issue concerns excessive sexual drive or desire. The DSM system has not considered this a diagnostic category, while ICD-10 introduces it without a specific diagnostic criteria set. As the concept of "sexual addiction" acquires significance in modern times, and as more empirical evidence accumulates to support its diagnostic reliability and validity (Sadock, 1995), this category becomes an important one to be considered for the new official schemas of the future.

Concerning orgasmic disorders, Vroege's group argues that in the last three versions of DSM, in contrast to ICD-10, a differentiation has been made between male and female orgasmic disorder. Thus, when a male patient does have an orgasm, but not an ejaculation, his disorder must go to the residual categories (Other sexual dysfunction, not caused by organic disorder or disease, in ICD-10; or Sexual dysfunction not otherwise specified, in DSM-IV). If, on the other hand, this same male patient has an ejaculation without the subjective enjoyment, it will go to "lack of sexual enjoyment" in ICD-10, but to the residual category in DSM-IV. Premature ejaculation remains along all systems. They finally call attention to the existence of a premature form of orgasm in females. This diagnosis is classified in the "Orgasmic dysfunction" by ICD-10 and in the "female orgasmic disorder" of DSM-IV.

Among sexual desire disorders, ICD-10 also has a category on "excessive sexual drive," which Vroege et al. (1998) propose should be changed to "excessive or hyperactive sexual desire." This group considers the surplus value of differentiating between the orgasmic disorders of men and women to be minimal. For them it is more important that the grouping of disorders of these phases do differentiate between the physiological and the psychological aspects of the sexual response. In their opinion, the DSM-IV "female sexual arousal disorder" and "male erectile dysfunction" could be merged into the category "genital arousal disorder." For cases in which only the subjective sense of sexual excitement is impaired, this could be supplemented with the category "sexual excitement disorder." In the same vein, the orgasmic disorders could be divided into "orgasmic disorder" and "anhedonic orgasm."

Diagnostic Criteria of the Specific Sexual Dysfunctions

F52.0.   Lack or Loss of Sexual Desire

Loss of sexual desire is the principal problem and is not secondary to other sexual difficulties, such as erectile failure or dyspareunia. It includes frigidity and hypoactive sexual desire disorder. Research diagnostic criteria include the following:

a. The general criteria for sexual dysfunction (F52) must be met.
b. Lack or loss of sexual desire, manifest by diminution of seeking out sexual cues, of thinking about sex with associated feelings of desire or appetite, or of sexual fantasies.
c. Lack of interest in initiating sexual activity either with partner or as solitary masturbation, resulting in a frequency of activity clearly lower than expected, taking into account age and context, or in a frequency very clearly reduced from previous much higher levels.

F52.1.   Sexual Aversion and Lack of Sexual Enjoyment

Either the prospect of sexual interaction produces sufficient fear or anxiety that sexual activity is avoided (sexual aversion) or sexual responses occur normally and orgasm is experienced but there is a lack of appropriate pleasure (lack of sexual enjoyment). Includes sexual anhedonia. Two variants of this disorder are considered in ICD-10:

F52.10.   Sexual Aversion

ICD-10 does not offer a clinical description of this disorder. However, it offers research diagnostic criteria. According to these, for a diagnosis of sexual aversion disorder to be made, it requires the following:

a. The general criteria for sexual dysfunction (F52) must be met.
b. The prospect of sexual interaction with a partner produces sufficient aversion, fear or anxiety that sexual activity is avoided or, if it occurs, is associated with strong negative feelings and an inability to experience any pleasure.
c. The aversion is not a result of performance anxiety (reaction to previous failure of sexual response).

F52.11. Lack of Sexual Enjoyment

No clinical criteria are provided; however, research diagnostic criteria indicate that for this diagnosis to be made the following must occur:

a. The general criteria for sexual dysfunction (F52) must be met.
b. Genital response (orgasm and/or ejaculation) occurs during sexual stimulation but is not accompanied by pleasurable sensations or feelings of pleasant excitement.
c. There is no manifest and persistent fear or anxiety during sexual activity (see F52.10, sexual aversion).

F52.2. Failure of Genital Response

The principal problem in men is erectile dysfunction (difficulty in developing or maintaining an erection suitable for satisfactory intercourse). In women, the principal problem is vaginal dryness or failure of lubrication. It includes female sexual arousal, male erectile disorder, and psychogenic impotence. It excludes impotence of organic origin. The research diagnostic criteria provided for this disorder by ICD-10 requires for this diagnosis to be made that the following occur:

a. The general criteria for sexual dysfunction (F52) must be met.

In addition, for men:
b. Erection, sufficient for intercourse fails to occur when intercourse is attempted. The dysfunction takes one of the following forms:
   1. Full erection occurs during the early stages of lovemaking but disappears or declines when intercourse is attempted (before ejaculation if it occurs).
   2. Erection does occur, but only at times when intercourse is not being considered.
   3. Partial erection, insufficient for intercourse, occurs, but not full erection.
   4. No penile tumescence occurs at all.

In addition, for women:
c. There is failure of genital response, experienced as failure of vaginal lubrication, together with inadequate tumescence of the labia. The dysfunction takes one of the following forms:
   1. General lubrication fails in all relevant circumstances.
   2. Lubrication may occur initially but fails to persist for long enough to allow comfortable penile entry.
   3. Situational: lubrication occurs only in some situations (e.g. with one partner but not another, or during masturbation, or when vaginal intercourse is not being contemplated).

F52.3.   Orgasmic Dysfunction

Orgasm either does not occur or is markedly delayed. It includes inhibited orgasm (male and female) and psychogenic anorgasmy. ICD-10's research diagnostic criteria require the following for the diagnosis to be made:

a.   The general criteria for sexual dysfunction (F52) must be met.
b.   There is orgasmic dysfunction (either absence or marked delay of orgasm) which takes one of the following forms:
   1.   Orgasm has never been experienced in any situation.
   2.   Orgasmic dysfunction has developed after a period of relatively normal response:
      (a)   General: orgasmic dysfunction occurs in all situations and with any partner.
      (b)   Situational:

For women: orgasm does occur in certain situations (e.g. when masturbating or with certain partners).

For men: one of the following can be applied: (i) Orgasm only occurs during sleep, never during the waking state; (ii) orgasm never occurs in the presence of the partner; (iii) orgasm occurs in the presence of the partner but not during intercourse.

F52.4.   Premature Ejaculation

Premature ejaculation or rapid ejaculation is the inability to control ejaculation sufficiently for both partners to enjoy sexual interaction. Research diagnostic criteria demand the following for this diagnosis to be made:

a.   The general criteria for sexual dysfunction (F52) must be met.
b.   There is an inability to delay ejaculation sufficiently to enjoy lovemaking, manifest as either of the following:
   1.   Occurrence of ejaculation before or very soon after the beginning of intercourse (if a time limit is required: before or within 15 seconds of the beginning of intercourse).
   2.   Ejaculation occurs in the absence of sufficient erection to make intercourse possible.
c.   The problem is not the result of prolonged abstinence from sexual activity.

F52.5.   Non-organic Vaginismus

Non-organic vaginismus is spasm of the pelvic floor muscles that surround the vagina, causing occlusion of the vaginal opening. Penile entry is either impossible or painful. It includes psychogenic vaginismus, and it excludes organic vaginismus (N94.2). Research diagnostic criteria demand for a diagnosis of this condition the following:

a.   The general criteria for sexual dysfunction (F52) must be made.
b.   There is spasm of the perivaginal muscles, sufficient to prevent entry or make it uncomfortable. The dysfunction takes one of the following forms:

1. Normal response has never been experienced.
2. Vaginismus has developed after a period of relatively normal response: (a) When vaginal entry is not attempted, a normal sexual response may occur; (b) any attempt at sexual contact leads to generalized fear and efforts to avoid vaginal entry (e.g., spasm of the adductor muscles of the thighs).

F52.6.   Non-organic Dyspareunia

Dyspareunia (pain during sexual intercourse) occurs in both women and men. It can often be attributed to local pathology and should then properly be categorized under the pathological condition. This category is to be used only if there is no primary non-organic sexual dysfunction (e.g., vaginismus or vaginal dryness). It includes psychogenic dyspareunia, and it excludes organic dyspareunia (N94.1). The research diagnostic criteria of the international system require the following for a diagnosis to be made:

a. The general criteria for sexual dysfunction (F52) must be met.

In addition, for women:
b. Pain is experienced at the entry of the vagina, either throughout sexual intercourse or only when deep thrusting of the penis occurs.
c. The disorder is attributable to vaginismus or failure of lubrication; dyspareunia of organic origin should be classified according to the underlying disorder.

In addition, for men:
a. Pain or discomfort is experienced during sexual response. (The timing of pain and the exact localization should be carefully recorded.)
b. The discomfort is not the result of local physical factors. If physical factors are found, the dysfunction should be classified elsewhere.

F52.7.   Excessive Sexual Drive

It includes nymphomania, and satyriasis. No clinical of research diagnostic criteria are provided by ICD-10; however, the system recommends that researchers studying this category are recommended to design their own criteria.

Two residual categories are included within the ICD-10 system:

F52.8   Other Sexual Dysfunction Not Caused by Organic Disorder or Disease

F52.9   Unspecified Sexual Dysfunction not Caused by Organic Disorder or Disease

The classification of sexual dysfunctions is presented in Table 2.2.2 according to the phases of the sexual response cycle. Additionally, sexual pain disorders are included.

2.2.1.3. Paraphilias or Disorders of Sexual Preference

Paraphilia is a technical word introduced in official psychiatric nosology by DSM-III to substitute for the terms previously used to describe abnormal patterns of sexual

Table 2.2.2 Classification of Sexual Dysfunctions according to Sexual Response Phases (Vroege, Gijs, and Hengeveld, 1998)

Group of Disorders	DSM-III	DSM-III-R	DSM-IV	ICD-10	Suggested Revisions
Sexual desire disorders	Inhibited sexual desire	Hypoactive sexual desire disorder	Hypoactive sexual desire disorder	Lack or loss of sexual desire	Diminished sexual desire
	—	Sexual aversion disorder	Sexual aversion disorder	Sexual aversion	Sexual aversion
	—	—	—	Excessive sexual drive	Excessive sexual desire
Sexual arousal disorders	Inhibited sexual excitement	Female sexual arousal disorder	Female sexual arousal disorder	Failure of genital response	Genital arousal disorder
	—	Male erectile disorder	Male erectile disorder	—	—
	—	—	—	Lack of sexual enjoyment	Sexual excitement disorder
Orgasm disorders	Inhibited female orgasm	Inhibited female orgasm	Female orgasmic disorder	Orgasmic dysfunction	Orgasmic disorder
	Inhibited male orgasm	Inhibited male orgasm	Male erectile disorder	—	—
	—	—	—	Lack of sexual enjoyment	Anhedonic orgasm
	Premature ejaculation	Premature ejaculation	Premature ejaculation	Premature ejaculation	Ejaculation disorder / Premature orgasm
Sexual pain disorders	Functional dyspareunia	Dyspareunia	Dyspareunia (not due to a general medical condition)	Nonorganic dyspareunia	Dyspareunia
	Functional vaginismus	Vaginismus	Vaginismus (not due to a general medical condition)	Nonorganic vaginismus	Vaginismus

preference. Such terms as "perversions" and "deviations" used in previous classification systems (e.g., ICD-9; World Health Organization, 1977) had reached pejorative, stigmatizing connotations impairing their use for purposes of diagnosis and treatment in medicine.

Sexual behaviors that deviate from intuitive notions of normality create uneasiness in large segments of the population (Levine, 2000). The very nature of these disorders ranging from the very bizarre to almost normative sexual behavior, or from the harmless to the obviously damaging to self or others, make issues of definition and classification a complicated task. Finally, it is likely that the clinician may find him- or herself trapped in the dilemmas brought by the responsibility to treat these behaviors and the social and legal consequences that they bring about. This makes issues of freedom of choice and confidentiality concerning treatment of these disorders very challenging ones for the clinical enterprise (Hernandez Serrano, 2000).

The fourth edition (text revised) of the U.S. psychiatric diagnostic system (DSM-IV-TR, American Psychiatric Association, 2000) preserves the term paraphilias and defines their diagnostic features as "recurrent, intense, sexually arousing fantasies, sexual urges, or behaviors generally involving (1) nonhuman objects, (2) the suffering or humiliation of onseself or one's partner, or (3) children or other nonconsenting persons that occur over a period of at least 6 months" (p. 566).

Chapter V of the ICD-10 labels these conditions "Disorders of Sexual Preference," provides the inclusion term "paraphilias," and classifies them as part of F6, Disorders of Adult Personality and Behavior. The general diagnostic criteria for research provided by the international systems (World Health Organization, 1993) are the following:

G1. The individual experiences recurrent intense sexual urges and fantasies involving unusual objects or activities.
G2. The individual either acts on the urges or is markedly distressed by them.
G3. The preference has been present for at least 6 months.

These criteria are fairly in line with criterion A of the U.S. nosological system, which in addition provides qualifiers in criterion B for each one of the specific paraphilias. Additional criteria include concepts such as acting out the fantasies, periodicity, impairment (social and occupational), distress, and interpersonal difficulties. Because of the nature of the international system as a "family of classifications," chapter V of ICD-10 does not include as part of the basic general criteria of mental health disorders, the concept of dysfunction. This is developed in detail in the International Classification of Functioning and Disability (WHO, 1999) and included as part of Axis II in the Multiaxial Presentation of ICD-10.

DSM-IV provides criteria for eight specified paraphilias and one residual category. These are exhibitionism, fetishism, frotteurism, pedophilia, sexual masochism, sexual sadism, transvestic fetishism, voyeurism, and paraphilia not otherwise specified. ICD-10, on its part, provides diagnostic criteria for eight specified disorders and one residual category, namely, fetishism, fetishistic transvestism, exhibitionism, voyeurism, pedophilia, sadomasochism, multiple disorders of sexual preference, other disorders of sexual preference, and disorders of sexual preference, unspecified.

Diagnostic Criteria for Disorders of Sexual Preference According to ICD-10

F65.0.   Fetishism

Fetishism is reliance on some nonliving object as a stimulus for sexual arousal and sexual gratification. Many fetishes are extensions of the human body, such as articles of clothing or footwear. Other common examples are characterized by some particular texture such as rubber, plastic, or leather. Fetish objects vary in their importance to the individual. In some cases they simply serve to enhance sexual excitement achieved in ordinary ways (e.g., having the partner wear a particular garment). Diagnostic criteria include the following:

    a. The general criteria for disorders of sexual preference (F65) must be met.
    b. The fetish (a nonliving object) is the most important source of sexual stimulation or is essential for satisfactory sexual response.

F61.1.   Fetishistic Transvestism

Fetishistic transvestism is the wearing of clothes of the opposite sex principally to obtain sexual excitement and to create the appearance of a person of the opposite sex. Fetishistic transvestism is distinguished from transsexual transvestism by its clear association with sexual arousal and the strong desire to remove the clothing once orgasm occurs and sexual arousal declines. It can occur as an earlier phase in the development of transsexualism. It includes transvestic fetishism. Diagnostic criteria include the following:

    a. The general criteria for disorders of sexual preference (F65) must be met.
    b. The individual wears articles of clothing of the opposite sex in order to create the appearance and feeling of being a member of the opposite sex.
    c. The cross-dressing is closely associated with sexual arousal. Once orgasm occurs and sexual arousal declines, there is a strong desire to remove the clothing.

F65.2.   Exhibitionism

Exhibitionism is a recurrent or persistent tendency to expose the genitalia to strangers (usually of the opposite sex) or to people in public places, without inviting or intending closer contact. There is usually, but not invariably, sexual excitement at the time of exposure and the act is commonly followed by masturbation. Diagnostic criteria include the following:

    a. The general criteria for disorders of sexual preference (F65) must be met.
    b. There is a recurrent or a persistent tendency to expose the genitalia to unsuspecting strangers (usually of the opposite sex), which is invariably associated with sexual arousal and masturbation.
    c. There is no intention to have sexual intercourse with the witnesses.

F65.3.   Voyeurism

Voyeurism is defined as a recurrent or persistent tendency to look at people engaging in sexual or intimate behavior such as undressing. This is carried out without the observed people being aware and usually leads to sexual excitement and masturbation. Diagnostic criteria include the following:

a. The general criteria for disorders of sexual preference (F65) must be met.
b. There is a recurrent or a persistent tendency to look at people engaging in sexual or intimate behavior such as undressing, which is associated with sexual excitement and masturbation.
c. There is no intention of sexual involvement with the person observed.

F65.4. Pedophilia

Pedophilia is defined as a sexual preference for children, boys and girls or both, usually of prepubertal or early pubertal age. Diagnostic criteria include the following:

a. The general criteria for disorders of sexual preference (F65) must be met.
b. There is a persistent or predominant preference for sexual activity with a prepubescent child or children
c. The individual is at least 16 years old and at least 5 years older than the child or children in criterion B.

F65.5. Sadomasochism

Sadomasochism is defined as a preference for sexual activity that involves the infliction of pain, humiliation, or bondage. If the subject prefers to be the recipient of such stimulation, it is masochism; if the provider, sadism. Often an individual obtains sexual excitement from both sadistic and masochistic activities. It includes masochism and sadism. Diagnostic criteria include the following:

a. The general criteria for disorders of sexual preference (F65) must be met.
b. There is a preference for sexual activity, as recipient (masochism) or provider (sadism), or both, which involves at least one of the following: (1) Pain, (2) Humiliation, (3) Bondage.
c. The sadomasochistic activity is the most important source of stimulation or is necessary for sexual classification.

F65.6. Multiple Disorders of Sexual Preference

Multiple disorders of sexual preference refers to situations where more than one abnormal sexual preference occurs in one person and there is none of first rank. The most common combination is fetishism, transvestism, and sadomasochism.

F65.8. Other Disorders of Sexual Preference

Other disorders of sexual preference refers to a variety of other patterns of sexual preference and activity, including making obscene telephone calls, rubbing up against people for sexual stimulation in crowded public places, sexual activity with animals, use of strangulation or anoxia for intensifying sexual excitement, and a preference for partners with some particular anatomical abnormality such as an amputated limb. It includes froteurism and necrophilia.

F65.9.   Disorders of Sexual Preference, Unspecified
Disorders of sexual preference, unspecified, includes sexual deviation NOS.

Factors Associated with the Phenomenology of Paraphilic Behaviors

Paraphilias in both fantasies and urges may begin in childhood or in early adolescence and once they are established they may continue over the lifetime and tend to be chronic. In some individuals, they often tend to diminish with advancing age. The frequency of paraphilic behaviors may increase in relation with psychosocial stressors. They can also increase as a consequence of other mental disorders and when the opportunity to engage in the paraphilia is available.

DSM-IV does not code F65.6, Multiple disorders of sexual preference, but on Sexual masochism (302.83) it states: "Some males with Sexual Masochism also have Fetishism, Transvestic Fetishism, or Sexual Sadism" (p. 529). Moreover, ICD's F65.5, sadomasochism has two separate diagnostic categories in the American system: 302.83 Sexual Masochism and 302.84 Sexual Sadism, as the clinicians' belief that sadistic and masochistic trends often occur together is not confirmed by some researchers (Chivers and Blanchard, 1996).

In the DSM-IV condition (302.9), Paraphilia not otherwise specified (NOS) and in the ICD-10 category F65.8, Other disorders of sexual preference, conditions such as obscene phone calls, zoophilia, necrophilia, and partialism are incorporated. ICD-10's F65.8 also includes frotteurism (touching and rubbing against a nonconsenting person), which is described as a specific condition in 302.89 by DSM-IV. Hypoxyphilia is included in the DSM-IV category 302.83 Sexual masochism as well as piercing, bondage, spanking, and infantilism. Klismaphilia (enemas), coprophilia, and urophilia are also mentioned in Paraphilia NOS. The coexistence of more than one paraphilia in the same individual patient is a well-known fact (APA, 1994; Chivers and Blanchard, 1996).

Paraphilia, to a certain degree, seems to transform people and relationships into objects to be manipulated. A similar functioning affects compulsive sexual behavior (CSB): a temporary relief of anxiety and distress is provided by sexual activity (Coleman, 1991). Forms of CSB include compulsive searching for multiple partners, compulsive masturbation, and repeated sexual relationships.

Money (1985, 1986), Langevin (1994), and Flores-Colombino (1999) underline the need for interdependent research on etiology, as well as on neuroendocrinological and physiological correlates of these clinical conditions. These authors propose that isolated theories of causality, such as psychoanalysis, family therapy, learning theory, endocrinology, or ethology, do not explain the presence of these disorders in their totality, and suggest that a multi-factorial model is more explanatory.

Sociocultural Aspects

The sociocultural importance of paraphilias is well accepted, especially as this concerns their symptomatic expression, the level of acceptance by society as a whole, and the legal implication of the symptoms. Thus, womanizing (also called Donjuanism in reference to the legendary Spanish nobleman) and machismo are accepted in certain social and cultural groups while in others are clearly rejected. As society evolves, peculiar sexual behaviors and new types of paraphilias may emerge (Hernández-Serrano, 2000).

2.2.1.4. Gender Identity Disorder

Core gender identity can be defined as the emotionally valued individual's recognition that he or she is a member of one sex, but not of the other (Zucker and Green, 1996)—the awareness that one is male or female (Stoller, 1964). How this awareness comes about in each individual, and the factors that affect its course, normal or otherwise, continue to be matters of debate among researchers and clinicians interested in the study of patterns of psychosexual differentiation in child development. Definite data to resolve etiological considerations of the disorders of gender identity beyond a reasonable doubt are still lacking. However, the factors influencing such development are considered complex and, according to evidence in the psychiatric literature, come from biological (Bailey et al., 1993; Goy et al., 1988; Hamer et al., 1993) as well as psychological (Coates and Person, 1985; Green, 1987; Stoller, 1985; Zucker and Bradley, 1995; Zucker and Green, 1996) and sociocultural (Masters, Johnson, and Kolodny, 1986, p. 189) roots.

The development of gender identity appears to follow a predictable pattern, even in individuals with ambiguous sexual anatomy (Money, 1957). By age two, a child can determine rather reliably the gender of other people, and by age three, his or her core gender identity is hypothesized to have reached a solid state (Masters, Johnson, and Kolodny, 1986). Around this age, and in response to socialization patterns heavily influenced by the child's own culture, he or she begins to develop an awareness of gender roles. With entrance to school, behavior consistent with gender-role expectations is consolidated.

Nosological Evolution of the Concept

The evolution of the nosology of gender identity disorders within the most important diagnostic systems in psychiatry reflect, in many ways, the changing conceptualizations of human sexuality in the recent history of Western psychiatry. This is also reflected in the changing terms such disorders are assigned in different editions of such systems.

Before DSM-III (1980), the term "gender identity disorder" was not included in the American nosological system. DSM-II in 1968 had included the diagnosis of "Transvestitism" (302.3) as part of its main category 302, Sexual Deviations, without providing a specific description or age boundaries for this disorder. A general description of Sexual Deviations in DSM-II indicated that:

> "This category is for individuals whose sexual interests are directed primarily toward objects other than people of the opposite sex, toward sexual acts not usually associated with coitus, or toward coitus performed under bizarre circumstances as in necrophilia, pedophilia, sexual sadism, and fetishism. Even though many find their practices distasteful, they remain unable to substitute normal sexual behavior for them. This diagnosis is not appropriate for individuals who perform deviant sexual acts because normal sexual objects are not available to them" (p. 44)

ICD-9—reflecting, evidently, the work in the classification of child psychiatric disorders by Rutter, Shaffer, and Shepherd (1975)—is the first to include the diagnostic term 302.6, Disorder of Psychosexual Identity, within the main category of 302, Sexual Deviations and Disorders. The other diagnoses included within such main category were

Homosexuality, Bestiality, Pedophilia, Transvestism, Exhibitionism, Trans-sexualism, and Frigidity and Impotence. ICD-9 provided a concise—and certainly incomplete—description of the disorder:

> "Behavior occurring in pre-adolescents of immature psychosexuality which is similar to that shown in the sexual deviations described under Transvestism (302.3) and Trans-sexualism (302.5). Cross-dressing is intermittent, although it may be frequent, and identification with the behavior and appearance of the opposite sex is not fixed. The commonest form is feminism in boys."

Gender identity disorder (GID), although first reported in the United States by Green and Money (1960) in young boys, only became incorporated into the "official" American psychiatric nosology, with the publication of DSM-III in the early 1980s. This was one of the three main categories of psychosexual disorders such manual contained, which included also the paraphilias and the sexual dysfunctions.

Consistent with its major advances in psychiatric classification, DSM-III defined GID as an "incongruence between anatomic sex and gender identity," provided a more complete set of diagnostic criteria, and defined in more accurate ways the age limits of the disorder, as well as its exclusionary criteria. DMS-III included within the gender identity disorders the following diagnostic labels: transsexualism, gender identity disorder of childhood, and atypical gender identity disorder.

DSM-III regarded transsexualism as a disorder of late adolescence and adulthood, leaving the category of Gender Identity Disorder of Childhood for those cases in which the disorder clearly shows an onset before puberty, and the residual term of Atypical Gender Identity Disorder, for those cases not fitting into any one of the former two. For a diagnosis of transsexualism to be made it was required that, in addition to the sense of discomfort about his or her anatomic sex and the wish to be rid of his or her genitals, the patient exhibited this disturbance continuously for at least two years. Also, the presence of physical intersex, genetic abnormality, or any other disorder explaining the abnormalities in gender discomfort, such as schizophrenia, were considered exclusionary criteria.

Gender Identity Disorder of Childhood was defined as "a persistent feeling of discomfort and inappropriateness in a child about his or her anatomic sex and the desire to be, or insistence that he or she is, of the other sex. In addition, there is a persistent repudiation of the individual's own anatomical attributes." To emphasize the importance of the severity of the disorder, DSM-III indicated "This is not merely the rejection of stereotypical sex role behavior as, for example, in 'tomboyishness' in girls or 'sissyish' behavior in boys, but rather a profound disturbance of the normal sense of maleness or femaleness" (p. 264).

DSM-III-R in 1987 introduced important, although ephemeral, changes in the nosography of this group of disorders. First, it removed Gender Identity Disorders from the main class of psychosexual disorders and located it in the section on "Disorders First Evident in Infancy, Childhood, or Adolescence." This emphasized the fact that many late adolescents or adults with the disorder reported an early onset of gender discomfort, and the importance child psychiatry had come to give this condition. DSM-III-R included among the Gender Identity Disorders the following diagnostic labels: (a) Gender Identity

Disorder of Childhood; (b) Transsexualism; (c) Gender Identity Disorder of Adolescence or Adulthood, Nontranssexual Type; and (d) Gender Identity Disorder, NOS.

DSM-III-R describes the essential feature of GID as "an incongruence between assigned sex (i.e., the sex that is recorded on the birth certificate) and gender identity" (p. 71), defining gender identity and gender role in the same way as DSM-III. It does provide a more defined developmental limit—puberty—for the use of either the childhood or the adolescent condition and provides a more specific set of diagnostic criteria for the diagnosis in children. Even more important, DSM-III-R does not mention physical intersex or genetic abnormality as exclusion criteria for the disorder at any age.

Consistent with DSM-III, DSM-III-R recommends specifying history of sexual orientation for transsexualism as well as for the nontranssexual condition in adolescents or adults, by using the additional labels of asexual, homosexual, heterosexual, or unspecified.

Gender Identity Disorders in the DSM System

DSM-IV in 1994 introduced again important changes in the classification of these disorders, which made its nosological organization more in line with DSM-III than with DSM-III-R. First, it returned the Gender Identity Disorders to the main class of Sexual and Gender Identity Disorders, and away from Disorders Usually First Diagnosed in Infancy, Childhood or Adolescence. Second, it reduces the number of diagnostic categories in this subclass to just one (Gender Identity Disorder), with two codes based on whether the individual is pre- or postpubertal: 302.6 Gender Identity Disorder in Children, and 302.85 Gender Identity Disorder in Adolescents or Adults.

As in DSM-III and in DSM-III-R, the fourth edition of the U.S. system continues to give diagnostic importance to the two main phenomenological components of the disorder, namely, the strong and persistent cross-gender identification (criterion A), and the persistent discomfort about one's assigned sex or a sense of inappropriateness in the role of that sex (criterion B). However, based on the reanalysis of available databases by the subcommittee on Gender Identity Disorders of Childhood (Zucker et al., 1998), the main diagnostic criteria were changed to a polythetic format collapsing the cross-sex wish—which in DSM-III and DSM-III-R had a decisive diagnostic importance—with other behavioral traits that represent important behavioral markers of cross-gender identification. This pays attention to the fact that, as clinical experience indicates, and the available empirical evidence tends to support, as the child grows older, he or she tends to not verbalize his or her cross-gender identification, even when other behaviors consistent with such desire continue to be present.

Another important feature of DSM-IV diagnostic organization is that the presence of nonpsychiatric medical conditions, such as hermaphroditism, congenital adrenal hyperplasia, or the androgen insensitivity syndrome, precludes the diagnosis of GID (criterion C). Finally, it introduces a criteria of dysfunction, requiring that for the diagnosis to be made, the patient must report "clinically significant distress or impairment in social, occupational, or other important areas of functioning" (p. 538), and omits the time course criteria introduced by DSM-III-R.

In line with the previous editions of the U.S. nosological system, DSM-IV requires, for sexually mature individuals, specification of the sexual orientation of the individual patient with GID; however, departing from the previous formats, it avoids the terms homosexual, asexual, and bisexual, and incorporates instead the subgroups Sexually Attracted to Males, Sexually Attracted to Females, Sexually Attracted to Both, and Sexually Attracted to Neither.

Gender Identity Disorders in the ICD System

ICD-10 follows a completely different organizational format when classifying gender identity disturbances. In F6, Disorders of Adult Personality and Behavior, ICD-10 locates F64, Gender Identity Disorders.

ICD-10 contains three specific and two residual categories of gender identity disorders. The specific disorders of this group include F64.0, Transsexualism; F64.1, Dual-Role Transvestism; and F64.2 Gender Identity Disorder of Childhood. As in other classes, the system includes F64.8, Other Gender Identity Disorders; and F64.9 Gender Identity Disorders Unspecified. In general the nosological organization of the ICD-10 system seems more in line with DSM-III-R, especially in the diagnostic criteria of transsexualism. The Dual Role Transvestism of ICD-10 closely resembles DSM-III-R's Gender Identity Disorder of Adolescence or Adulthood, Nontranssexual Type.

Gender Identity Disorder of Childhood is classified in F64, instead of F9 (Behavioral and Emotional Disorders with Onset Usually Occurring in Childhood or Adolescence) "because [it] has many features in common with the disorders in this section" (World Health Organization, 1996). The diagnostic criteria of this disorder is rather consistent with those of the same disorder in DSM-IV, although in the clinical version of ICD-10 less diagnostic weight is attributed to the repudiation of anatomical structures of the patient's own sex, which is considered very rare in children of either sex. This varies slightly with the more strict diagnostic criteria for research (World Health Organization, 1993), where the persistent repudiation of anatomical sex is an important component of the disorder, although its absence does not preclude the diagnosis.

ICD-10 offers diagnostic criteria for the following conditions within the three-character category of Gender Identity Disorder:

F64.0.   Transsexualism

Transsexualism is a desire to live and be accepted as a member of the opposite sex, usually accompanied by a sense of discomfort with, or inappropriateness of, one's anatomic sex and a wish to have surgery and hormonal treatment to make one's body as congruent as possible with one's preferred sex. ICD-10 criteria for research read as follows:

a. The individual desires to live and be accepted as a member of the opposite sex, usually accompanied by the wish to make his or her body as congruent as possible with the preferred sex through surgery and hormonal treatment.
b. The transsexual identity has been present persistently for at least 2 years.
c. The disorder is not a symptom of another mental disorder, such as schizophrenia, nor is it associated with chromosome abnormality.

F64.1.   Dual-Role Transvestism

Dual-role transvestism refers to the wearing of clothes of the opposite sex for part of the individual's existence in order to enjoy the temporary experience of membership of the opposite sex, but without any desire for a more permanent sex change or associated surgical reassignment, and without sexual excitement accompanying the cross-dressing. It includes the Gender Identity Disorder of Adolescence or Adulthood, Non-Transsexual Type. It excludes Fetishistic Transvestism (F65.1). The diagnostic criteria for research demand that for a diagnosis of this condition to be made:

a. The individual wears clothes of the opposite sex in order to experience temporarily membership of the opposite sex.
b. There is no sexual motivation for the cross-dressing.
c. The individual has no desire for a permanent change to the opposite sex.

F64.2. Gender Identity Disorder of Childhood

This is a disorder which is usually first manifested during early childhood (and always well before puberty), characterized by a persistent and intense distress about assigned sex, together with a desire to be (or insistence that one is) of the other sex. There is a persistent preoccupation with the dress and activities of the opposite sex and repudiation of the individual's own sex. The diagnosis requires that there be a profound disturbance of the normal gender identity; mere tomboyishness in girls or girlish behavior in boys is not sufficient. Gender identity disorders in individuals who have reached or are entering puberty should not be classified here but in F66. It excludes Egodystonic Sexual Orientation (F66.1) and Sexual Maturation Disorder (F66.0). The diagnostic criteria for research indicate that a diagnosis of this condition is likely when:

For girls:
a. The individual shows persistent and intense distress about being a girl, and has a stated desire to be a boy (not merely a desire for any perceived cultural advantages to being a boy), or insists that she is a boy.
b. Either of the following:
   1. Persistent marked aversion to normative feminine clothing and insistence on wearing stereotypical masculine clothing, e.g. boys' underwear and other accessories.
   2. Persistent repudiation of female anatomical structures, as evidenced by at least one of the following:
      (a) An assertion that she has, or will grow, a penis.
      (b) Rejection of urinating in a sitting position.
      (c) Assertion that she does not want to grow breasts or menstruate.
c. The girl has not yet reached puberty.
d. The disorder must have been present for at least 6 months.

For boys:
a. The individual shows persistent and intense distress about being a boy, and has a desire to be a girl or, more rarely, insists that he is a girl.
   Either of the following must be present:
   1. Preoccupation with stereotypic female activities, as shown by a preference for either cross-dressing or stimulating female attire, or by an intense desire

to participate in the games and pastimes of girls and rejection of stereotypical male toys, games and activities.
2. Persistent repudiation of male anatomical structures, as indicated by at least one of the following repeated assertions:
    (a) That he will grow up to become a woman (not merely in role).
    (b) That his penis or testes are disgusting or will disappear.
    (c) That it would be better not to have a penis or testes.
b. The boy has not yet reached puberty.
c. The disorder must have been present for at least 6 months.

The system allows for two additional residual conditions without providing diagnostic criteria for them:

F64.8. **Other Gender Identity Disorders**
F64.9. **Gender Identity Disorder, Unspecified**

2.2.1.5. Psychological and Behavioral Disorders Associated with Sexual Development and Orientation

ICD-10 advises that "sexual orientation by itself is not to be regarded as a disorder" (WHO, 1997, p. 90). This section includes the following categories:

F66. **Psychological and Behavioral Disorders Associated with Sexual Development and Orientation**
F66.0. **Sexual Maturation disorder**
F66.1. **Egodystonic sexual orientation**
F66.2. **Sexual relationship disorder**
F66.8 **Other psychosexual development disorders**
F66.9 **Psychosexual development disorder, unspecified**

2.2.1.6. Categories Proposed for Further Study

The professional literature presents a number of conditions not included presently in official diagnostic systems. (ICD-10, DSM-IV). These proposals include the following:

Relational Sexual Dysfunction

Relational sexual dysfunction refers to conditions in which a sexual disorder in one partner induces a sexual disorder in the other (Schnarch, 2000). For example, in some couples, premature ejaculation in the male partner may induce lack of sexual desire in the female partner.

When the "traditional" sex therapy was introduced (Masters and Johnson, 1970) the emphasis on both partners being involved in the therapeutic situation was strongly advocated. Furthermore, therapists of each sex were supposed to participate in the sessions.

Clearly, it was an ideal goal, but it could not be followed in an ordinary daily practice where one person would come and present his or her problems to a clinical practitioner.

A highly prestigious private clinic or an academic department may survive by adding such demands to a given referral but ordinary daily clinical life cannot. In the extreme, certain clinics in the Western world have even refused to take in a partner if the spouse could or would not participate. Furthermore, the relative scarcity of professionals dealing with sexual disorders limits the ideal situation considerably.

Epidemiological studies indicate that the experience of sexual difficulties is not always to be considered a serious sexual problem or disorder. For example, Sweden (1998) showed that among sexually active men who had experienced erectile failure quite often during the preceding year, only 69% stated that this was a significant problem. Among these subjects, 75% reported low level of overall satisfaction with sexual life.

It should be considered that a dysfunction may be a problem for the individual only, the partner only, or both. Hence great effort should be made to get knowledge of the reaction of the partner. It will quite often show that it is the couple that is sexually dysfunctional.

Sexual Compulsivity/Addiction

This condition is expressed through recurrent intense sexually arousing fantasies, urges, or behaviors involving essentially normative aspects of sexual expressions, which increase in frequency or intensity to the extent that they significantly interfere with the sexual relationship with the partner. Such behaviors as compulsive masturbation, uncontrolled promiscuity, and dependence on pornography, including Internet pornography or telephone sex, are included under this heading (Kafka, 2000).

The concept of compulsive sexual behavior, or sex addiction, developed over the past two decades to describe persons who compulsively seek out sexual experiences and whose behavior becomes impaired if they cannot gratify their sexual impulses (Carnes, 1983, 1989, 1991).

DSM-IV does not include as part of its nosology the terms "sex addiction" or "compulsive sexual behavior," but it provides a place where such conditions can be classified (302.9, Sexual Disorder NOS). This disorder is not universally recognized or accepted. Some clinicians regard these behaviors as part of the spectrum of obsessive-compulsive disorders or affective disorders. However, the person whose entire life revolves around sex-seeking behavior and activities is well known to clinicians (Sadock, V., 2000). Such persons show repeated and increasingly frequent attempts to have a sexual experience, and deprivation evokes symptoms of distress. Virginia Sadock (2000) has proposed that "sex addiction is a useful concept heuristically because it can alert the clinician to seek an underlying cause for the manifest behavior" (p. 1599).

Individuals referred to as "sex addicts" seem to have considerable difficulties controlling their sexual impulses, regardless of serious consequences to their loved ones and to themselves (Schneider, 1988). Such impulses are frequently expressed through multiple types of behaviors, motivated largely by the persistent desire to experience the sex act. The history usually reveals a long-standing pattern of such behavior, which the person repeatedly tried to stop without success (Sadock, 2000). Although feelings of guilt and remorse may exist after the act, they do not prevent its recurrence. The patient may report that the need to act out is most severe during stressful periods or when angry, depressed, anxious, or otherwise dysphoric. Eventually, the sexual activity interferes with the person's social, vocational, or marital life, which begins to deteriorate (Sadock, 2000).

Sexual Dysfunctions of the Resolution Phase

These disorders only recently have been recognized as disorders deserving a place in the official nosological systems. A brief description of some of these not well-defined conditions follows.

Post-Coital Dysphoria Postcoital dysphoria is not included in either DSM-IV or ICD-10. According to Virginia Sadock (2000), this disorder occurs during the resolution phase of sexual activity, when persons normally experience a sense of general well-being and muscular and psychological relaxation. Some persons, however, after an otherwise satisfactory sexual experience, become depressed, tense, anxious, and irritable and show psychomotor agitation. They may show irritable and abuse behavior mostly against the sexual partner, which may lead to relational pathology. The incidence of the disorder is unknown, but clinicians tend to report it more commonly in men than in women. Although there are not reliable studies concerning etiology, the fear of AIDS seems to play a role. Treatment requires insight-oriented psychotherapy to help patients understand the unconscious antecedents to their behavior and attitudes (Sadock, 2000).

Post-Coital Headache Post-coital headache is another condition not considered as part of the most visible diagnostic systems so far. The disorder is characterized by a headache immediately after coitus and may last for several hours. The cause is unknown but may be vascular, muscle contraction (tension), or psychogenic (Sadock, 2000). As in the other disorders of the resolution phase, neither the etiology nor the epidemiology is known at this time.

2.2.2. Axis I.B: Comorbidities of Sexual Disorders

The discussion of comorbidities of sexual disorders requires a discussion of three separate comorbidities: the interrelationships of sexual disorders with each other, the psychiatric comorbidities, and the medical comorbidities. For most of these topics, there is more information regarding male than female disorders. When appropriate studies have been conducted, usually male and female comorbidities have been found to be similar.

The largest published study of the interrelationships between the sexual disorders was obtained by an analysis of a large multisite drug trial of a proposed pharmacological treatment for sexual disorders. In this study, 901 patients with sexual disorders were recruited from 15 investigational sites. Operationalized DSM-III criteria were used, and all subjects also had to be rated on a multidimensional instrument, which included all phases of the sexual response cycle. To minimize the influence of extraneous factors, all patients had to be in a stable monogamous heterosexual relationship and free of psychiatric illness. Patients could not have a medical problem known to cause sexual dysfunction nor to be on any drug known to cause sexual problems. Significant relationships were found between the presence of arousal disorder and hypoactive sexual desire disorder. Of female patients with a primary diagnosis of female arousal disorder, 89% had a secondary diagnosis of hypoactive sexual desire disorder (HSDD) (Segraves and Segraves, 1991). Of the men with a diagnosis of male erectile disorder (MED), 20% had a secondary diagnosis of HSDD. Similarly, of men with a primary diagnosis of HSDD,

47% had a secondary diagnosis of MED. This information is important as it suggests that multiaxial diagnoses may be necessary in studies of sexual disorders. A recent population survey of sexual behavior in Sweden found significant intercorrelation between different sexual dysfunctions.

Table 2.2.3 summarizes much of the information discussed here.

Table 2.2.3. Major Sexual Comorbidities

Sexual Disorders of Reference	Other Sexual Disorders	Other Psychiatric Disorders	General Medical Disorders	Iatrogenic Drugs and Procedures
		Comorbid Conditions		
Desire disorders	Arousal disorders	Affective disorders Alcoholism Drug abuse Anorexia nervosa Schizophrenia Anxiety disorders	Hypogonadism Hyperprolactinemia	SSRIs Antihypertensives LiCO3 Benzodiazepines Digoxin MAOIs TCAs
Arousal disorders	Desire disorders	Affective disorders Alcoholism Drug abuse Anorexia nervosa Schizophrenia Anxiety disorders	Diabetes mellitus Multiple sclerosis Hyperlipidemia	SSRIs Antipsychotics Antihypertensives H2 blockers Cancer chemotherapy Pelvic radiation Hypolipidemics Antiarrythmics Beta blocker Protocolectomy Radical prostatectomy Colectomy
Orgasm disorders		Affective disorders Anorexia nervosa Schizophrenia Anxiety disorders Alcoholism Drug abuse	Tabes dorsalis Peripheral neuropathy	Alpha blockers Antipsychotics SSRIs TCAs Benzodiazepines Aortoiliac surgery Retroperitoneal Lymphadenectomy Sympathectomy

A number of studies have suggested the presence of sexual problems in various psychiatric syndromes, especially depression. Lindal and Stefansson (1993) studied the relationship between the lifetime prevalence of sexual disorders and psychiatric disorder in a random sample of the population of Iceland born in 1931. Notably, it has been reported that patients of either sex who had a diagnosis of hypoactive sexual desire disorder had an increased lifetime prevalence of affective disorder. Significant comorbidities were noted between sexual diagnoses and depression and anxiety disorders. A number of other studies have found relationships between measures of depression and sexual function. In a random sample of 40–70 men living in cities near Boston, Massachusetts, significant relationships were found between measures of depressive symptoms and erectile disorder (Feldman et al., 1994). Other studies have confirmed the association between depression and erectile disorder (Shabsigh et al., 1998; Lustman and Clouse, 1990). Studies of men with major depressive disorder have found both decreased magnitude, frequency, and turgidity of nocturnal erections (Thase et al., 1987; Thase et al., 1988; Nofzinger et al., 1993; Thase et al., 1999; Steiger et al., 1993). A number of studies have shown that loss of libido is a common manifestation of both major depressive disorder and dysthymic disorder in both men and women (Kivela et al., 1989; Kivela and Pahkala, 1988; Casper et al., 1985). Other investigators have noted the presence of hypoactive sexual desire disorder in patients with schizophrenia (Raboch, 1984) and anorexia nervosa (Raboch and Faltus, 1991).

A recent population study in the United Kingdom found that female problems with arousal and orgasm were associated with marital difficulties, anxiety, and depression (Dunn et al., 1999). In a recent study, Meana and associates (1998) found that rating of severity of dyspareunia correlated with measures of marital adjustment and depression. As one might expect, symptoms of sexual dysfunction are associated with correlates of low quality of life (Laumann et al., 1999) and return of sexual function in men has been associated with an improvement in quality of life for men with erectile failure (Willke et al., 1997).

Sexual dysfunction can be associated with a variety of pharmacological agents. Antihypertensive drugs and psychiatric drugs are among the main drugs associated with sexual dysfunction (Broderick and Foreman, 1999). Antidepressant drugs, especially the serotonin reuptake inhibitors, may be associated with anorgasmia and decreased libido in both sexes (Rosen et al., 1999). A small number of patients may experience decreased lubrication or erectile problems on antidepressant agents (Segraves, 1998). Antipsychotic agents have also been reported to be associated with decreased libido and anorgasmia.

It is unclear whether the newer prolactin sparing antipsychotics will have a different profile of sexual side effects. Lithium carbonate may be associated with decreased libido (Segraves, 1995), and there is controlled evidence that benzodiazepines may inhibit orgasm attainment in females (Riley and Riley, 1986).

Sexual problems may be associated with changes in endocrine status. It is fairly well established that hypogonadism or hyperprolactinemia in men is frequently associated with decreased libido (Randeva et al., 1999). There is some evidence in females that low testosterone levels may be associated with decreased libido (Sarrell et al., 1998; Redmond, 1999).

Diseases associated with impaired blood flow to the genitalia such as advanced vascular disease are often associated with arousal disorders. Diseases that interrupt the autonomic nervous system innervation of the genitalia may be associated with both erectile disorders and orgasm disorders. These disorders include diabetes mellitus and multiple sclerosis.

Various medical and surgical interventions may also interrupt the nervous innervation to the genitalia. Common examples include retroperitoneal lymph node resection, radical bowel surgery, aorto-iliac surgery, kidney transplant, and pelvic radiation (Broderick and Foreman, 1999).

In summary, a large number of psychiatric and general medical diseases are associated with sexual dysfunction.

2.2.3. Axis II: Disabilities (Social Functioning)

Introduction

By definition, sexual disorders, acute or chronic, organic or psychosocial in nature, impair multiple areas of functioning in the individual patient. The understanding of how sexual dysfunctions impact social functioning in a more direct way remains an area where empirical evidence is still lacking. In recognition of this, DSM-IV requires that for the disorder to be identified that the disturbance must "cause marked distress and interpersonal difficulty" (p. 493).

Sadock (1995), on her part, has indicated that sexual dysfunctions may lead to or result from relational problems, and patients "invariably develop an increasing fear of failure and self-consciousness about their sexual performance" (p. 1301). To make matters even more complicated, sexual dysfunctions are frequently associated with other mental disorders, such as depressive disorders, anxiety disorders, personality disorders, and schizophrenia; therefore, isolating a sexual disorder as a single variable to be studied in its impact upon social functioning is not an easy task.

Multidimensional assessment models are widely used in psychiatry, particularly in the evaluation of male erectile dysfunction and sexual pain disorders (Rosen and Leiblum, 1995), and a multiaxial formulation of the clinical condition of the patient tends to dominate the general clinical practice of the specialty (Mezzich, Berganza, von Cranach, et al., 2003, Section VII).

A multiaxial formulation of the patient's clinical condition facilitates the understanding of the complexity of such condition and allows the formulation of a treatment program that is less arbitrary and more addressed at the important complaints the patient brings to the clinical encounter (Mezzich, 1991).

Given the fact that, as it is accepted now, sexual problems may be the expression of difficulties in other areas of psychosocial functioning, it seems evident that history taking with these individuals must cover a wide assessment of functioning, such as patterns of interaction with people, sexual partners, dating patterns, and expectations about marriage and sexual partnership. Of paramount importance concerning attitudes toward sex are history of relationship with peers, parents, and other significant authority figures. Particular attention must be paid to ways in which the individual has learned to express affection, as well as the degree of physical contact that was allowed in the individual's family (Sadock, 1995).

Since culture influences behavior in general, and sexuality is clearly influenced by cultural patterns, the therapist must remain attentive to specific events in the patient's life that could have led to nonadaptive patterns of sexual expression, such as rigid religious practices, abuse, or gross distortion in the way sexual matters were modeled for the patient either in the family environment or in the immediate social and cultural group.

Initiation in sexuality, for instance, may be differentially approached by different sociocultural groups and may constitute areas of concern for patients either by commission or by omission. It is likely that for a young girl, for instance, from a Hispanic group, losing her virginity may become a reason to be ostracized, whereas keeping her virginity in an Anglo group may lead to the same social rejection or pressure. Also, attitudes toward abortion are heavily influenced by social and cultural factors, and an unwanted pregnancy leading to abortion may lead to rejection or scapegoating either by the family or the social group. An experience of this nature may lead to anxiety about sexual practices and be the source of sexual dysfunctions in some patients.

A very important area of sexuality related to difficulties in psychosocial functioning may be the so-called midlife crisis of the adult. In their chapter on adult sexuality, Masters, Johnson, and Kolodny (1986) describe changes in sexuality around the age of forty for men and women. The turning toward younger sexual partners in the case of the male, or the redirection of talents and energy in the case of women, may flag important difficulties in the sexual life of the married couple and give way to dysfunction in other areas, such as communication, childrearing, work, friendships, and entertainment.

An important component of the midlife crisis is what these authors call "sexual burnout," which, according to them, affects as many as 20% of people in this stage of the life cycle and is the result of tedium and satiation with the same sexual routine. An important consequence of this problem may be a reversal in roles exhibited by male and female partners, with an increase in extramarital affairs, leading to increasing tensions in the marriage that can end up in divorce. It has been suggested that it may be more stressing for the couple when it is the wife that is involved in an extramarital relationship, probably due to the fact that women tend to become more emotionally involved in their affairs (McCarthy, 1982).

How to Indicate Level of Social Functioning

DSM-IV and ICD-10, the two most visible systems of diagnostic classification in psychiatry, differ in the way they approach social functioning. DSM-IV, in the first place, as it has been customary in the American diagnostic system, includes impairment of functioning as one of the criteria for defining a mental disorder. However, it advises that "Neither deviant behavior (e.g., political, religious, or sexual) nor conflicts that are primarily between the individual and society are mental disorders unless the deviance or conflict is a symptom of a dysfunction in the individual."

As regards functioning, DSM-IV offers a global assessment of functioning on a scale that goes from scores of 0 to 100, based on the perception of the clinician on the overall functioning of the individual patient in areas of self-care, communication, social and occupational functioning (see table 2.2.4).

Table 2.2.4. **Global Assessment of Functioning Based on DSM-IV**

100	Superior functioning in a wide range of activities; life's problems never seem to get out of hand; is sought out by others because of his or her many positive qualities.
91	No symptoms.
90	Absent or minimal symptoms (e.g., mild anxiety before an exam); good functioning in all areas; interested and involved in a wide range of activities; socially effective;
81	generally satisfied with life; no more than everyday problems or concerns (e.g., an occasional argument with family members).
80	If symptoms are present, they are transient and expectable reactions to psychosocial stressors (e.g., difficulty concentrating after family argument); no more than slight
71	impairment in social, occupational, or school functioning (e.g., temporarily falling behind in schoolwork).
70	Some mild symptoms (e.g., depressed mood and mild insomnia), or some difficulty in social, occupational, or school functioning (e.g., occasional truancy, or theft
61	within the household), but generally functioning pretty well; has some meaningful interpersonal relationships.
60	Moderate symptoms (e.g., flat affect and circumstantial speech, occasional panic attacks), or moderate difficulty in social, occupational, or school functioning
51	(e.g., few friends, conflicts with peers or coworkers).
50	Serious symptoms (e.g., suicidal ideation, severe obsessional rituals, frequent shoplifting) or any serious impairment in social, occupational, or school functioning
41	(e.g., no friends, unable to keep a job).
40	Some impairment in reality testing or communication (e.g., speech is at times illogical, obscure, or irrelevant), or major impairment in several areas, such as work
31	or school, family relations, judgment, thinking, or mood (e.g., depressed man avoids friends, neglects family, and is unable to work; child frequently beats up younger children, is defiant at home, and is failing at school).
30	Behavior is considerably influenced by delusions or hallucinations, or serious impairment in communications or judgment (e.g., sometimes incoherent, acts
21	grossly inappropriately, suicidal preoccupation), or inability to function in almost all areas (e.g., stays in bed all day; no job, home, or friends).
20	Some danger of hurting self or others (e.g., suicide attempts without clear expectation of death; frequently violent/manic excitement), or occasionally fails
11	to maintain minimal personal hygiene (e.g., smears feces), or gross impairment in communication (e.g., largely incoherent or mute).
10	Persistent danger of severely hurting self or others (e.g., recurrent violence), or persistent inability to maintain minimal personal hygiene, or serious suicidal act with clear expectation of death.
0	Inadequate information.

(Continued)

Table 2.2.4. CONTINUED

Consider psychological, social, and occupational functioning on a hypothetical continuum of mental health-illness. Do not include impairment in functioning due to physical (or environmental) limitations.

Use intermediate codes when appropriate, e.g., 45, 68, 72.

The rating of overall psychological functioning on a scale of 0-100 was operationalized by Luborsky in the Health-Sickness Rating Scale (Luborsky, L. "Clinicians' Judgments of Mental Health." *Archives of General Psychiatry* 7:407–417, 1962). Spitzer and colleagues developed a revision of the Health-Sickness Rating Scale called the Global Assessment Scale (GAS) (Endicott, J., Spitzer, R. L., Fleiss, J. L., Cohen, J. "The Global Assessment Scale: A Procedure for Measuring Overall Severity of Psychiatric Disturbance." *Archives of General Psychiatry* 33: 766–771, 1976). A modified version of the GAS was included in DSM-III-R as the Global Assessment of Functioning (GAF) Scale.

Concerning functioning, in 1982 the World Health Organization developed the International Classification of Impairments, Disabilities and Handicaps. This has been recently reformulated as the International Classification of Functioning, Disabilities and Health (WHO, 2001). Its chapter on interpersonal behaviors (pp. 170–176) relates to the adoption of behaviors that constitute a person's engagement in social situations. Such situations may range from the familiar to the unfamiliar, may involve few or many people, and may be predictable or unpredictable.

A practical way of rating functioning has been proposed as part of a formulation for ICD-10 (Janca et al., 1996b); Kastrup, 1993; WHO, 1999) and involves a global assessment of the degree of disability using a diagnostic instrument comprised by one global scale and four subscales. The subscales considered are (1) personal care and survival; (2) occupational functioning (i.e., performance of expected roles as worker, student or homemaker); (3) functioning with family (interaction with spouse, parents, children, and other relatives); and (4) broader social behavior (i.e., interaction with other individuals and the community at large, including leisure activities).

In line with this, the Axis II (disabilities of the IGDA multiaxial schema) records impairments in four separate areas of functioning, as follows:

- Personal care and survival.
- Occupational functioning, including roles as paid or volunteer worker, student, or homemaker.
- Family functioning, including interactions with spouse, children, parents, and other relatives.
- Broad social functioning, including roles, activities, and interactions with other individuals and groups in the community at large.

Ratings are made for each area of functioning, using a semi-quantitative 6–point scale based on frequency and intensity of impairments. Table 2.2.5 summarizes such a rating scale. The use of this scale is illustrated in Section 2.4. Format for Comprehensive

Table 2.2.5. Degrees of Disability according to the WPA International Guidelines for Diagnostic Assessment

Score	Degree	Criteria
0	None	No disability identifiable in this area
1	Minimal	Perceptible, but low in intensity and frequency
2	Moderate	Middle in intensity or frequency, low in the other one
3	Substantial	Middle in intensity and frequency
4	Severe	High in intensity or frequency, middle in the other one
5	Massive	High in intensity and frequency

Source: Mezzich, Berganza, von Cranach, et al., 2003.

Diagnostic Formulation, and in the corresponding Illustrative Clinical Case (see Appendix 1).

In summary, social functioning must be assessed in each individual patient presenting with a sexual complaint, in order to appraise more fully the clinical condition and provide information conducive to effective planning and management.

2.2.4. Axis III: Contextual Factors

In modern diagnosis and classification, contextual factors concern the psychosocial problems or situations, acute or chronic, that affect the emergence and course of the illnesses and that are subject to clinical attention. They also include personal problems that do not amount to a disorder proper, but are of clinical significance (e.g., accentuated personality, hazardous substance use) (World Psychiatric Association, 2001).

The role of contextual factors in sexual functioning has long been subjected to much discussion. For instance, in their study on sexual deviations Lorand and Schneer (1967) tended to deemphasize the role of the cultural context upon sexuality by stating that "the fact that certain sexual practices which are considered deviant by our cultural standards are acceptable in other cultures can not alter the pathological significance of such behavior. The fact remains that, whatever the cultural attitude toward such practices, sexuality which does not find expression in mature, genital union must be considered deviant" (p. 979). For his part, Bieber (1967) indicates that "Each society determines what behavior shall be deemed normal and what abnormal, based on how it fits into the social context. . . . This point of view contrasts sharply with the argument advanced here— that the health or pathology of behavior must ultimately be assessed in relation to optimal individual and group development and continuity, not on the basis of conformity to a cultural norm" (p. 959).

Several years later, Rosen and Leiblum (1989), in discussing sexual desire disorders, called attention to the "increasing pressure in our society for couples to maintain a high level of sexual interest in their primary relationship," which contributes to create potentially unrealistic expectations. These authors also point out the negative effects that "labeling" may have upon the individual with supposedly low sexual desire. They recommend that this diagnosis be applied judiciously, since "sexual desire problems are always present in the context of a couple's relationship" (p. 25); therefore, they propose, the clinician needs to consider the possible role of the "high desire" partner in defining the problem as well as the likelihood that symptoms of low desire may reflect problems of intimacy, power, or territoriality in the relationship.

Rosen and Leiblum (1989) also suggest that the majority of cases seen in clinical practices with sexual desire disorders are due to problems with self-esteem, adequacy, conflict in the partner relationship, difficulties with intimacy, trust and territoriality, performance anxiety frequently compounded by the pressure to be sexually available, and the negative reactions of the sexual partner to lack of sexual desire. In fact, they argue that in each one of the cases that present as examples of desire disorders, the "problem was inextricably associated with dissatisfaction with other aspects of the relationship" and that therapeutic success was clearly associated to "successful conflict resolution among couples" (p. 32).

More recently, Sadock (2000) has stressed that sexual function can be affected by stress of any kind, by emotional disorders, and by a lack of sexual knowledge. In describing the important domains to consider during the evaluation process of the patient with a sexual complaint, she includes premarital expectations, mutual physical attraction, periods of separation, type of contraception used, the effect of children on the couple's sexual life, the satisfying aspects of the marriage, and the partner's contribution to the present distress.

A competent assessment of all contextual factors that affect the clinical condition should inform planning for treatment and for health promotion.

An immediate question the clinician may be confronted with when identifying contextual factors concerns the number and types of these factors that are relevant to record when assessing a patient presenting with a sexual disorder. Each case must be assessed according to the particular circumstances and needs of the patient and his or her family. In this regard, the World Health Organization (1992) has developed a listing of all factors that are relevant for health care in chapter 21 of the *International Classification of Diseases and Related Health Problems*. This listing has been reduced further to a grouping of eleven areas for use in mental health (Janca et al., 1996b). These areas include problems related to (1) negative events in childhood and upbringing, (2) education and literacy, (3) primary support group, (4) social environment, (5) housing or economic circumstances, (6) (un)employment, (7) physical environment, (8) psychosocial circumstances, (9) legal circumstances, (10) family history of diseases, and (11) lifestyle and life-management.

It has been suggested in the World Psychiatric Association's International Guidelines for Diagnostic Assessment (Mezzich, Berganza, von Cranach, et al., 2003), that at least five contextual areas must be appropriately assessed and recorded, as it is illustrated in the diagnostic format provided in this volume for comprehensive diagnosis (see figure 2.4.1). These include circumstances related to family/house, education/work, economic/ legal, cultural/environmental, and personal (e.g., internal factors of the patient him- or herself, such as hazardous, violent, abusive, and suicidal behaviors, that do not amount to a standard disorder but impinge upon the emergence, course and prognosis of the overall clinical condition).

Another important question is the time frame according to which the relevant factors have been operative and influential. Although there are differences in opinion in this area, it is generally considered that the year preceding the current evaluation is most pertinent (Janca et al., 1997).

2.2.5. Axis IV: Quality of Life

Quality of life is becoming one of the key concepts in the health field. Since the 1970s, interest in the assessment of quality of life has been growing with reference to individuals experiencing oncological and other chronic medical illnesses. In more recent years such interest has also become conspicuous in psychiatry and mental health (Katschnig, 1997).

Concern with quality of life can be inscribed within an expanding movement to complement the traditional focus of health on pathology or illness with an additional focus on positive aspects of health. These aspects include, most prominently, adaptive functioning, social supports, and quality of life.

Sexuality is being increasingly perceived as a significant quality of life issue, even into advanced age (Bortz and Wallace, 1999). Furthermore, it has been argued that sexuality should be viewed as a health issue that has an impact on quality of life (Butler et al, 1998).

While the notion of quality of life is acquiring a prominent place in the health field, its definition and the approaches to its assessment are still under intense discussion and investigation. The sections that follow review critical topics for the appraisal of quality of life.

2.2.5.1. Key Issues for the Appraisal of Quality of Life

The following are widely acknowledged as crucial issues for the proper assessment of quality of life:

Simplicity vs. Multidimensionality

Responses to simple questions such as "How is the quality of your life?" have proven to be highly interesting, for example, through the Medical Outcomes Study SF-36 Form (Ware et al., 1993). On the other hand, it has been argued (Ferrans and Powers, 1992; Ruiz and Baca, 1993) that understanding the concept requires a comprehensive and multidimensional framework. Such complexity may range from concrete and conventional aspects such as physical stamina to much subtler facets such as self- actualization and spirituality.

Fundamental and Complementary Evaluators

Quality of life, its meaning and scope, are eminently a personal matter. Therefore, the main evaluator of this concept must be the subject himself or herself. There is little argument on this point (e.g., Osoba, 1994). At the same time, it has been noted that there are circumstances (e.g., clinical depression), which may greatly bias the subjective assessment of quality of life (Katschnig and Angermeyer, 1997). This observation is leading to proposals for complementing the views of the subject with those of external evaluators such as the family, the clinician and the caregiver.

Cultural Suitability

The subjectivity of quality of life assessment noted above brings up cultural suitability as a fundamental issue to be addressed. As Guarnaccia (1996) points out, quality of life is inherently a cultural construct. Thus, instead of attempting in vain to attain a culture-free appraisal of quality of life, it may be wiser to strive for a culture- informed assessment.

Generic vs. Specific Instrumentation

Perhaps because the concept of quality of life emerged initially with reference to particular illnesses, such as cancer or diabetes, many of the instruments designed for its assessment have been disease-specific (Spilker, 1990). While such specificity emphasizes relevance to certain clinical conditions or problems, it may not be appropriate for a large number of situations and uses, such as the care of individuals experiencing multiple illnesses (comorbidity is prominent whenever health is impaired) and nonclinical populations. For these many situations, generic measures of quality of life are in order (Aaronson, 1988). This is also in line with the notion that quality of life involves the totality of the person of the patient.

Efficiency

The fluidity, fast pace and time pressures of clinical care require that assessment tools be efficient and simple if they are to be usable in a clinical setting (Mezzich, Dow, and Coffman, 1981). This does not mean, of course, that superficial approaches are called for. Instead, efforts at compressing thorough and well-thought-out appraisals into brief and easy-to-use procedures are likely to be most effective and helpful.

Validation

Any new quality of life measure, as any other health assessment procedure, is to be considered a hypothesis waiting to be tested. Such careful approach can enhance, first, the conceptualization, content, and structure of the instrument at hand. Furthermore, empirical validation may delineate the extent to which and the circumstances under which the new instrument may be used. Broad validation parameters often include reliability or generalizability, validity or usefulness, and feasibility (Anastasi, 1982).

2.2.5.2. Designing an Approach to Assess Quality of Life

Identification of Key Dimensions

In order to design an approach to the evaluation of quality of life, it is helpful to conduct a review of the pertinent literature. Such a literature review (e.g., Mezzich et al., 2000) suggests the relevance and value of the following dimensions:

- Physical well-being
- Psychological/emotional well-being
- Self-care and independence
- Occupational functioning
- Interpersonal functioning

- Social emotional support
- Community and services support
- Personal fulfillment
- Spiritual fulfillment

Rating Options

The appraisal and formulation of the quality of life of a given person could involve the use of a multidimensional instrument, for example, the WHO Quality of Life Instrument (Kuyken and Orley, 1995) and the Quality of Life Index (Mezzich et al., 2000). Alternatively, a probably less reliable but a simpler approach based on the global estimation by the subject of his or her total quality of life could be considered.

The form for the proposed Standardized Multiaxial Diagnostic Formulation presents for Axis IV a linear approach for the rating of quality of life, from poor to excellent. This can be facilitated by using a formal quality of life scale, as outlined above, or be completed by direct global rating.

Idiographic Diagnostic Formulation

Comprehensive diagnosis of individuals experiencing sexual disorders should involve first a standardized multiaxial formulation that concisely and codifiably, through official typologies and scales, describes sexual disorders and their mental and general medical paraphilias, associated disabilities or impairments in social functioning, and contextual factors (stressors and supports) that may influence the emergence of disease, its course, and resolution. Comprehensive diagnosis should also include a personalized idiographic formulation that addresses, in a narrative way, what is unique in the condition of the patient and couple experiencing sexual disorders, with an emphasis on biographical understanding and the meaning, for this patient and couple, of illness, health, and quality of life.

Since the comprehensive diagnosis of the patient with sexual disorders—as with any other health problem—entails the appropriate assessment of all the elements relevant for effective treatment, including the positive aspects of the patient and his or her circumstances, this axis should record, in addition to conditions contributing to ill health, those factors within the patient and in his or her immediate surroundings that promote healthy adaptation. These may include personality maturity, skills, talents, social resources, and supports, as well as personal and spiritual aspirations (Mezzich, Berganza, von Cranach et al., 2003).

The features of an idiographic personalized formulation, as part of a comprehensive diagnostic formulation, would do the following:

- Articulate the perspectives of the clinician with those of the patient, couple, and family.
- Be based on the establishment of a thoughtful and respectful relationship between the participants, which shall extend throughout the course of clinical care.
- Include the joint formulation of comprehensive diagnosis and a plan for treatment and promotion of health.
- Have a qualitative character to be obtained through an approach akin to an ethnographic investigation and that involves a process that is interactive (among clinicians, patient, couple and family) and diachronic (dynamic and longitudinal) in nature.

- Be presented in a narrative form, either oral or written, to take advantage of the flexibility and richness of natural language (see figure 2.4.1, the sections and guidelines for a usual written presentation are outlined; its length may vary according to the circumstances, setting, and purposes of the diagnostic evaluation).

In addition, the formulation should include the following sections:

- *Clinical problems and their contextualization.* This involves the shared formulation (by the clinician, the patient, the couple, and the family) of clinical problems, the summarization of complementary information, and the elucidation of mechanisms and explanations, from biological, psychological, social and cultural perspectives. Important disagreements among these perspectives should be mentioned.
- *Patient's positive factors* pertinent to clinical treatment and promotion of health, e.g., personality maturity, abilities and talents, social supports and resources, and personal and spiritual aspirations.
- *Expectations on health restoration and promotion* (concerning the realistically desirable types and goals of treatment as well as aspirations about status of health and quality of life in the foreseeable future).

Format for Comprehensive Diagnostic Formulation

I n order to facilitate and optimize the completion of the comprehensive diagnostic formulation for persons experiencing sexual disorders, an ad hoc form was designed. This form is modeled on the one produced by the World Psychiatric Association at the core of the International Guidelines for Diagnostic Assessment (Mezzich, Berganza, von Cranach, et al., 2003). The new form highlights sexual disorders in the context of a variety of health problems, and also pays particular attention to the situation of couples. The form is presented as figure 2.4.1.

Figure 2.4.1. COMPREHENSIVE DIAGNOSTIC FORMULATION FORM FOR PERSONS WITH SEXUAL DISORDERS (BLANK).

Comprehensive Diagnostic Formulation Form
for Persons with Sexual Disorders
(Based on the WPA International Guidelines for Diagnostic Assessment)

Name: _____ Code: _____

Date: _____

Age: _____ Sex: M F Marital Status: _____

Occupation: _____

First Component: Standardized Multiaxial Formulation (*Sexual Health Version*)

Axis I. Clinical disorders (as classified in ICD-10)

A. Sexual disorders (sexual dysfunctions, paraphilias, and gender identity disorders)

Disorders	Codes

B. Comorbidities (coexisting mental and general medical disorders)

Disorders	Codes

Axis II: Disabilities

	Disability Scale*						
Areas of Functioning	0	1	2	3	4	5	U
A Personal care							
B Occupational (wage earner, student, etc.)							
C With spouse or partner							
D With other relatives							
E Social in general							

0 = None; 1 = Minimal; 2 = Moderate; 3 = Substantial; 4 = Severe; 5 = Massive; U = Unknown; according to the intensity and frequency of the recent presence of the different types of disabilities

Axis III: Contextual factors (psychosocial problems pertinent to the presentation, course, or treatment of the patient's disorders or relevant to clinical care, as well as personal problems that do not amount to a standard disorder)

Problem Areas (to be specified)	Codes Z
1. Family/house:	
2. Education/work:	
3. Economic/legal:	
4. Cultural/environmental:	
5. Personal:	

(Continued)

Figure 2.4.1. CONTINUED

Comprehensive Diagnostic Formulation Form
for Persons with Sexual Disorders

Axis IV: Quality of life (indicates the perceived level of quality of life, from poor to excellent; patient marks one of the 10 points in the line below; this level can be determined through an appropriate multidimensional instrument or by direct global rating)

Poor   Excellent

| 0 | 1 | 2 | 3 | 4 | 5 | 6 | 7 | 8 | 9 | 10 |

Second Component: Idiographic Formulation

I: Clinical problems and their contextualization (Include disorders and problems, extracted from the Standardized Multiaxial Formulation, and formulated in language shared by the clinician, patient, partner, and family, as well as complementary key information, mechanisms, and explanations from biological, psychological, social, and cultural perspectives.)

_____

_____

_____

_____

_____

_____

_____

II: Positive factors of the patient (Include resources pertinent to treatment and health promotion, e.g., maturity of personality, abilities and talents, self-awareness, motivation for change, capacity for sexual fantasies and playfulness, social supports and resources, personal and spiritual aspirations.)

_____

_____

_____

_____

_____

_____

_____

III: Expectations on restoration and promotion of health (Include specific expectations on types of treatment and outcome as well as aspirations on health status and quality of life in the foreseeable future.)

_____

_____

_____

_____

_____

_____

_____

PART 3

COMPREHENSIVE TREATMENT AND HEALTH PROMOTION OF PERSONS WITH SEXUAL DISORDERS

Introduction to Treatment and Health Promotion

Treatment and health promotion of persons with sexual disorders is both a science and an art, and it should be informed by the conceptual bases of sexual health, comprehensive diagnostic procedures, and formulation presented in parts 1 and 2, respectively.

There is a growing body of literature substantiating available approaches to care. It includes biological, psychological, and social clinical patterns and treatment techniques as well as considerations of patients' sexual health attitudes and practices, patient expectations of sexual professionals, and professionals' attitudes and practice.

A brief summary of factors involved in treatment includes the following:

- Sexual concerns and problems are common; virtually all individuals have concerns about sexuality at some point in their lives.
- Many sexual problems are hidden, or masked as nonsexual psychosomatic complaints, and medical and mental health professionals need to help discover them. Such skills require specialized training.
- The more common sexual dysfunctions for women are lack of sexual desire, difficulty with orgasm, and arousal disorder, while for men, sexual dysfunctions seem to be premature ejaculation, erectile dysfunction, lack of sexual desire, and inhibited ejaculation.
- People with sexual concerns want their common hesitation to initiate discussion of sexual matters to be accepted and understood with empathy and a nonjudgmental attitude by the professional, and look to them to initiate a respectful discussion in a professional way.
- The sexual health professional should base his or her understanding of sexuality on credible scientific terms and conduct professional practice with respect and sensitivity to the patient's beliefs and values.
- Empathetic interviewing by the professional, rather than alienating patients, may actually be a rapport-building professional skill.
- There is a relatively high prevalence of multiple sexual dysfunction (sexual comorbidity)—for example, low sexual desire and difficulty achieving orgasm, or erectile dysfunction and premature ejaculation.

- In recent years, increasing attention has also been drawn to diagnosis and treatment of other sexual disorders such as the sexual paraphilias, sexually compulsive behavior, ego-dystonic sexual orientation, the psychological impact of sexually transmitted diseases, gender identity issues, and sexual dysfunction among same-sex couples. Other important issues that need to be considered include domestic violence, rape, childhood sexual abuse, treatment of sex offenders, teenage pregnancy, abortion, and female mutilations, among other controversial topics.

Contemporary sex therapy has developed to humanely treat those sexual problems that may cause individual anguish, distress, and relationship problems. Sexual therapy is directed to not only correct functional sexual deficits but ultimately to enrich and enhance the personal welfare of the individual and couple. Studies for several decades now suggest that men and women in a variety of countries and cultures commonly experience sexual concerns and sexual problems. Surveys of different populations, as well as more rigorous representative samples, generally report that virtually every individual has concerns about one's thoughts, feelings, and behaviors about sexuality at some point in their life. A survey (Laumann et al., 1999) found that approximately 43% of women and 31% of men in the U.S. population reported sexual problems in the previous year.

Most individuals report they prefer to address such concerns with their medical physician (Metz and Seifert, 1993; Holzapfel, 1998). Probably because of the reserved nature of people in most cultures regarding human sexuality and the subsequent lack of openness in interpersonal and public discussion of sexuality, it is often difficult for many—even sexual health professionals—to believe that the epidemiological data of the high prevalence of sexual dysfunction are accurate. Talking about personal sexual concerns is a new experience for most adults. Many talk about sex in general, but few discuss their own sexuality and behavior. Nevertheless primary care physicians and other mental health professionals rarely recognize the sexual dysfunctions, often because many sexual problems are masked as nonsexual psychosomatic complaints.

These sexual dysfunction prevalence data are supplemented with data that suggest that many sexual problems have both hidden and medical roots; therefore mental health professionals need to help identify them. However, many professionals work with the common assumption that if sexual concerns are important to the patient, the patient will initiate discussion about it, while at the same time, many patients similarly think that if the professional is open to discussion and has the professional training and ability to help with sexual problems, then the professional will lead the discussion and inquiry. Unfortunately, such common attitudes may serve to continue a silent avoidance of sexual concerns, leaving many to privately worry or rarely receive help for their sexual concerns. In addition, other studies report that although patients may feel some anxiety to talk and subsequently hesitate to initiate discussion of sexual concerns, most have a positive view of the appropriateness of the professional to ask sensitive and suitable questions about sexual concerns and taking a sexual history; and they want the professional to provide professional leadership. These findings suggest that sex history-taking and problem management not only is a professional behavior with low risk of alienating one's patient but may actually be a rapport-building behavior. The permission to talk openly and confidentially that is implied by the professional's empathetic inquiry itself would likely be valued by patients. It appears that many patients look to the professional for an understanding and tolerance of their anxieties about sexuality, and they want them to professionally and warmly lead discussion focused on possible sexual concerns. Therefore, nesting specific sexual inquiries within the patient's general relationship or personal medical concerns offers a more comfortable context within which to talk specifically about sex for some. The synopsis of research data regarding the relationship between the sexual health professional and their patients or clients serves as a welcoming and positive guide for professionals in their addressing sexual concerns.

Once sexual problems are discovered, the professional needs to know how to manage these disorders effectively. Such skill requires specialized training. The professional must understand not only his or her professional role in addressing and treating sexual disorders, but also the causes of sexual disorders, their pathogenesis, and how to evaluate them thoroughly, initiate management, and refer to other appropriate professionals when the problem is beyond their expertise or interest.

A number of studies have suggested that when patients are asked, they clearly want the professional to initiate and respectfully lead inquiry into their experience and concerns about human sexuality. In regard to the personal qualities that the patients prefer in the professional, both women and men almost universally reported that they strongly want empathy and personal warmth, professional excellence in knowledge and skill in treating sexual problems or the ability to refer to another professional who can help, and confidentiality and trust, especially in small or rural communities. These professional qualities are desired even more so than the patient's comfort, or nonembarrassment on the part of the professional. Patients want professional consultation and assistance in addressing sexual concerns even though such discussion may involve some anxiousness.

It is important for the professional to consider that establishing good rapport, which includes openness, empathy for the patient's sexual concerns, and willingness to assist at whatever level of his or her ability, is the initial and often the most important stage in the treatment of sexual problems; if the patient is not even able to openly communicate with the professional, the specific and technical therapies will be blocked. Therefore, it is important to remember that sex therapy treatment begins at the moment that the professional, with knowledge and skill, initiates discussion with the patient about sexual concerns, in an empathetic, warm, and respectful manner. Sex therapy, then, may be as brief as a simple question and discussion or as intensive as formal traditional sexual therapy by a professional sex therapist.

Sexual health professionals should base their understanding of sexuality on credible scientific knowledge from anthropology, physiology, medicine, psychology, theology, pedagogy, sociology, zoology, and other branches of disciplined inquiry and science, and they should discuss patients' problems with respect and sensitivity to the patient's beliefs and values. Healthy sexual functioning is based on (1) accurate and adequate knowledge about sexuality, sexual function, and sex behavior; (2) a positive value of human sexuality; (3) general physical and psychological health; and (4) positive and cooperative relationship values and skills.

It is especially important that the health professional consciously consider his or her role in addressing and helping with the sexual problems of the patient or client. While often the focus is upon the patient, it is also of critical importance that the professional be self-aware of his or her attitudes about sex, feelings about sex, and convictions about what is appropriate or healthy sexual behavior.

It is particularly important that the professional respect the sexual beliefs and values of the patient, even when they are different. "Professionalism" within the health care field expects that the caretakers can differentiate their own values and beliefs from the patient's, when different, and not impose the professional's beliefs upon the patient. It is well for the professionals to be clear with themselves, and when unable to separate their values from those presented by the patient, it is appropriate to explain the perceived values conflict and to refer to another professional who is capable of working with the patient's values. While professionals are not required to violate their own values, religious beliefs, or principles, it is unethical for them to impose their values, religious beliefs, or principles upon the patient. Rather than struggle with any conflicts, it is usually healthier to refer the patient to another professional.

It is also important that health professionals, through comprehensive training, become comfortable in dealing with sexual problems. Health professionals are themselves the product of their own culture. As there is a wide diversity across the world in the experience, expression, meaning, and regulations concerning sexuality and its difficulties, it is important that the professional both appreciate and honor his or her own emotional discomfort as well as over time take advantage of academic training and skills education to improve the professional's comfort dealing with patients with sexual concerns. For example, there are several educational programs that have been developed (e.g., the Sexual Attitude Reassessment program developed at the Institute for Human Sexuality in San Francisco in the 1970s), which provide the educational opportunity to replace one's learned negative feelings about sexuality with more comfortable feelings through "desensitization." Most cultures deeply respect the importance and meaning that human sexuality holds for individuals and couples, and this respect is frequently manifested as private respect and even social control of sexual behavior.

To the extent that the sexual health professional understands his or her own feelings about sexuality and sexual behavior, affirms the healthy nature of human sexuality, and endeavors to develop greater comfort talking and dealing with the sexual concerns and problems of one's patients, the professional will demonstrate the empathy, acceptance, and care sought by the patient who is commonly uncomfortable as well.

In addition to developing increasing professional comfort, the professional also must learn specialized knowledge and skills to treat sexual problems comprehensively. Sexual knowledge and understanding are increasing at a rapid pace, and the professional does well to pursue continuing professional development in the area of sexuality. This WPA program itself is intended to offer some assistance in this area. An international survey conducted by Mezzich and Hernández (1999) (see Appendix 5) showed clearly the need for continuous sexual education, even for psychiatrists and sexologists. For example, it revealed the very low frequency with which both health professionals and patients address sexual questions in the initial interview.

It is important that the sexual health professional develop a reliable and quality network of other professionals to whom he or she may refer patients for specialized treatment of sexual problems that arise, or to treat sexual conditions that the professional is not comfortable with or not skilled at treating. Referral networks can help professionals find competent sexual therapists. Some such networks include the World Psychiatric Association (WPA), World Association for Sexual Health (WAS) (formerly the World Association for Sexology [WAS]), Latin American Federation of Societies of Sexual Education and Sexology (FLASSES), Robert Koch Institute (RKI), American Association for Sex Education and Therapy (AASECT), Society for Sex Therapy and Research (SSTAR), and the Society for the Scientific Study of Sexuality (SSSS), as well as a number of national and regional sexology professional associations.

Treatment is based on comprehensive differential diagnosis. It is particularly important that the sexual health professional rule out or distinguish psychiatric disorders that may be concealed behind a sexual complaint. Professionals must differentiate sexual complaints that warrant therapeutic attention from psychiatric syndromes that, among other symptoms, manifest with sexual features. For example, one common feature of major affective disorder (depression) is the loss of sexual desire (low libido) or inhibited sexual arousal (difficulty lubricating for women or erectile dysfunction among men). Even more important, treatment must include consideration of the larger system within which the patient experiences his or her sexual problem. The interaction between the person with the sexual problem and the partner, for example, is of critical importance; characteristics of either individual partner in a sexual relationship can contribute to a sexual dysfunction. Some individuals bring to their couple relationships a personal legacy of painful experiences, such as childhood physical and/or sexual abuse. The long-term negative effects of such prior trauma on the person's adult functioning (Gold, 1986; McCarthy, 1997; Talmadge and Wallace, 1991) can result in tension, disappointment, and hurt between the partners, which can then decrease their sense of intimacy and cohesion and precipitate sexual problems. Other individuals have personality characteristics or psychopathology symptoms that directly interfere with sexual functioning and thereby affect the couple's sexual and overall relationship. For example, individuals with panic disorder commonly fear any bodily symptoms of arousal (Barlow, 1988), including those associated with sexual arousal and physical exertion during sex with their partners (Sbrocco et al., 1997). In addition, individuals who grew up in families or environments characterized by stressful experiences such as community war, violence, or substance abuse are at increased risk for adult relationship problems and sexual dysfunction (Seilhamer and Jacob, 1990).

Differential diagnosis seeks to accurately identify the sexual concerns. For example, some men will attribute their sexual problem to erectile dysfunction, when in fact they have suffered chronic premature ejaculation without understanding that when one ejaculates, an erection will detumesce, and observing this they believe and say that they have erectile dysfunction. The professional is wise to be open to all possibilities and to base the assessment, history, and treatment plan on a comprehensive understanding of the patient's sexual situation and activity.

Another concern for the preparation of a treatment plan is to determine sexual comorbidities. There is a relatively high prevalence of multiple sexual dysfunctions. For example, in the clinic, careful interview and history has suggested that one-third or more of men whose chief complaint was premature ejaculation (PE) or erectile dysfunction (ED) had simultaneous ED and PE (Loudon, 1998; Metz et al., 2000); the same is true of women who reported hypoactive sexual desire (HSD) or inhibited orgasm (IO) (Verma, Khaitan, and Singh, 1998).

Sexual disorders also need to be distinguished from sexual difficulties. The traditional model for classifying the sexual dysfunctions and disorders originated in the 1960s with Masters and Johnson and has been subsequently modified by others. This model is based in the psychophysiological patterns characterizing normal sexual response. The complete sexual response cycle usually consists of six phases: desire, excitement or arousal, plateau, orgasm, resolution, and satisfaction following a mutual, reinforcing circular model. The sexual dysfunctions are distinguished by their effect on these phases of the response cycle. Other dysfunctions, such as sexual pain, may affect a number of these phases.

In clinical practice, a number of problems may present as a "sexual" concern (e.g., sexual jealousy, worry about a biological concern such as nocturnal emissions or "wet dreams," penis or breast size), which in the absence of physical findings may be one of a number of symptoms of a psychiatric disorder such as Generalized Anxiety Disorder (GAD), Obsessive-Compulsive Disorder (OCD), or Schizophrenia.

In the past twenty-five years, the emphasis in differential diagnosis has shifted from presumed psychogenic etiology for sexual dysfunction to the role of biomedical and organic factors in the etiology of sexual dysfunction (Rosen and Leiblum, 2000). With advances in medical understanding, current estimates of etiology are usually comparable for biological and psychological factors. With this increased attention to physiological features, there appears to be a trend toward the "medicalization" of sexual dysfunction (Rosen, 1996). At the same time, more attention is warranted and is being drawn to the psychological impact or "toll" from biogenic sex dysfunction on the individual's psychological health and the couple's general welfare.

Comprehensive Diagnosis of Sexual Disorders: The Integrative Biopsychosocial Model

An integrative, biopsychosocial model for understanding sexual problems (figure 3.1.1) comprises four broad factors. The philosophy of this approach is to recognize the potential complexity of sex disorders, understand the multiple potential causes and effects, and use and integrate all available resources—medical, pharmacological, psychological, relational, and psychosexual skills—to increase relationship intimacy, pleasure, and satisfaction as well as adequate (not perfect) sexual function. It emphasizes that four essential factors require equivalent attention for sexual health: the biophysical foundation of sexual function, the psychological dimensions (cognitions, behaviors, emotions), relationship dynamics (such as ability for cooperation and emotional intimacy), and the psychosexual skills of lovemaking.

The clinician also needs to distinguish the subtypes of sexual disorders. One approach to subtyping (e.g., for premature ejaculation) is based on phenomenological features (Rowland and Slob, 1995). Both the ICD-10 and the DSM-IV-TR distinguish organic and psychological phenomenological types. Another approach identifies subtypes inferred from the known or hypothesized causes and effects of sex dysfunction reported in research reports and clinical observations (e.g., Metz and Pryor, 2000). The literature discusses not only etiology or causes but also manifestations or effects that result from other causes and can interact to maintain a sexual dysfunction.

Figure 3.1.1. Components of an integrative, biopsychosocial, multidimensional model of sexual dysfunction.

Components of an Integrative, Biopsychosocial, Multidimensional Model of SD

Biological factors: physiologic dimensions of sexual function: vascular, neurologic, hormonal, and lifestyle aspects.

Psychological CBE dimensions (CBE):
Cognitions: assumptions; beliefs or standards; perceptions; attributions; expectancies.
Behaviors: actions.
Emotions: feelings, for example, confidence; resentments.

Relationship dimensions (ICI):
Identity: relationship cognitions, for example, couple expectations such as autonomy, cohesion, commitment.
Cooperation: interactions, for example, mutual conflict resolution.
Emotional intimacy: relationship feelings, especially empathy.

Psychosexual skills: cognitive, behavioral, emotional, and interpersonal aspects of love making.

Organic or physiological causes for sex dysfunction include the following

1. Physiological system conditions (e.g., neurological system)
2. Physical illness (e.g., diabetes, cardiovascular disease)
3. Physical injury (e.g., abdominal surgery)
4. Drug side-effects (e.g., antihypertensive medication; alcohol)
5. Lifestyle issues (e.g., smoking, obesity)

Psychological causes and effects of sex dysfunction may include these:

1. Psychological system problems (e.g., bipolar mood disorder)
2. Psychological distress (e.g., adjustment disorders)
3. Relationship distress (e.g., unresolved conflicts)
4. Psychosexual skills deficits (e.g., unrealistic expectations)
5. "Mixed" sexual dysfunction, which occurs with concomitant, multiple sex dysfunctions (e.g., erectile dysfunction or low desire with his partner's dyspareunia)

Appreciating the potentially multiple biopsychosocial factors of sexual dysfunction serves as the basis for an individualized, comprehensive treatment plan. To overlook a contributing or maintaining cause, or a detrimental effect, will sabotage treatment effectiveness and frustrate both the couple and the clinician.

Figure 3.1.2 presents the "Sexual Dysfunction Diagnostic Decision Tree: Assessing the Causes/Effects (Types)" to assess the potential physical and psychosocial causes and effects of SD. The "Clinical Worksheet: Evaluating the Possible Causes and Effects of a

Figure 3.1.2. SEXUAL DYSFUNCTION DIAGNOSTIC DECISION TREE: ASSESSING THE CAUSES AND EFFECTS (TYPES).

Sexual Dysfunction Diagnostic Decision Tree

Initial differential:
(1) Is the onset of SD lifelong or acquired? If lifelong, go to Step 1; if acquired, go to Step 4.
(2) Is the context of SD generalized to all sexual situations or a single situation?

Lifelong onset: If lifelong onset and generalized context:

Step 1: Is there also a history and evidence of a physiological condition associated with SD such as congenital, genetic, circulatory, neurologic, hormonal, or urologic system problem, and no evidence of psychopathology?

Yes: Physical system SD   Treatment: medical options, pharmaco-therapy, and CB sex therapy for adaptation.

No: Go to Step 2.

Step 2: Is there evidence of chronic psychopathology or a psychological character pattern that predisposes to SD such as bipolar, obsessive/compulsive, dysthymia, or generalized anxiety disorders, etc.?

Yes: Psychological system SD   Treatment: individual psychotherapy, psychotropic pharmaco-therapy, and CD sex therapy.

No: Go to Step 3.

If lifelong onset and either generalized or situational context SD:

Step 3: Is there evidence of the person's cognitive and behavioral inability to physiologically relax during sexual arousal, focus on specific pleasure/arousal of one's own bodily sensations, and manage desire and arousal?

Yes: Psychosexual skills SD   Treatment: CB psychosexual skills training; judicious use of prosexual medications.

No: Go to Step 4.

Acquired onset: If acquired onset and generalized context SD:

Step 4: Is there a current physical illness that is known to cause SD such as one of the following?

Diabetes mellitus	Cardiac disease	Vascular disease
Multiple sclerosis	Sleep apnea	Peyronie's disease
Hypothyroidism	Hypopituitarism	Hypogonadism
Polyneuropathy	Systemic lupus	Sexually transmitted disease (STD)
Lipid abnormalities	Chronic renal failure	Epilepsy
Prostatitis	Hypertension	Cancer (and its treatments)

Yes: Physical illness SD   Treatment: medical treatment, if possible; consider CB sex therapy to rebalance.

Figure 3.1.2. Continued

No: Go to Step 5.

Step 5: Has there been a physical injury, pelvic surgery, or neurologic trauma that may reasonably cause SD?

Yes: Physical injury SD   Treatment: medical treatment if possible; pharmacotherapy; consider CB sex therapy.

No: Go to Step 6.

Step 6: Has the person begun taking (or withdrawn from) a chemical agent known to cause SD such as an antihypertensive, psychotropic medications, chemotherapy?

Yes: Drug side effect SD   Treatment: discontinue agent if safe; try alternatives or antidotes; CB sex therapy.

No: Go to Step 7.

Step 7: Are there physiologic lifestyle patterns that are known to precipitate detrimental effects on sexual function such as obesity, smoking, poor cardiovascular conditioning, marathon athletics, sleep deprivation, and so on?

Yes: Physiologic lifestyle SD   Treatment: address patterns with programs such as weight loss, physical conditioning, adaptation sex therapy.

No: Go to Step 8.

If acquired onset and either generalized or situational context SD:

Step 8: Is there history and objective psychological test evidence that the person is experiencing current psychological stress?

Yes: Psychological distress SD   Treatment: psychotherapy; consider psychotropic medication; CB sex therapy.

No: Go to Step 9.

Step 9: Is there interview, history, and relationship test evidence of relationship distress associated with SD such as emotional conflict, infertility stresses, infidelity?

Yes: Relationship distress SD   Treatment: relationship therapy and CB sex therapy.
No: Go to Step 10.

Step 10: Is there also a complaint of another SD with the person and/or partner?

Yes: Multiple sex dysfunction   Treatment: comprehensive treatment of the causes and effects of the multiple sex dysfunctions ("mixed SD"). Reconsider Steps 1, 2, 7, and 8.
No: If acquired SD, consider Step 3, psychosexual skills deficit. Reconsider and reevaluate the case.

(Source: Metz & Pryor, 2000)

Figure 3.1.3. Clinical worksheet: evaluating the possible causes and effects of a sexual dysfunction.

Clinical Worksheet:
Evaluating the Possible Causes and Effects of a Sexual Dysfunction

Type of SD	If this is a feature	If a feature, % of total
A. Physiological SD (biogenic):		
1. *Bio-neuro-hormonal system*	_____	_____
2. *Physical disease / illness*	_____	_____
(Illness: _____)		
3. *Physical injury*	_____	_____
(Injury: _____)		
4. *Pharmacological side effect*	_____	_____
(Agent: _____)		
5. *Lifestyle issues*	_____	_____
(Issue: _____)		
B. Psychological SD (Psychogenic):		
1. *Psychological system*	_____	_____
2. *Individual psychological issues*	_____	_____
(Issues: _____)		
3. *Relationship issues*	_____	_____
(Issues: _____)		
4. *Psychosexual skills deficit*	_____	_____
(Issues: _____)		
5. "Mixed" SD	_____	_____
(Other dysfunction: _____)		
Number of causes / effects:	_____	100% _____

Sexual Dysfunction" (figure 3.1.3) is a convenient "log" to list the potential subtypes of SD suspected in the SD decision tree evaluation. These subtypes, then, are included as clinical problems in the comprehensive "Treatment Plan Format" (figure 3.1.4).

Figure 3.1.4, "Treatment Plan Format," presents a treatment plan worksheet and orientation for its use. Integrated sex therapy incorporates attention to biopsychosocial assessment and treatments as outlined in this chapter in order to specifically address the detailed features of the disorder. It is important that the treatment plan include identified sexual problems, concomitant general medical disorders, and other health-related biopsychosocial problems so that treatment addresses all relevant pathology and also contributes to enhancing the patient's quality of life.

General Principles of Contemporary Sex Therapy

While the techniques of contemporary sex therapy are fairly straightforward and simple in their cognitive and behavioral structure, they represent a multifaceted package with many different theoretical approaches and treatment components. They are unified as a therapeutic approach by a number of principles or theoretical guides that direct the therapist's attention and judgment although they may not be formally presented to the patient(s). Most clinicians who employ the more direct, cognitive-behavioral treatment approaches follow these principles, as appropriate to the clinical need and in varying degrees. The guiding principles of comprehensive sexual therapy include instilling positive attitudes about human sexuality; offering basic sexual education; attending to basic sexual enrichment and growth; training the patient in basic physiological relaxation as the foundation for adequate sexual functioning; inviting the patient to adopt personal responsibility for one's sexual self; centering therapy in the essential foundation of relationship intimacy; building mutual cooperation with the partner; facilitating adaptation by means of behavioral interventions; and concluding sex therapy with relapse prevention.

Positive Attitudes toward Human Sexuality

The principle of positive sexual attitudes acknowledges every patient's right to sexual health. It incorporates such basic tenets as the belief that the body and sexuality are good, that patients have a right to know about their sexuality, and that sexuality is a respectable and decent physiological and psychological process. Negative societal and family attitudes toward sexual concerns, expression, and past traumatic sexual experiences may combine to make the dysfunctional patient feel anxiety and, in extreme cases, even disgust and revulsion. Given that it is common that a patient has a negative value or attitude toward sex, the therapist's positive attitude and encouragement—that healthy sexuality includes developing a positive attitude and respect for human sexuality as decent, moral, and enjoyable—is essential to treatment. For example, many religions promote the view that sexuality is good, even a gift from God, although as with other areas of life it may be misused or abused. A positive attitude toward sexuality is a fundamental principle of effective and helpful sexual therapy.

Figure 3.1.4. TREATMENT PLAN FORMAT.

Treatment Plan Format
(Based on the WPA International Guidelines for Diagnostic Assessment)

Name: _____ Record N°: _____

Date (d/m/y): _____

Age: _____ Gender: M F Marital Status: _____

Occupation: _____

Clinicians Involved: _____

Setting: _____

INSTRUCTIONS:

Under **Clinical Problems** list as targets for care key clinical disorders, disabilities, and contextual problems presented in the multiaxial diagnostic formulation, as well as problems noted in the idiographic formulation. Keep the list as simple and short as possible. Consolidate into one encompassing term all those problems that share the same intervention.

Interventions should list diagnostic studies as well as treatment and health promotion activities pertinent to each clinical problem. Be as specific as possible in identifying modalities planned, doses and schedules, amounts, and time frames, as well as the corresponding responsible clinicians.

The space for **Observations** may be used in a flexible way as needed. Illustratively, it could include target dates for problem resolution, dates of scheduled reassessments, and notes that a problem has been resolved or has become inactive.

Clinical Problems	Interventions	Observations
1.		
2.		
3.		
4.		
5.		
6.		
7.		

Basic Sexual Information and Education

Most patients suffering from sexual disorders are regrettably unaware of basic sexual anatomy and physiology, as well as effective sexual techniques. In contemporary sex therapy, then, the therapist ensures that the patient has accurate and adequate knowledge about the body and reasonable expectations about how men's and women's bodies commonly function during the human sexual response cycle. While this specific information alone is not usually sufficient to produce improvement, it is often a necessary part of the overall sexual therapy—and its absence may be a common feature in treatment failures.

Basic Sexual Enrichment and Health Promotion

Ultimately sexual therapy intends to enrich the sexual lives of patients. The sexual enrichment or sexual growth part of sex therapy involves teaching psychosexual skills for discovering higher levels of erotic response. These skills for conscious loving include such features as (1) deep breathing, (2) eye contact during sexual interaction, (3) slower and more paced style of touching and sensual expression, and (4) a personalized, interactive, and explorative attitude towards sensual and sexual experiences. Such development includes a more deliberate discovery and mapping of one's own and the partner's erotic geography. Each partner embraces more deliberate and specific communication of one's erotic wishes and responses. Overall, sexual enrichment works to establish a climate between the partners that is less goal-oriented and more focused upon exploration and enhancement. One example of this enrichment approach is tantric love-making as practiced in India, Thailand, and other South Asian countries. Different features of sexual enrichment or sexual growth training are frequently incorporated into various stages of overall sex therapy for the various sexual problems. A number of programs have been developed to encourage positive sexual development, such as the Sexual Attitude Reassessment (SAR) workshop, adult-level sex education courses, body-image workshops, massage training, and even physical exercise classes (e.g., aerobics). Bibliotherapy, utilizing self-help sexual enrichment and self-help sexual therapy books, is another common adjunct to sex therapy. Because of continuing misinformation among many adults, even books on basic anatomy and physiology are usually helpful.

The Importance of Physiological Relaxation Training

Training in physiological relaxation is a primary goal of psychological sex therapy. Adequate and satisfying sexual performance depends on physical relaxation as the foundation for more natural physiological and psychological sexual excitement. Because anxiety is a common element in patients with sexual problems, whether as a cause or effect of the sexual problem, specific training in physiological relaxation is common to all therapeutic approaches. Such focus is designed in part to eliminate the "performance anxiety"—the cultural and psychological demand for sexual competence, expertise, and perfection that has been identified as both ubiquitous with, and a likely cause of, sexual dysfunctions. Relaxation training that focuses on deep muscle relaxation, biofeedback, hypnotic relaxation, yoga, or tai chi may be useful, in addition to frequent, progressively intense and endorphin-generating physical exercise. Especially useful are techniques that draw the patient's attention to the physical sensations in his or her own body. Relaxation training is a basic tool in any program of sexual therapy. In severe sex dysfunction cases, anxiolytic medicines, if properly prescribed, may also be useful particularly at the beginning of the therapeutic process.

Personal Responsibility for Self

The central principle undergirding most contemporary sex therapy is the principle of being sexually responsible for one's self and one's sexual enhancement. Partners are commonly enlisted to provide therapeutic support and to deal with relationship issues, but each partner is encouraged to claim actively his or her own sexuality and to be responsible for one's own sexual growth. After months or even years of experiences of sexual failure, individuals frequently feel confused about what or how to overcome their dysfunction and feel powerless to make changes. Avoidance of the sexual situation, then, becomes recurrent. One of the essential principles of sexual therapy is to invite the patient to accept responsibility for leading the changes in attitude and behavior that will bring about improvement, inspired by the encouragement and direction of the therapist. The therapist offers realistic confidence and guidance and uses graduated cognitive-behavioral techniques that produce the patient's progress by taking small, manageable steps in sequence.

Mutual Cooperation with the Partner

At the same time the patients are encouraged to take personal responsibility for their own sexual growth, both partners in a relationship are responsible for future change and for the resolution of the problem. It is typically important to assist couples to distinguish "blame" (retrospective focus on the "causes") from "responsibility" (the power to take steps to improve the situation) so that they are not paralyzed by a negative focus on the past. Cooperation between the partners in sex therapy is not only required for successful completion of the therapeutic techniques that may be prescribed, but cooperation is at the heart of healthy and satisfying mature sexual interaction. Partners need to feel that each is fully accepted, cared for, and positively regarded for his or her feelings even when there are difficulties. Such affirmation is central to the emotional "glue" in an intimate, sexually satisfying relationship (Jacobson and Christensen, 1996). In addition, encouraging fundamental interpersonal cooperation in the pursuit of the sexual goals—working together as an "intimate team"—can enhance the couple's relationship and is required to resolve the sexual problem to the partners' mutual satisfaction. In successful sex therapy, couples are helped to be protagonists in enhancing their sexual life.

The Essential Role of Relationship Intimacy

The concept of interdependence and intimacy in the sexual relationship (Parra, De Vries, and Hernández Serrano, 1995) is essential to comprehensive sex therapy. It is important to consider a comprehensive concept of sexual health as discussed in part 1. The World

Association for Sexology (WAS) has adopted a Declaration of Human Sexual Rights (Valencia, 1997; Hong Kong 1999), which is presented in the appendix and serves as the foundation for a new definition of sexual health and is incorporated in the WPA Sexual Health Education Program (see chapter 1.1 of this volume) and Pan American Health Organization (PAHO) documents. Commitment, intimacy, and love are essential variables in healthy sexual functioning.

Often couples with sexual dysfunction are found to be unable to clearly communicate their sexual likes and dislikes to each other due to inhibitions about discussing one's sexual feelings, excessive sensitivity to what is perceived as criticism by the partner, inhibitions about trying new sexual techniques, and erroneous assumptions that a person's sexual responsiveness does not vary (that is, does not vary in pleasure and desire from one time to the next). Accordingly, specific sexual therapy programs encourage the partner's respectful, mutual experimentation within open and positive communication about techniques and responses in order to enhance emotional intimacy.

The Importance of Relapse Prevention

A final principle of effective sex therapy is that the gains affected by formal sexual therapy commonly are lost over time unless the therapist also develops a plan to maintain the therapeutic gains. Creating a cognitive-behavioral understanding of what has helped bring about the improvement and developing a couple plan including small steps that will maintain the improvements is essential to long-term sexual improvement (McCarthy, 2001).

The General Organizational Plan for Sex Therapy

Comprehensive treatment for sexual dysfunctions and disorders recognizes the overall role and opportunity that the professional brings to the patient's distress. While often professionals focus upon the "techniques" (sensate focus) or specific "interventions" (e.g., medications) of sex therapy, it is important that the professional appreciate one's role throughout the entire process of providing assistance. Therapeutic techniques cannot be employed without the patient first interacting with the professional who understands and caringly carries out his or her professional role.

The well-known PLISSIT model, initially developed by Annon (1973) and later expanded by Lerer et al. (1999), describes the professional's role in sex therapy treatment by offering guidance for four different levels of involvement: "P" represents permission, "LI" denotes limited information, "SS" stands for specific suggestions, while "IT" represents intensive therapy. These four levels of involvement in patient care describe the roles the professional may provide depending upon practice, skills, and comfort. It is appropriate for every professional to be aware of the level of treatment of sexual problems that he or she is comfortable with and committed to provide. For those who—for whatever reason—are not willing or capable of providing some level of professional assistance with sexual difficulties, referral to other professionals who are willing and able is a necessity.

The initial role, permission, entails asking about sexual concerns, conducting a simple sexual inquiry involving several brief questions, and offering basic sexual information. All health care professionals, even those not specifically skilled in sexual medicine, can encourage patients to discuss sex, accept their patients' sexual concerns, and make appropriate referral. Some look at this role as that of an evaluator and empathetic listener. Patient surveys have suggested that this is the most commonly sought trait desired of the professional.

At the limited information (LI) level, the professional gives normalizing information to reassure patients regarding a specific concern, such as "Yes, almost all men have 'wet dreams' (nocturnal penile emissions) at some time in their lives, and this is the body's way of self-care." This limited information level is the professional role of providing sexual education.

"Specific suggestions" (SS) means offering options for managing a specific sexual concern such as medication choices or sexual therapy by another professional. This role is one of sexual counselor, and commonly that of the marital therapist.

"Intensive therapy" (IT) refers to providing professional sexual, marital, and psychological therapy. Most professionals are not specifically trained in providing intensive psychotherapy, but refer for this type of treatment. The IT professional role here is that of a formal sex therapist.

It is important that all professionals consider which role or level of involvement in sexual problems that they are both interested and capable of providing for patients. A commitment to providing sexual health services at an appropriate level of involvement is possible for every professional.

When actually interviewing and addressing patient concerns, the LAB (Learning/Attitudes/Behavior) model is also useful to many professionals. Accepting that some patients may feel some initial discomfort discussing in detail their sexual concerns, an anxiety-reducing approach for asking questions about the patient's sexuality is to ask for discussion in three levels, which proceeds from the less revealing personally to the more revealing—that is, from the less anxious to the more uncomfortable area.

First, the professional asks about what the patient may have learned ("L") about the topic (e.g., "What have you learned about sexual self-pleasuring or masturbation?"). Second, the professional invites the patient to describe what one's attitude ("A") or belief may be about the concern under discussion (e.g., "What do you believe about masturbation?"). Finally, the professional may ask the patient what actual behaviors ("B") he or she may have engaged in (e.g., "How old were you when you first masturbated?" or "How frequently do you masturbate now?"). The advantage of this approach is to therapeutically allow the patient to gradually describe his or her concerns, provide a nonthreatening environment in which to discuss them, and demonstrate the professional's sensitivity and respect for the patient and his or her values. Such rapport building or gentle engaging with the patient is the first major therapeutic endeavor and sets the stage for formal sexual therapy work.

Biological Treatment

A number of biological treatments are available to ameliorate specific biogenic sources of sexual disorders that arise from specific medical problems. Biogenic causes include the following:

1. *Physiological system:* innate, chronic biological system conditions such as congenital or genetic sexual physiological problems, neurological, circulatory, endocrine, or myotonic systems disorders
2. *Physical illness:* acute illness such as urinary tract infection, sleep apnea, cardiovascular disease, diabetes, and respiratory disease
3. *Physical injury:* temporary or permanent physical impairment such as head trauma, spinal cord injury, bikers' ED, abdominal surgery, stroke
4. *Drug/pharmacological side-effect:* chemical side-effects of antihypertensive medications, ethyl alcohol abuse, some psychotropic medications, recreational drug abuse, or withdrawal from agents such as the opiates
5. *Lifestyle issues:* detrimental effects of smoking, poor physical conditioning, excessive physiological stress, and obesity

3.2.1. General Perspectives

Sexual dysfunctions are invariably multidetermined; a single cause is uncommon. Even when an organic factor is present, it is essential to treat the principal psychological factors that can complicate the organic problem or that could have resulted from it. As described in part 2, organic problems affect all phases of the sexual response cycle. For example, according to current estimates, the cause of at least 50% of erectile dysfunction cases is primarily organic, with some estimates ranging as high as 75%–85% (Vliet and Meyer, 1982; Kaplan and Sadock, 1994). A total of 30% of surgical procedures on the female genital tract result in temporary dyspareunia, and 30%–40% of the women seen in sex therapy clinics for dyspareunia have pathological pelvic condition (Fordney, 1978). The common general organic factors that affect sexual function include chronic illness, pregnancy, pharmacological agents, endocrine alterations, and chemical abuse. A variety of other medical, surgical, and traumatic factors can be implicated in specific dysfunctions.

From the biopsychosocial perspective, while treatment should address biological, psychological, and interpersonal areas, whether cause or effect of the sexual problem, initial treatment for sexual problems addresses the biological or physiological features that may have been discovered in the biophysiological assessment.

Experienced sexual therapists have learned that presuming that a sexual problem is psychological in nature, even when there are psychological symptoms, may lead the therapist to provide psychological sex therapy that is doomed to failure because the primary cause is physical, thereby iatrogenically creating a disheartening experience for the patient (Halvorson et al., 1988). The safer clinical presumption is to pursue organic etiology first and rule out this feature as carefully as possible before proceeding with psychological or relationship therapies, although psychological sex therapy designed to repair any psychological damage from an organic cause is also necessary. Generally, sexual medicine is directed toward managing those organic conditions that could contribute to almost all sexual dysfunctions. Any existing chronic systemic disease must be comprehensively managed. Diabetes should be meticulously controlled, thyroid dysfunctions corrected, pharmacological therapies altered, and bad lifestyle habits involving chemical abuse, poor nutrition, obesity, and inadequate rest and exercise changed.

3.2.2. Pharmacological Treatments

A host of prescription therapies are available for the treatment of male sexual disorders; however, comparable medications for women are quite limited. Traditionally, female sexual dysfunction has been viewed as secondary to either estrogen deficiency or psychological inhibitions. Thus, women presenting with sexual problems typically were referred to either a gynecologist for hormone replacement therapy or to a psychotherapist. Men with analogous complaints generally receive a battery of physical tests to rule out physiological causes, including hormonal, neurophysiological, hemodynamic, and other studies. However, owing to the momentum generated by sildenafil's impact upon male erectile disorder, researchers have also been looking at the physiological factors that underlie women's sexual disorders, as well as corresponding medical therapies. In addition to pharmacological therapies, there are a number of medical sexual devices or aides available to treat sexual dysfunctions, and in some cases, surgical alternatives.

In the sections below we describe the pharmacological and other biological treatments available for women and for men.

Pharmacological Treatments for Women

The following section discusses medications that have been suggested by some clinicians as potentially beneficial to women with sexual dysfunction. However, none have been thoroughly studied as yet. For example, none of them have been approved for use in women by the U.S. Food and Drug Administration. Clinicians should exercise caution in recommending any of the following medications because they are associated with side effects and their safety and efficacy have not been determined.

Vasoactive Medications

There is no evidence to date that vasoactive drugs improve sexual functioning in women. More specifics are discussed below for various medications.

Phosphodiesterase inhibitors (sildenafil, tadalafil, vardenafil) are oral medications for erectile disorder. Phosphodiesterase inhibitors have similar efficacy. The major difference between the three products is that tadalafil has a longer duration of action. It has a thirty-six-hour duration of action whereas sildenafil and vardenafil have a four-hour duration of action. Extreme caution should be used if phophodiesterase inhibitors are combined with alpha-blockers because of the risk of dangerous hypotension. This is important because alpha-blockers are commonly used to treat benign prostatic hypertrophy, a common disorder in the age group which need to utilize phosphodiesterase type 5 inhibitors.

Their mechanism of action involves inhibition of phosphodiesterase type 5, which results in smooth muscle relaxation and increased blood flow to the corpus cavernosum. It is described more fully in the section on Biological Treatment of Male Sexual Disorders.

As in the male, the female genitalia contain ample amounts of erectile tissue. Theoretically, sildenafil should enhance the vaginal engorgement/lubrication response in women just as it enhances erection in men, through localized genital vasodilation. In one small, uncontrolled study, all 9 women who took sildenafil an hour before sexual activity experienced a reversal of antidepressant-induced dysfunction (Nurnberg et al., 1999). In another uncontrolled study with 14 consecutive cases of women and men with antidepressant-induced sexual dysfunction, all measures of sexual functioning in all patients demonstrated significant improvement (Fava, 1998). However, another open label study in postmenopausal women with sexual dysfunction showed no significant improvement on sildenafil (Kaplan S. et al., 1999). In another study, which was double blind and controlled, utilizing Doppler ultrasonography and vaginal pH levels, sildenafil appeared to enhance physiological sexual response in posthysterectomy and menopausal women (Berman et al., 1999). However, it should be mentioned with emphasis that the first large-scale, placebo-controlled study involving 583 postmenopausal women with a broad range of sexual dysfunctions demonstrated no significant improvement with sildenafil (Basson, 2000).

Psychotropic Medications

Many antidepressants are known to have negative sexual side effects; however, some may do the reverse, particularly at the beginning of treatment. Some antidepressants and anxiolytics actually may have a positive effect on sexual functioning (Kaplan et al., 1987).

Nefazodone is an antidepressant chemically similar to trazodone. It has been characterized by a relative lack of negative sexual effects, but it has been associated with liver toxicity.

Bupropion is an unconventional antidepressant with primary dopamine reuptake and secondary noradrenaline reuptake actions. Prior to its approval as an antidepressant in the late 1980s, bupropion was tested in a 60-patient controlled, double-blind, 32-week trial for the treatment of low sexual desire and other sexual response deficits in nondepressed women and men (30 female, 30 male) (Crenshaw, Goldberg, and Stem, 1987). Statistically significant sexual improvement was found in over 60% of patients treated with bupropion but in less than 10% treated with placebo. Recent clinical trials have found that use of bupropion is associated with a lesser impairment of sexual functioning than SSRIs (Segraves et al., 2000). It also appears that, used in combination with SSRIs, bupropion may minimize antidepressant-induced sexual side effects (Bodkin et al., 1998). A recent double-blind study has shown that bupropion increases orgasmic capacity in women with low sexual desire (Segraves et al., at press).

Anxiety over sexual activity may be alleviated with a number of antidepressants and anxiolytics. Benzodiazepines are helpful in temporarily reducing sexual anxiety when prescribed on as needed basis, although sustained use may be habit-forming and lead to sexual dysfunction (Kaplan, 1974).

Buspirone, a 5HT-1A agonist prescribed for treatment of generalized anxiety disorder, may reverse antidepressant-induced sexual dysfunction. Depression contributes to interpersonal friction and sexual problems between couples. Moreover, depression and other psychiatric disorders are known to be associated with sexual dysfunction. Though antidepressants relieve the symptoms of depression, they can cause sexual side effects, such as diminished desire, impaired arousal, and inhibited or delayed orgasm. The more serotonergic the antidepressant is, the greater the sexual side effects.

Strategies for coping with sexual side effects include reducing the dosage, taking a brief drug holiday, changing to a less serotonergic antidepressant, or using one of the medications purported to counteract sexual side effects. These include cyproheptadine, buspirone, gingko biloba, psychostimulants, nefazodone, bupropion, amantadine, and sildenafil. Out of these, only sildenafil, buspirone, and bupropion have been subjected to controlled studies.

Psychostimulants, which augment dopaminergic activity, theoretically have the potential to enhance sexual functioning (Bartlik, Kaplan, and Kocsis, 1995). When taken in low dosages on an occasional basis, psychostimulants such as dextroamphetamine and methylphenidate have been reported to improve sexual responsivity (Kaplan, 1974). However, sustained high dosages can be habit-forming and may inhibit sexual functioning.

Adrenergic Agonists

The benefit of adrenergic agents in treating female arousal problems is unclear. While these agents increase physiological arousal, it should be kept in mind that psychological and physiological arousal in the female are not always linked (Meston and Heiman, 1998).

Ephedrine, an alpha- and beta-adrenergic agonist, facilitates sexual behavior in female rats (Yanase, 1977). Ephedrine has also been found, in double-blind, controlled studies of sexually healthy women, to increase plethysmographic measures of vaginal engorgement during the viewing of erotic video (Meston and Heiman, 1998). Although ephedrine may facilitate sexual arousal and orgasm, its capacity to cause nervousness and vasoconstriction may limit its usefulness as a treatment of sexual dysfunction.

Hormonal Therapies

Testosterone   Women whose levels of circulating testosterone are below normal often experience sexual dysfunction. Symptoms of testosterone deficiency may include diminished sexual desire and fantasies; reduced sensitivity to stimulation of the nipples, vagina, and clitoris; and the inability to become aroused and to achieve orgasm. When orgasms occur, they may be briefer, more localized, and less pleasurable (Bartlik and Kaplan, 1999). Testosterone deficiency also may cause a diminished sense of well-being as well as a loss of muscle tone and pubic hair, genital atrophy, and dry skin (Rako S., 1996). The normal range for testosterone in women is .7 to 2 pg per ml (unbound or free), and 25 to 70 ng per dl total (bound and unbound); however, the clinician should be aware that laboratory values are often inaccurate.

It has been found that exogenous testosterone that caused serum levels of androgens to exceed or be at the upper end of normal values restored sexual functioning in women who had experienced hysterectomy and bilateral oophorectomy. It should also be noted that exogenous testosterone use can lead to androgenization. Consultation with an endocrinologist is recommended. Studies show that women who receive both supplemental estrogen and testosterone after a total hysterectomy have greater libido than those given either estrogen alone or a placebo (Sherwin and Gelfand, 1985).

Women with testosterone deficiency may not respond to supplemental testosterone at first because of atrophy or a lack of testosterone receptors in the genitalia (Rako S., 1996). Therefore, it might be desirable to begin therapy by applying testosterone or methyltestosterone directly to the vulva once a day in a cream base. After a week or two, the cream can be applied to the inner thigh or wrist five days a week, alternating with the vulva twice a week, at a dosage of .25 to 1 mg per day (Bartlik and Goldstein, 2000). Some patients prefer to switch to either a fraction of an oral methyltestosterone pill designed for men, a specially compounded methyltestosterone pill in dosages suitable for women (.25 to 1 mg per day), or a testosterone skin patch (Testoderm TTS) for men, which delivers 5 mg in a 24-hour period. Women need wear the patch for one to four hours a day. Unlike methyltestosterone, which confounds laboratory assays, testosterone itself has the advantage of allowing for the measurement of blood levels.

For women at risk of breast cancer who need to avoid estrogen intake, methyltestoterone taken orally is preferable because it cannot be converted as easily to estrogen as testosterone itself. A combination pill of methyltestosterone and conjugated estrogens is also available.

Dosages of testosterone must be kept as low as possible to avoid side effects, which may include not only enlargement of the clitoris but also weight gain, liver damage, reduced levels of high density (good) cholesterol, acne, irritability, and male secondary sexual characteristics such as facial hair, lowered voice, and male pattern hair loss. These side effects rarely occur at the low doses necessary for women. Clinical experience has shown that if the response wanes after a few weeks or months, a two-week drug holiday may restore the hormone's effectiveness.

Some women will need testosterone supplementation for the rest of their lives to maintain sexual functioning, whereas others may require it for a year or less. Information on long-term effects, optimal doses, routes of delivery, and potential risks (including cancer and cardiovascular disease) are lacking, and research in these areas is urgently needed. Because female sexual dysfunction is not yet an approved indication for use of any form of testosterone, patients should sign consent forms and be monitored frequently.

DHEA Dihydroepiandrosterone (DHEA) is a precursor of both estrogen and testosterone. It is available over the counter and has been touted to have sex positive effects in both men and women. However, scientific evaluation of this is missing. DHEA replacement therapy in women with adrenal insufficiency resulted in improved sexual functioning in all phases of the sexual response cycle (Casson et al., 1996). The effect of DHEA on the sexuality of women with normal adrenal functioning has been minimally studied.

Estrogen   Women vary considerably in their sexual response to exogenous estrogen. The use of hormonal replacement therapy has been said to cause both increases and decreases in libido and sexual functioning (Crenshaw and Goldberg, 1996). The sex-positive effect may in part be psychological due to the feminizing effect of estrogen on the skin, breasts, and vagina. Improved self-confidence and mood, which also may occur, can lead to increases in libido indirectly. Certainly, it is essential to correct dyspareunia secondary to estrogen deficiency, as this may inhibit sexual desire.

On the other hand, many women who are given exogenous estrogen (with or without progesterone) often report a diminution in desire and arousability. This may be due to the effect of synthetic progesterone or to elevations in blood proteins that bind to the hormones (including testosterone) and inactivate them. Thus, taking exogenous estrogen may actually lead to sexual dysfunction by precipitating a testosterone deficiency of free testosterone (Rako, 1996). Estrogen is now available through a number of routes of administration, including oral, transdermal patch, vaginal cream, and an intravaginal ring that remains in place for three months. Given the FDA warnings about the use of estrogen for other than severe menopausal symptoms in the lowest dose and for the shortest time possible, vaginal cream may be the optimal route of administration for sexual dysfunction. More research is needed to clarify the effect of estrogen and other sex hormones on female sexuality.

Progesterone   Natural progesterone has been reported to stimulate libido (Lee, 1997) and to do the reverse (Crenshaw and Goldberg, 1996) as well. The increase in sex drive that some women experience during the late stages of pregnancy and premenstrual has been said to be linked with elevated progesterone levels at these times (Laux and Conrad, 1997).

Pharmacological Treatments for Men

Erectile Dysfunction (ED)
Erectile dysfunction may be the result of a number of causes. In cases of clear and exclusive organicity, the treatment may be singular and targeted to the physical problem. In other cases, integrated therapies are considered, combining individual psychotherapy, individual or couple sexual therapies, oral or injectable pharmacological therapies, prosthetic implantation, or vascular corrective surgery. The pharmacological options include oral medications such as phosphodiesterase (PDE) inhibitors (e.g., sildenafil, tadalafil, vardenafil); alpha-adrenergic antagonists (e.g., phentolamine); serotonergic agonists (e.g., trazodone); and dopaminergic agonists (e.g., apomorphine).

Sildenafil   Sildenafil is a phosphodiesterase (PDE) inhibitor and is a powerful selective and specific inhibitor of the type 5 phosphodiesterase, which is present in high concentration in the corpus cavernosum. At a lesser concentration, the 5-phosphodiesterase is also present in the visceral and vascular smooth muscle. The recommended initial dose is 50 mg. According to the results, it can be reduced to 25 mg or, in case of failure, switched to 100 mg per dose. With respect to the mechanism of erection, this medicine acts on the nitric oxide/cGMP system. It promotes the maintenance of the relaxation of the corpus cavernosum smooth muscle and avoids the cGMP degradation. It facilitates the initiation of erection and its maintenance. Sexual stimulation or reflex responses give raise to the release of nitric oxide at the NANC (nonadrenergic/noncholinergic) nervous endings and the vascular endothelium, which leads to the penile erection mechanisms. Sildenafil has been used for therapy for ED when its etiology is organic, psychological, or drug induced. The favorable global response has been reported to be greater than 80% positive results, with better results noted in functional (psychological) patients and in patients with neurogenic spinal lesions. Among the most frequently observed adverse effects are headache, facial redness, dyspepsia, visual disturbances, and nasal congestion, each of them presenting in approximately 10%–15 % of patients.

Contraindication for use includes simultaneous ingestion of nitrates (generally used as coronary vasodilators) or nitrite spenders. In those patients using high-dosed antihypertensive agents or who are at cardiac risk associated to effort, it is administered cautiously, requiring cardiac assessment. Deaths reported due to its use are likely linked to the absence of an accurate cardiac evaluation of these patients or its use without taking into account the cautions previously mentioned. One of its practical values is that it may be taken one hour before the probable sexual intercourse. It is encouraged that it be combined with psychological sex therapy for those individuals or couples who appeared particularly distressed with their experience of erectile dysfunction. The clinician should be aware that there are reports of marital discord associated with use of sildenafil for erectile disorder.

Vardenafil and Tadalafil Since the release of sildenafil, two other phosphodiesterase inhibitors have become available to treat ED. As yet there are few good scientific studies that compare the relative effectiveness and side effects of these three medications. It appears that they are approximately equal in efficacy. Effectiveness studies suggest that when the man takes the drug and has adequate penile stimulation, he will have a sufficient erection for intercourse 40%–80% of the time (depending on the severity of ED).

There are some differences in the medications (see table 3.2.1). For example, sildenafil and vardenafil work in about thirty to sixty minutes while tadalafil works in as little as thirty minutes. The erection enhancing effect may last for approximately four hours with sildenafil and four to five hours with vardenafil, while tadalafil effectiveness may last for up to thirty-six hours.

Each pill sometimes (5%–15% of men) produces side effects like headache, facial redness, upset stomach, back pain, and sinus congestion. The blue vision or light sensitivity some men experience with sildenafil does not occur with vardenafil and tadalafil. Each medication has a warning about use with alpha-blocker antihypertensive (blood pressure) medications that are often used to treat enlargement of the prostate. Vardenafil cannot be safely taken with any alpha-blocker (e.g., Hytrin [terazosin], Flomax [tamsulosin], and Cardura [doxazosin mesylate]) while for sildenafil in doses above 25 mg there is a warning to stagger the dose of sildenafil by four hours after taking an alpha-blocker.

Tadalafil also is not to be taken with most alpha-blockers although it may be used with Flomax (0.4 mg per day) with no staggering of doses. While none of these medications has been shown to increase the risk of heart attack, the three medications can not be taken safely with nitrates (such as Imdur [isosorbide] or nitroglycerine) for chest pain due to angina.

Apomorphine   This is a dopaminergic agonist that acts directly on the D2-receptors at the central nervous system. It has been shown to be effective in psychogenic EDs and in some varieties of organic ED. The recommended dose varies between 4 and 6 mg per day. Its side effects include nausea, vomiting, and syncope. The results of the use of the drug in clinical practice were not very positive, and in most countries the drug has been discontinued.

Yohimbine   This is a central and peripheral acting agent that blocks the alpha-2 receptors at the corpus cavernosum (most of the adrenergic receptors at this site are alpha-1 receptors). This medicine, used for many years, shows a relative efficacy and aphrodisiac effect on many men and women. Among the most commonly observed adverse effects are tachycardia, high blood pressure, nervousness, excitability, oliguria, and slight tremor, which occasionally give rise to the interruption of therapy.

Phentolamine Mesylate   This is a central and peripheral acting alpha-1 and alpha-2 adrenergic blocker. The drug is rapidly absorbed and peak concentrations are reached after thirty minutes and its effect lasts for one hour. The usual dose is 40 mg. Among the reported adverse effects are rhinitis (21%), dizziness and tachycardia (7%), headache (4.5%), nausea (3%), and hypotension (2%). Oral phentolamine is less effective than oral PDE5 inhibitors.

Trazodone   This is a serotonergic agonist antidepressant agent that blocks the alpha-adrenergic receptors. It was thought it could help patients with erectile dysfunction, as there were reports of a few cases of priapism associated with its use. However, recent double-blind studies have shown that it does not have an effect on erectile dysfunction.

Intracavernous Drugs   There are several intracavernous drug therapies for erectile dysfunction. By means of an injection in the cavernous tissue, vasoactive drugs acting on the penile arterial and venous smooth muscle and on spongiosum and cavernous tissues induce their contraction or relaxation, thus modifying their volume and producing the erection. They are also called peripheral erection-promoting drugs. Such vasoactive drugs are classified as inductive drugs, which act directly on the smooth muscle cell (papaverine, PGE1-prostaglandin, linsidomine), and facilitating drugs, which require endogenous mechanisms to produce their action (VIP, phentolamine, and linsidomine). The most commonly used is E1-prostaglandin (PGE1, alprostadil). PGE1 stimulates the adenyl cyclase supporting the synthesis of cAMP. It also inhibits the release of noradrenaline. It is considered a drug of election, as it is a molecule that is present in the body, its metabolism is fast, it has few adverse effects, and it shows a high bioavailability for its active metabolite PGE0. Dosage varies from 2.5 mcg to 40 mcg. It is useful for the treatment

Table 3.2.1. COMPARISON OF ORAL TREATMENTS FOR ERECTILE DYSFUNCTION

Drug	Launching Year	Time for Effect (Mins.)	Effect (Hrs.)	T Max. (Hrs.)	Efficacy	Mechanism of Action	Contra-indications	Main Side Effects	Dosage Range
Sildenafil citrate	1998	40	> 4	0.8	High	PDE 5 INH	Nitrates	Headache	25/50/100 mg
Tadalafil	2002	45	> 36	2.0+	High	PDE 5 INH	Nitrates	Backache	20 mg
Vardenafil	2002	30	> 4	0.7	High	PDE 5 INH	Nitrates	Headache	10/20 mg
Phentolamine	1998	20	> 3		Low	Peripheral nonselective A Blocker	—	Stuffiness Congestion	20 mg
Apomorphine	2001	15	> ?		Low	Central active dopamine agonist	—	Nausea Syncope Dizziness	2/4 mg

References:
Padma-Nathan et al. (2004), Rosen (2000), Gresser et al. (2002), Rosen and McKenna (2002), Saenz de Tejada (2002), Carrier (2003), Porst et al. (2003), Stroberg et al. (2003), Francis and Corbin (2003).

of neurogenic impotence and mild to moderate vascular erectile dysfunction. There is a high dropout rate from these treatments presumably because of their inconvenient delivery system.

Papaverine   Papaverine acts through inhibition of the phosphodiesterase, thus supporting the accumulation of cAMP and cGMP and the relaxation of the smooth muscle at the helicine arteries and the sinusoids. It is inexpensive, but its risks include immediate (greater propensity to priapism) and late adverse effects (fibrosis). Recommended doses are 5 to 90 mg. Phentolamine acts by alpha-adrenergic blocking, thus facilitating erection. Its erection-facilitating effects are very useful, enhancing the effects of alprostadil and papaverine. Most used is Trimix (papaverine 75 mg + phentolamine mesylate 2.5 mg + PGE1 25 mcg in 4.25 ml) (0.2 to 0.5 ml). The different drugs are injected alone or in combination in the penile corpus cavernosum. They produce vasodilation and hardness in impotent, diabetic, or drug-induced subjects. When they are adequately applied and controlled by the physician, they do not show secondary effects. When testing has not been done and the drugs are applied without any control, drug-induced priapism can be the consequence. The initial trial with injection should be prescribed by a specialized physician trained in the management of complications. He or she has to show the patient how to apply the required dose himself a few minutes before sexual intercourse. Recommended frequency of application is up to two or three times a week. Complications include pain (especially with PGE1), hematomae, ecchymosis, and urethral puncture. The most important complication is the prolonged erection (which persists between two and six hours after administration of the vasoactive agent) and drug-induced priapism (which persists more than six hours). According to different authors and to the diverse drugs used, the incidence of this complication varies between 1% and 10%.

MUSE   Medicated Urethral System for Erection (MUSE) is a galenic form to apply vasoactive drugs in the penis using the transurethral route. The active substance is alprostadil, in concentrations of 125, 250, 500, and 1,000 mcg, in a vehicle of polyethylene glycol, which facilitates the tissular penetration of the active drug. In the literature there are reports of efficacy varying between 7% and 65%. The most common adverse effects are penile pain (36%), urethral burning (13%), dizziness (4%), orthostatic hypotension (3%), and syncope (0.4%). Priapism is very rare.

Testosterone   In the medical literature, the incidence of ED caused by endocrine disorders varies between 1% and 35%. Testosterone replacement therapy does not benefit men with normal serum levels. In fact, in impotent men with normal serum levels, testosterone can compound the problem by increasing sexual desire without increasing performance. Testosterone therapy is indicated in hypogonadal men whose testosterone values are below normal levels. Androgens are necessary for sexual functioning. About 60% of testosterone circulates bound to the steroid hormone binding globulin (SHBG), 38% bound to albumin, and the remaining 1%–2% is free. Both first mentioned types are the bioavailable testosterone, which is the really useful hormone for sexual functioning. Hypogonadism is characterized by the decrease of blood testosterone. It can be caused by a testicular defect or a failure at the hypothalamus-hypophyseal unit. This deficit is seen in 4%–7% of men with erectile dysfunction, and frequency may increase with age. Iatrogenic hypogonadism is induced by antiandrogens and finasteride and the use of estrogens and hair lotions by bald persons. High prolactin (PRL) levels are also associated with ED, as they induce a hypogonadotrophic hypogonadism. High PRL could also exert a direct action on the CNS, as the simple reposition of testosterone in hyperprolactinemia patients does not ameliorate sexual functioning. Most frequent causes of the PRL increase are drugs, tumors, and idiopathic features. Hyperprolactinemia has been reported in some ED patients.

Hormonal replacement therapy with testosterone in patients with hypotestosteronemia ED requires the diagnosis of hypogonadism (low testosterone). The determination of bioavailable testosterone levels is significantly important, as they have to be lower than the reference values by age. When they are lower than or equal to normal values, and especially when there is also an erectile dysfunction, an attempt of replacement therapy is recommended after the prostatic function has been assessed with a prostatic specific antigen (PSA). Contraindications include prostatic cancer; severe benign prostatic hyperplasia; abnormalities of the rectal tract; echographic or PSA changes; sleep disturbances; and hematocrit greater than 50%. Most commonly used are testosterone esters (enantate and cipionate). Initial dose is 250 mg i.m. every fourteen days. When there is a partial deficit of testosterone, lower doses may be used (50–100 mg every two weeks). Testosterone transdermal patches may also be employed, which are applied at the skin, releasing the hormone progressively. Advantages are that they maintain physiological testosterone levels, they are easy to apply for the patient, and the discomfort of the intramuscular administration is avoided. The drug therapy to be employed has to be selected according to the cause of PRL increase (bromoergocriptine, lisuride, and cabergoline); surgery could be selected in order to resect a prolactinoma.

Premature Ejaculation (PE)

There are a number of pharmacological agents used "off label" to ameliorate premature ejaculation (Balon and Segraves, 2003). Table 3.2.2 summarizes some of the agents reported in the literature in case examples and double-blind studies. These reports suggest that clomipramine, paroxetine, sertraline, and fluoxetine are preferred for positive effect, with paroxetine being first-rated among SSRIs. Positive effects generally range from 60% to 80%; positive placebo effect, 20% to 30%. Effect appears to be dosage dependent. With such medications, reports, for example, indicate intravaginal time improvement from approximately 45 seconds to 2.5 minutes with placebo, 4.27 minutes with sertraline, to as much as 5.75 minutes with clomipramine for as many as 70% of men (clomipramine). The response rate in different studies may also be dosage related. Side-effects typical of SSRIs may be a problem for some men. New agents are under development (e.g., dapoxetine) that may be approved specifically to treat PE.

While the SSRIs are the most commonly used pharmacological agents to prolong ejaculatory latency, other agents are also utilized (see table 3.2.2). In cases where PE is concomitant with ED, a combination of agents are sometimes used experimentally. For example, clomipramine may be combined with sildenafil or a topical agent (lidocaine). Research has not yet established the effectiveness of these treatments.

Table 3.2.2. Pharmacological Agents Used "Off Label" to Ameliorate Premature Ejaculation

Type of Agent	Generic Name	Commercial Name	Dosage Range
Heterocyclic antidepressants			
	Amitriptyline	Elavil	10–150 mg
	Clomipramine	Anafranil	20–50 mg
	Desipramine	Norpramin	10–150 mg
SSRI antidepressants			
	Fluoxetine	Prozac	20 mg
	Sertraline	Zoloft	50–200 mg
	Paroxetine	Paxil	20–40 mg
	Citalopram	Celexa	20–40 mg
	Fluvoxamine	Luvox	25–100 mg
In development	Dapoxetine	Dapoxetine	—
Atypical antidepressant			
	Nefazodone	Serzone	100–250 mg
Antianxiety			
	Lorazepam	Ativan	0.5–1 mg
Topical agents			
	Prilocaine		
	Lidocaine	EMLA cream	25 mg of each/g of cream

Source: Segraves, R. T., and Balon, R., (2003). *Sexual Pharmacology Fast Facts*. New York: W. W. Norton & Company.

Integrating Medications and Other Treatments into a Couple's Sexual Style

An integrative approach to SD emphasizes the use of all available resources, including sexual performance–enhancing medications, especially when SD has an organic etiology. In some cases, even when the SD cause is psychogenic and severe, medications and other medical treatments (e.g., vacuum device) may be helpful. The medication or device must be integrated into the couple sexual styles. As is evident from research and clinical experience with the pro-erection medications (e.g., sildenafil), these medications are rarely effective as stand alone treatments. The drop out rate is relatively high, perhaps 40%–80% (McCarthy and Fucito, 2005; Brock et al., 2002). This is due to a failure to integrate medication with the partner, failure of the medication to alleviate low sexual self-esteem, medication side-effects, or disappointment that the drug was not the miracle cure as shown on the TV advertisements.

Medication is likely to succeed best when used along with a psychosexual skills program and integrated into the couple sexual style of intimacy, pleasuring, and eroticism (McCarthy and Fucito, 2005; Lieblum, 2002; Metz and McCarthy, 2004). If the man depends on a medication to establish 100% erections or ejaculatory delay every time, he sets himself and the relationship up for failure. Sex is an interpersonal experience. Striving for perfect sexual performance subverts sexual function and satisfaction.

3.2.3. Other Biological Treatments

Devices for Women

Eros-CTD

Eros-CTD (Clitoral Therapy Device) is the first prescription device for women with sexual dysfunction that has been approved as safe by the U.S. Food and Drug Administration (FDA). The device is a tiny, flexible cup that fits over the clitoris, providing gentle suction and facilitating blood flow to the clitoris. Initial studies, while limited, suggest the device may be of some benefit to postmenopausal women (Billips et al., 2002).

Vibrators

Electric and battery operated vibrators are very effective in enhancing female sexual desire, arousal, and orgasm. The intense stimulation they provide can help to overcome psychological inhibitions and medical causes of inhibited arousal. They may be incorporated into therapeutic exercises performed individually or with the partner (Kaplan, 1983). Vibrators come in various shapes and sizes. In addition to the traditional phallic-shaped vibrators, there are powerful but small "lipstick" size models, "palm-of-hand" shaped models designed specifically for clitoral stimulation, and curved wands for "G-spot" (Graffenberg spot) stimulation. Many vibrators are now fitted with expendable silicone sleeves for greater comfort and cleanliness (Bartlik and Goldstein, 2000).

Lubricants

The addition of artificial lubrication may be helpful not only for menopausal and postpartum women but for those with adequate sex hormone levels. Many of the new water-based lubricants have improved in recent years and are silkier and longer lasting. They are preferable to oil-based lubricants because they will not damage latex condoms and are less likely to cause infection. Silicon-based lubricants are preferable for sex in water or for particularly vigorous activity; however, they tend to be more expensive. Though they improve safety, lubricants containing the antiviral spermicidal nonoxynol-9 can be irritating to some patients. In general, the fewer the number of additives, the lower the risk of allergic reaction (Bartlik and Goldstein, 2000).

Devices for Men

Devices for Erectile Dysfunction

The penile vacuum device (e.g., Erecaid) is a mechanical therapeutic alternative for treating ED. The device produces an acceptable penile erection in some cases. Its action mechanism works by generating a negative pressure that facilitates the passive filling of the corpus cavernosum. The erection is maintained by placing elastic rings on the penile base in order to avoid the venous return. It includes a cylindrical acrylic chamber with an end open (where the flaccid penis is introduced); at the other end the vacuum pump is connected (a mechanical pneumatic system that is set on manually or by an electronic device). Patients are told not to maintain the compression for a period longer than twenty or thirty minutes in order to avoid complications (Bianco, 1998). This device is indicated for patients with erectile dysfunction who seek a non-intrusive alternative to other ED treatments.

Devices for Premature Ejaculation

The testicular restraint is a physiological aid to delaying orgasm if the testicles are restrained from ascending to the perineum. Cuffing the testicles in the hand and gently pulling or holding down helps some men to not ejaculate. Although not approved for use by the Food and Drug Administration (FDA), there are Velcro-type devices that gently restrain the testicles.

The penile rubber ring device was tested in a small pilot study by Wise and Watson (2002); in this study, men used a latex rubber ring on the base of the penis daily for no more than thirty minutes, but not during sex. Some of the men reported that they improved ejaculatory control within a week of using the device. It may be that the device desensitized or stressed the penile nerves or operated as a placebo.

Surgical Interventions for Women

There are no accepted surgical treatments for sexual dysfunctions in women at this time. In certain cases where medical problems affect sexual quality—such as endometriosis, cervical cancer, uterine tumors, and uterine prolapse—corrective surgery may be palliative therapy.

Surgical Interventions for Men

Penile Prosthesis Implantation

The intracavernous implant with silicone prosthesis represented one of the first effective resources to treat ED. From the earliest medical publications in 1973, the penile prosthetic implant was a breakthrough in the therapeutic armamentarium for ED. With the introduction of the intra-penile vasoactive drugs and the oral vasodilators, its prescription was notably reduced. A commonly used penile prosthesis is the malleable prosthesis which is composed of a firm silicon cylinder with a central axis made of flexible metal (silver or steel multifilaments). Advantages of the malleable prosthesis are that it is a simple device with few mechanical failures; the surgical procedure is less complicated and costs are lower; the complication rate is low; and the prosthesis provides good hardness and satisfaction of patients and couples. Disadvantages of the malleable prosthesis include a persisting nonnatural erection; an erection that is difficult to dissimulate in public changing rooms; and the fact that performance of transurethral endoscopic procedures is difficult or even impossible.

Hydraulic or inflatable prostheses are hollow silicon cylinders with liquid contents and hydraulic transfer systems that are implanted in the penis. They are composed of various parts including the principal body, reservoirs, valves, and conducts. An advantage of these models is their easy mechanical ability to inflate and disinflate. These models are readily accepted because of their good erectile results and their easy management.

Indications for a penile prosthetic implant may include patients with severe organic erectile sexual dysfunction who do not respond to other simpler and less invasive therapeutic alternatives. Penile prosthetic implants are good therapeutic options to treat certain severe cases of ED. However, the consequences of implantation are irreversible, and no other therapy can be applied in the future.

Arterial and Vascular Reconstruction Surgery

While still considered experimental, arterial vascular surgery (neoarterialization) of the penile arterial arbor or arterialization procedures at the profound dorsal vein in known arterial lesions have been sometimes considered in cases of arteriosclerotic or traumatic origin, and venous vascular surgery for venous surgery in the failure of the veno-occlusive system. In both cases, long-term results of these surgical procedures show a low efficacy rate (less than 30% good long-term results). A possible exception would be cases of arterial lesions due to trauma.

To some extent the above review may serve as an historical review of the medical biological and pharmacological treatment options that have been developed in the past thirty-five years. While these developments are remarkable, treatments currently under development promise an increasing number of treatment options for men and women who suffer sexual problems.

Penile Dorsal Nerve Severance and Verumontanum Impairment to Prevent PE

There have been reports that neurotomy of the penile dorsal nerve (Santos, Vieira, and Fischer, 1999; Tullii et al., 1994) or cauterizing the verumontanum in the prostate gland (Schapiro, 1943) effectively slows rapid ejaculation, although the appropriateness of such intrusive, radical, and irreversible methods need extensive study and ethical justification. Pharmacotherapy and careful training in the cognitive-behavioral psychosexual arousal management skills are invariably adequate treatment without the permanent obliteration of penile sensation and pleasure.

Psychological Treatment

3.3.1. General Perspectives

Comprehensive sex therapy not only addresses the physical causes first because of the constitutional priority of biology but also pursues treatment choices guided by the principle of the least intrusive or less complicated technique before proceeding to more involved treatment(s) should the lesser options not ameliorate the problem. It is valuable to consider that the most helpful therapy for the patient may not be the newest, more expensive, or more sophisticated of the options available. This principle is particularly important for medical physicians who have increasingly more biomechanical options, with the plethora of pharmacological and surgical treatments at their disposal. While it may be tempting to use the most impressive techniques, it is essential that the professional offer the patient all of the options available and inform him or her of the honest experiences and results of others who have selected each option.

The overall personal satisfaction of the patient must be the ultimate determinant. When this is the guiding principle, often the more simple and straightforward technique is more helpful for the patient. This important principle of integrative sexual therapy is to provide the minimal and least intrusive treatment that will effectively ameliorate the problem of the patient and achieve his or her treatment goals. For example, surgical implantation of a penile prosthesis may be contraindicated when psychological sex therapy or pharmacological therapy may be effective. The patient's informed decision, safety, and general well-being must be the highest priority.

Psychological sex therapy is warranted for all but the most simple sex problems. General medical professionals should be alert for possible psychological and relationship distress that may result from an organically caused sexual disorder. When the cause of the sexual problem is psychological, psychological sex therapy is the treatment of choice. For psychogenic sexual dysfunction, psychosexual therapy offers reasonably effective treatment. In the medical management of organic sexual problems, psychological sex therapy can help patients adjust to any adverse impact on their normal sexuality caused by physical limitations, as well as develop alternative ways to achieve sexual satisfaction (e.g., manual pleasuring when intercourse is precluded). The advantages of psychosexual therapy include its noninvasive nature and broad applicability. The disadvantages of psychosexual therapy include its variable efficacy in treating the multiple sexual problems, cost acceptability by the patient or the couple, and the often limited availability of qualified sex therapists.

The psychological component of sexual problems varies in content and severity. The psychological component may (1) cause, (2) exacerbate, or (3) be an effect of an organic sexual disorder. The level of psychological etiology/sequelae directly influences the type of psychological treatment and its effectiveness (e.g., Metz and Pryor, 2000). There are four basic psychological components:

1. *Psychological system* or constitution: When there are significant and chronic individual psychological disorders (e.g., panic disorder, obsessive-compulsive disorder, dysthymic depression, bipolar mood disorder, generalized anxiety disorder, or a personality disorder) concomitant with the sexual dysfunction, the psychological problem is likely etiological and warrants primary attention in comprehensive treatment. Prevalence of such is thought to be infrequent.

2. *Psychological distress*: Temporary psychological difficulties (e.g., situational adjustment disorder, reactive depression, sexual shame, etc.) precipitate sexual difficulty or result from it. Such dynamics are thought to be common in the clinical situation. With psychological distress, attention to addressing the negative cognitive, behavioral, and emotional features associated with the sexual dysfunction is important.

3. *Relationship distress*: Relationship stresses such as unresolved emotional relationship conflicts cause reactive sexual disorders. The sexual problem, then, manifests as (a) acquired and (b) generalized. This dynamic is observed to be common in the clinical situation.

4. *Psychosexual skills deficits*: Lack of sexual experience and skill, difficulty focusing on one's own sensations, deficits at physiological relaxation during arousal, lack of awareness of physical self-regulation ability during sexual arousal, and other skills deficits psychologically hinder the adequate management of the body (e.g., "performance anxiety") and cause sexual problems as well as interpersonal problems. The resulting sexual dysfunction, then, is commonly present as (a) lifelong and (b) usually generalized. Such psychosexual skills limitations are thought to be very common in the clinical situation. Frequently this feature is due to a lack of adequate sexual education, especially about sexual physiology and sexual functioning. Surveys of sexual scientists and therapists commonly indicate that the professionals who treat sexual problems view adequate sex education as the priority for treatment (e.g., Apt, Hurlbert, and Clark, 1994).

The therapies described in this chapter represent what is known from the current scientific and psychotherapeutic state of knowledge. In utilizing these treatments, care should be taken to work respectfully with patients and with sensitivity for their values, beliefs, and spirituality when they seek help for their sexual concerns.

3.3.2. Professional Approaches to Treatment

There is a wealth of professional theoretical approaches to treating mental health problems. Depending on the patient's personal, family, and relationship history, a number of professional approaches may be useful in sex therapy. Contemporary sex therapy relies on this wealth of approaches such as cognitive, behavioral, psychodynamic, humanistic, and integrative therapies, as well as utilizes a number of treatment modalities or treatment environments (individual, couple, family, group) to comprehensively treat sexual problems. Individuals and couples who have better general relationships, less psychopathology, and greater motivation for treatment than others who enter therapy are more successful in treatment outcome (Vansteenwegen, 1996; Stravynski et al., 1997).

Contemporary sexual therapy utilizes a number of clinically useful models or therapeutic approaches to treat sexual dysfunction and sexual disorders (e.g., Heiman and Verhulst, 1990; Leiblum and Rosen, 2000). Psychoanalytic therapy, useful for insight therapy, declined in use for sex therapy in the United States after Masters and Johnson, Helen Singer Kaplan, Harold Lief, and others made classic contributions to behavioral sex therapy (Masters and Johnson, 1966, 1970; Leif, 1982; Kaplan, 1974). Current treatments have expanded to incorporate cognitive therapy (e.g., McCarthy, 1988; Berg and Snyder, 1981; Metz and McCarthy, 2003, 2004), family systems theory (e.g., Schnarch, 1997), integrative marital therapy (Jacobson and Christensen, 1996), and also a number of adjunctive therapies including sexual education, relaxation training, yoga, acupuncture, biofeedback training, hypnosis (e.g., Fishbein, 1985), desensitization, and aversive therapy. As a result, sex therapies and effectiveness may vary considerably. Over time, cognitive-behavioral sex therapy has become the treatment of choice for most sexual problems. Cognitive-behavioral and interpersonal treatment approaches have been shown to be effective in a number of studies of sexual dysfunction treatment (e.g., Gregoire and Dhugra, 1996; Heiman and Verhulst, 1990; McCarthy, 1988).

One definition of psychotherapy is: helping patients to do those things they could not do by themselves. The sexual therapist—operating from one's own theoretical perspective—also needs to know the basics and models of marital psychotherapy, group psychotherapy, cognitive-behavioral psychotherapy, assertiveness training, and self-esteem reinforcement techniques.

Adequate training in general psychopathology is important for sex therapists in order to recognize deeper psychiatric problems that may manifest with a sexual symptom. Without this background, the sex therapist could mistakenly attempt to treat a sexual problem that is only a symptom of a larger psychological problem, subsequently fail to help the patient, and create frustration for both the patient and professional. For example, the depressed patient more often than not has sexual problems. Treatment with an antidepressive medication may serve as the initial and most effective treatment not only for the depression but also for the sexual dysfunction if it is actually the result of depression. On the other hand, not every patient with a sexual problem may be depressed.

The treatment of sexual difficulties has evolved considerably since the pioneering work of Masters and Johnson (1970). Their highly structured method has incorporated over the years a panoply of concepts and techniques that reflect the wide range of psychological determinants and biopsychosocial conditions. Aided by psychopharmacology and biological treatment, sex therapy can effectively resolve specific sexual problems in a short span of time. Awareness of the contribution of medical and pharmacological factors to sexual disorders has stimulated important research that has underscored the multifactorial causation of sexual problems and the importance of integrative treatment.

3.3.2.1. Psychodynamic Therapy

One of the strengths of sex therapy since its inception more than four decades ago has been its integration of behavioral techniques with various psychotherapeutic approaches in order to effectively treat sexual dysfunction. Prior to this addition, the rationale of treatment of sexual problems was to bring the deeper childhood roots of each dysfunction to consciousness from the unconscious mind, which was hoped to then spontaneously resolve the sexual problem. However, this occurred in only a minority of cases. With the addition of a more behavioral approach in the 1960s, techniques were developed to address what then began to be called the immediate rather than the deeper causes of sexual dysfunction. The immediate causes are the current obstacles to good sexual functioning that are reported or inferred by the patient as he or she describes a typical sexual experience. Without the obliteration of these immediate causes and positive improvement of psychosexual skills, irrespective of how deeper causes are addressed, there will most likely be no cure. When these immediate causes are resistant to change, however, addressing the remote (deeper) causes with the richness of psychodynamic psychotherapy can help to overcome resistance; synthesize the role of developmental issues that shape the dysfunction; reduce current anxiety, depression, guilt, and shame; and improve social adjustment (Leiblum and Rosen, 2000).

For comorbid sex problems involving major affective disorder, generalized anxiety disorder, and other major psychopathologies, psychodynamic therapy may be useful in addressing these features and may need to take precedence over addressing the secondary sexual problem. In the sexual therapy itself, psychodynamic theory has evolved over the years and yields multiple therapies that can be employed notably to deal with unusually resistant sex therapy cases. Based upon the premise that sexual problems may express unconscious conflicts deriving from developmental problems in the patient's childhood and emphasis upon various emotional and projective techniques can sometimes be effective in treating the resistances that may gridlock sexual growth and recovery. The exclusive use of psychodynamic therapies to treat basic sexual dysfunctions, however, has not been shown to be particularly effective unless combined with straightforward cognitive-behavioral interventions.

3.3.2.2. Cognitive-Behavioral Therapy

Sex therapy in the past thirty years has relied on the behavioral domain as the primary medium for improving sexual functioning. In recent years, this behavioral tradition in sex therapy has been notably enhanced with the integration of cognitive therapy theory and practice into behavioral sex therapy. Together with recent medical advances, contemporary sexual therapy offers improving benefit to an increasing number of sexual problems.

There appear to be two major reasons for the current trend toward cognitive-behavioral interventions with sexual problems. First, sexual problems frequently include concomitant individual features that are typically treated with cognitive-behavioral therapies, such as depression, anxiety, and obsessiveness. The behavioral interventions such as those developed by Masters and Johnson were practical strategies designed to address the specific cognitive-behavioral features of sexual dysfunction. For example, "spectatoring" is a cognitive preoccupation or obsessiveness, and "performance anxiety" is anxiety that would respond to common behavioral anxiety treatment. The cognitive-behavioral techniques were "applied" with anxiety management strategies (such as systematic desensitization) to the sexual disorder, which was viewed as a specific form of anxiety. Sex therapists also identified common cognitions or unreasonable expectations about sexual functioning among sex dysfunction patients, and they attempted to address them with already established cognitive techniques such as cognitive restructuring.

A sophisticated approach is the cognitive-interpersonal treatment model. The five key elements of this paradigm include (1) psychoeducational remediation, (2) reduction of sexual and performance anxiety, (3) script modification techniques, (4) relationship enhancement and conflict resolution strategies, and (5) relapse prevention procedures (Leiblum and Rosen, 2000, p. 252).

3.3.2.3. Contemporary Sex Therapy

Comprehensive sexual therapy addresses the whole person—thoughts or cognitive features, behaviors, and emotional or affective features. Different theoretical models for psychological understanding and treatment address these three domains differently and with different emphasis. The emotional dimension has been traditionally addressed therapeutically by psychodynamic-based therapies (e.g., Gestalt, insight-oriented analytic therapy) designed to ameliorate emotionally based conflicts. The behavioral dimension (such as couple communication, erectile performance, orgasm) in sex therapy is primarily addressed with behavioral therapy. The cognitive dimension is principally addressed with types of cognitive therapy designed to ameliorate the problem by reorganizing the way the patient analyzes and thinks about the problem. While each is important, each emphasizes a different avenue to address a problem and facilitate change. The cognitive therapist recommends that the more expeditious path to change is to change the way the patient thinks, and that this cognitive change will subsequently change one's feelings and then behavior. The behavioral therapist, on the other hand, proposes that changing the patient's behavior will subsequently alter the patient's thoughts and feelings. Each dimension—cognition, behavior, feelings—may have an important role depending on the causes of the sexual disorder, comorbidity, and the severity of the problem. While there are differing psychological theories to integrate the paths between cognitive, behavioral, and affective, current sexual therapy has developed as a hybrid of cognitive-behavioral-emotional strategies and interventions.

Theory, practice, and outcome research suggests that cognitive-behavioral sex therapy is the treatment of choice for the treatment of uncomplicated sexual dysfunction and other sexual disorders. There are a number of cognitive-behavioral treatment approaches utilizing individual, couple, family, and group therapeutic modalities. Most recently, some integrative therapies (for example, integrative couples therapy) attempt to address each of the cognitive-behavioral-affective domains together. There is some empirical evidence that such combined treatments—and notably the cognitive-behavioral blend—are more effective than single domain therapies (e.g., psychodynamic or behavior therapy alone). Research also suggests that the integration of cognitive-behavioral sex therapies with appropriate biomedical treatments, notably pharmacological therapy, is most effective. Comprehensive assessment and treatment integrates the biological/physiological, psychological (cognitive, behavioral, and emotional), interpersonal, and cultural aspects in order to address the sexual concern in an inclusive way for the benefit of the person and his or her sexual relationship.

Because of the inherently relational nature of human sexuality, couples, family, and group therapies are often preferred to individual therapy or are used as powerful adjunctive treatments to individual therapy. Depending upon the psychological features and interpersonal circumstances of distinctive cases, couples, family, or group therapy may provide the treatment of choice. Research suggests that sexual dysfunction therapy is likely more effective conducted with couples rather than individual therapy and that group therapy appears to be particularly helpful in treating sex offenders (enacted paraphilia), gender dysphoria, and sexual abuse cases. Current comprehensive sexual therapy attempts to design treatment that addresses the circumstances and needs of the particular patient and his or her situation.

The principles of contemporary sex therapy outlined above guide the professional sex therapist who conducts specific and detailed sexual therapy with a patient. The techniques employed are utilized in the therapeutic environment wherein the professional supports a positive attitude toward sex; teaches accurate sexual physiology; encourages the patient to take personal responsibility for pursuing sexual growth and improvement; explains the importance of physical relaxation and teaches physiologically focused relaxation techniques; facilitates the cooperation of the sexual partners; centers the sexual relationship within the general interpersonal relationship of the couple and endeavors to enhance their overall as well as sexual relationship; utilizes cognitive-behavioral interventions to facilitate the sexual growth; and establishes a maintenance plan at the end of the specific therapy in order to better ensure lasting results.

Contemporary Sex Therapy Features

Current sex therapy is integrative. It is grounded in the biopsychosocial perspective that considers the biological, psychological, and interpersonal etiological sources. Treatment is obliged to specifically address each contributing feature. From the human perspective, sex problems are a simultaneous interaction between physiological, psychological, and relational features, and each aspect warrants attention. In treating the patient's problem, for example, the biological features (e.g., erectile dysfunction subsequent to medication use for high blood pressure), the psychological features (mild depression due to the erectile dysfunction), and the relational features (distressed marital intimacy subsequent to the sexual problem and avoidance) each need therapeutic focus.

The most common sexual therapy techniques or interventions are described below, including basic sex education, physiological relaxation training, attention to cognitive distortions or myths that impede healthy sexual functioning, arousal pacing techniques, "sensate focus" exercises, as well as interpersonal skills (e.g., communication) and relationship intimacy interventions (e.g., conflict resolution). Contemporary sex therapy selects a combination of strategies from the extensive array of techniques and tailors them into a comprehensive plan to specifically deal with the detailed features of the individual or couple's sexual difficulty.

Sexual Education about Sexual Physiology

Accurate knowledge about the basic physiology of sexual arousal is essential to relaxed and confident sexual interaction. Physiological and sexual misunderstandings are often the source of unreasonable expectations about sexual performance and satisfaction. For example, the expectation that all women are capable of orgasm from intercourse alone (when research suggests that only 20%–30% of women report orgasm with intercourse alone while many more report orgasm with intercourse supplemented with manual clitoral stimulation or other supplemental stimulation) may set unreasonable demands and performance anxiety for both partners.

It is important to understand that general knowledge and advanced education do not assure adequate sexual knowledge and that knowledge about sexual anatomy does not ensure adequate knowledge about sexual physiology. Experienced sexual therapists are well aware that even well-educated leaders and professionals do not possess equivalent knowledge about sexual physiology. Many cultures and countries now enjoy readily available and professionally accurate publications (books and audiovisuals) as well as computer internet resources about human sexuality, and these can serve as an important adjunct to sexual therapy. The availability of such resources, however, does not ensure that many take advantage of such assets, and therapists should wisely incorporate basic sexual education into the standard sex therapy protocol.

Basic Sex Education Interventions

Accurate sexual knowledge and education are major priorities and components of sex therapy. Adequate sexual information includes knowledge about the male and female physiological sexual functioning, developmental sexual changes over the life cycle, and knowledge and skills for cooperative interpersonal relationships. Psychosexual skills include awareness of and cooperation with the partner regarding such features as the basic purposes of sex (reproduction, pleasure, anxiety reduction, individual self-esteem, and relationship intimacy) and the styles of sexual arousal (sensual entrancement, partner/interaction, and role enactment focus; see Mosher, 1980).

Teaching the "Purposes" of Sexual Activity

Clinical experience suggests that sexual difficulties commonly arise from misunderstandings and differences about the purposes of sexual activity and about the different styles of sexual arousal and their accompanying behavioral patterns. As a result, teaching about such features is useful and serves as the foundation for understanding a number of features of typical sexual therapy.

There are five general functions or purposes for sexual activity:

1. Reproduction or procreation (biological)
2. Physical pleasure or sensual enjoyment (physiological)
3. Anxiety reduction or tension release (physiological/psychological)
4. Individual self-esteem and confidence (psychological)
5. Relationship intimacy, closeness, and satisfaction (interpersonal/social)

Reproduction or procreation is the "natural" or biological function of sex. Physical pleasure is thought to be the basic function of sex in long-term satisfying sexual relationships—it's what keeps partners interactive. A third purpose is tension release or reduction of stress and anxiety, a common psychophysiological purpose of sex for both men and women. Individuals may also seek enhancement of their self-esteem through sex and pursue feelings of self-worth, confidence, or satisfaction in being and functioning as a sexual person. The fifth function is to use sex to both create and celebrate a variety of relationship qualities such as love, intimacy, affection, and joy. In healthy relationships, these are positive purposes. In dysfunctional relationships, the purposes are more negative, such as manipulation, destructive control, or hurt.

It appears that individuals typically pursue each of these five purposes for sex at one time or another in their lives. Often multiple purposes are pursued simultaneously. In fact, when the focus becomes too singular—for example, to reproduce—sex can become distressing and dysfunctional.

It also appears that the priority or ratio of one purpose to another can fluctuate significantly from time to time—even day-to-day. For example, one partner may engage in sex with 40% of the purpose to feel the physical pleasure, 40% out of a sense of love, 10% for self-esteem, and 10% for procreation. The other partner may seek sex for 60% tension release, 20% self-esteem, 10% love, and 10% for pleasure. The potential for conflicted sexual interaction then exists as the partners may feel this difference in agenda. Realizing and accepting that we have sex for multiple and fluctuating purposes, clarifying the sexual agenda, and developing more partner congruence is helpful.

Teaching about the Types or Styles of Sexual Arousal

There are many ways of sexual arousal. However, for classification simplicity, there are three basic styles of sexual arousal (see: Mosher, 1980):

1. Sensual entrancement arousal: becoming aroused by focusing upon one's own body, the sensations, the pleasure, and self-abandonment
2. Partner interaction arousal: becoming aroused by focusing upon the partner, his/her body, his/her responses, and the "romantic" interaction with the partner
3. Role enactment arousal: becoming aroused by other erotic stimuli (e.g., erotic video), role playing, or acting out feelings or fantasies

These styles behaviorally look different. An individual pursuing arousal primarily by "sensual entrancement," may typically be immersed in one's sensory exposure and may close one's eyes, go within, become quiet, and look detached and passive. Routine, sameness, and stylized touch help this person to get turned on. The person who pursues arousal by partner interaction is very active, with eyes open, looking at the partner, talkative (romantic talk), and energetic. This is the sexual style portrayed on television and in movies—passionate and impulsive sex. This person gets pleasure and is turned on by focusing attention outside one's self—such as seeing the partner respond—and getting carried away in passion and heat. (It is a common feature of men and women who suffer sexual dysfunction, that they principally utilize partner interaction arousal to the detriment of sensual entrancement arousal focus.) The person aroused by role enactment finds variety and experimentation arousing, such as dressing in sexy lingerie, role playing being tough or hard to get, acting out a scene from a movie or fantasy, having sex in new places (e.g., vacation), or using toys such as massage oil, a vibrator, or a dildo. By trying new things, this person finds excitement and arousal through sexual playfulness—feeling a sense of trust, freedom, and uniqueness with the lover.

While individuals appear to have a preference for one style, every person has the capacity for arousal by each style and may use them interchangeably. For example, an individual may begin lovemaking with role enactment, change to partner involvement, and then switch to entrancement. An individual's use of the three styles seems to vary over time. It is likely that there are developmental stages which individuals and couples go through. For example, early in a couple's sexual life, partner involvement seems common, giving way to individual entrancement and a more "sedate" sexuality for a while, then enlivened with role enactment, or a resurgence of partner involvement. Many individuals report that they may pursue a different type of arousal even from one sexual meeting to the next: Tuesday, entrancement, "because I was very tired"; and Saturday, partner involvement "because I was really appreciating my partner."

Sexual partners who may not realize that there are different kinds of arousal may misinterpret their partner's behavior in a hurtful, personalized way. For example, the entrancement-focused individual having sex with a partner involvement person would likely find the partner involvement individual's love-making efforts distracting (the looking, talking, heavy breathing, interacting, being expressive and passionate), and wonder why the lover is "interrupting" or seeming to work against their arousal. The partner involvement person, on the other hand, might interpret the entrancement partner as disinterested, rejecting, or bored. The potential for misunderstanding and hurt is evident.

Learning that people have different purposes and ways of getting aroused helps couples appreciate their differences and accept them. It also helps couples to cooperate so that both partners may feel respect and caring from the other as they mutually pursue satisfying sex for each other and their preferred ways of getting aroused. Sharing and discussing one's sexual feelings, cooperating, and collaborating in pleasure are perhaps the most crucial sexual skills.

The Use of Questionnaires and Audio-Visual Materials

The use of questionnaires to assess various aspects of sexual thoughts, feelings, and behaviors are not only an aide to assessment and diagnosis but can serve as powerful tools for basic sexual education. For example, a survey that invites the respondent to indicate the frequency of masturbation, or the frequency of orgasm, when reviewed with the patient, provides a natural opportunity for the sexual therapist to offer supplemental information and data regarding the current state of scientific understanding. For example, to explain that reliable research regarding sexual behavior suggests that nine of ten men and seven of ten women masturbate at some point in their lives may serve as a reference point for the patient to understand the sexual behavior of others as a marker for his or her own behavior. Other surveys may yield objective information that can further guide the patient in such areas as the extent of sexual experience, role of fantasy, body image, positive versus negative feelings about sex, or global sexual satisfaction (e.g., Derogatis Sexual Functioning Inventory, DSFI). There are a number of established surveys and inventories that are useful for teaching as well as assessment purposes (Davis et al., 1998; Rosen, Riley, et al., 1997).

The use of audiovisual materials—tape recordings, films, videos, the Internet—can provide validating sexual information for individuals and couples. When used during sex therapy, such tools can provide visually vivid portrayals of such therapeutic features as relaxation techniques, relaxed massaging, guided touch, or relaxed intercourse. For many individual and couples, such educational material can provide a more healthy, realistic, and encouraging image of how couples act during mature sexuality, which can serve to counter the more commonly available pornographic images from magazines and Hollywood movies. The positive use of such educational sexual materials is well researched and considered a quite useful tool in sex education and sex therapy programs. Audiovisual aids developed in the context of a particular culture may not be appropriate or well received in another culture. Furthermore, use of these aids may have different legal status across the world.

In contemporary sex therapy, then, the therapist ensures that the patients have accurate and adequate knowledge of the human sexual response cycle through verbal discussion, reading materials, films or other audiovisual materials. In addition, specific information is often provided on the general principles of effective sexual techniques of kissing, manual and oral pleasuring, erotic features of men's and women's bodies, positions of intercourse, and so forth.

Sex Therapy Techniques

Generally, couples treatment is the preferred treatment modality for most sexual dysfunctions, although combining individual, conjoint, and even group treatments has value. Each treatment modality offers unique values. For example, the individual modality may encourage the treatment principle of responsibility for one's self, while couples therapy promotes partner cooperation.

Sex therapy integrates the basic principles and common sex education features into basic behavioral interventions commonly called "sensate focus" exercises. These interventions, initially described by William Masters and Virginia Johnson, Helen Singer Kaplan, and Joseph LoPiccolo, were designed to address the impediments to adequate sexual functioning. These strategies have been developed and expanded over the years to produce a blend of cognitive-behavioral psychosexual skills for individuals and couples (e.g., Metz and McCarthy, 2003, 2004).

Current cognitive-behavioral sex therapy interventions utilized in both individual and couples comprehensive sex therapy are listed in figure 3.3.1.

Psychosexual Interventions for the Individual and the Couple
These "homework exercises" or interventions are designed to overcome psychogenic dysfunction and comprise a typical, graduated psychosexual skills approach for individuals and couples. The therapist individualizes treatment by selecting interventions appropriate to the causes, effects, and severity of the sexual problem, as well as drawing from

Figure 3.3.1. FREQUENTLY USED COGNITIVE-BEHAVIORAL SEX THERAPY STRATEGIES.

Cognitive-Behavioral Sex Therapy Strategies

This figure outlines some common strategies in contemporary sexual therapy. By design these exercises are graduated, that is, one builds upon the satisfactory learning or completion of the preceding exercise. Commonly, other techniques are readily incorporated into the appropriate phase of treatment that may amplify or serve as helpful alternatives to these interventions.

Phase One: Developing emotional comfort and physical relaxation:

1. Realistic sexual expectations: correcting sexual "myths"
2. Couple communication skills enhancement
3. Couple cooperation skills: working as an "intimate team"
4. Physiological relaxation and sensual training for the individual
5. Kegel/pelvic muscle (PM) relaxation training for the individual

Phase Two: Enhancing pleasure and erotic flow:

6. Sensual entrancement arousal for the individual: genital focus
7. Cognitive pacing techniques for the individual
8. Couple "sensual entrancement" relaxation (e.g., sensate focus)
9. Couple genital exploration relaxation training
10. Couple arousal pacing training:
    a. Manual stimulation by partner with sensual entrancement focus only
    b. Manual stimulation by partner with erotic fantasy but not of intercourse
    c. Manual stimulation by partner with lubricant with erotic fantasy of intercourse (intercourse "rehearsal")

Phase Three: Enjoying confident, flexible, and intimate intercourse:

11. Intercourse "acclimation" technique
12. Progressive intercourse: alternative scenarios

Phase Four: Promoting long-term satisfaction:

13. Maintenance plan and agreement

his or her therapeutic repertoire to bring about healthy sexual function and satisfaction. While each exercise may be particularly helpful, invariably individuals and couples must blend several (five or six) for the best result.

1. Realistic Sexual Expectations: Correcting Sexual "Myths"   Because it is common that individuals and couples experiencing sexual dysfunctions lack adequate knowledge about sexual lovemaking physiology, they may have unrealistic expectations of their sexual interactions. For example, some believe that because they may live in a more sexually "open" or "liberated" culture they are automatically very comfortable with sex. However, they may be emotionally self-deceived because it is almost invariably the case that sexual dysfunction includes some anxiety that is contributing to the sexual problem.

In other cases, there is subtle pressure in the sexual relationship as one or both partners may believe that all touching is sexual or should lead to sex, which both stresses the sexual relationship and may serve to inhibit nonsexual affections. Other unrealistic beliefs may be that men are always interested in and always ready for sex; that sex is centered on a hard penis and what's done with it; that sex equals intercourse; that good sex requires orgasm; that good sex is spontaneous, with no planning and no talking; or that real men don't have sex problems.

Sexual therapy frequently identifies such unrealistic beliefs and pressures, and addresses them by providing corrective information and the opportunity for the couples to work through such stresses that may undermine the physiological relaxation essential to healthy sexual functioning. Realistic expectations of sexual performance are the cognitive precursors of physiological relaxation.

2. Couple Communication Skills Enhancement   Communications training that focuses on the direct discussion of specific sexual feelings and desires is another standard feature of sex therapy. Direct discussion decreases feelings of shame, guilt, or embarrassment about sex; helps patients clarify their own feelings and those of their partners; and establishes a communication process for discussing sexual problems in the future. While some couples may communicate their thoughts and feelings with skill and sensitivity in their general relationship, it is not automatic that they will manifest the same level of skill and openness in their sexual relationship. The natural and learned embarrassment about one's own sexual thoughts, feelings, and desires is a common deterrent to openness and expressiveness in one's relationship.

Sex therapy with couples invariably includes attention to their comfort and sensitivity communicating together about their sexual thoughts, wishes, and feelings because the ability to openly discuss qualities of their personal sexual interaction is a feature of comfortable and relaxed sexuality. The ability to conduct such interpersonal communication is predicated on confident self-acceptance of one's sexuality, positive valuing of sex, and freedom and respect to express one's feelings about sexual relations.

Attention to communication in couples therapy may include basic teaching and coaching of basic communications skills such as using "I" messages to personalize and avoid "blame" messages, "paraphrasing" or "reflective listening" to focus on patience and understanding, and coaching the couple in empathy and cooperative understanding.

The primary goal of communication skills training is to enhance the partners' ability to empathize and learn about their partner, as well as support the relaxation that is essential to healthy sexual functioning. Empathy between the partners is the emotional "glue" or adhesive in their general as well as sexual relationship. Successful sexual skills learning requires the couple operate as an intimate team, cooperating with mutual giving and receiving with mutual pleasure.

3. Couple Cooperation Skills: Working as an "Intimate Team"   Supportive communication is the starting point for a couple to resolve their disagreements—whether general or sexual—cooperatively. While positive conflict resolution can facilitate positive sexual feelings in a relationship, a negative process of conflict resolution can play a direct or indirect negative role in sexual dysfunction through its injurious effect on the emotional environment of sexual activity as well as the couple's general relationship. In turn, it is also thought that sexual dysfunction, which may at times be caused by a physical cause, may undermine a couple's overall sense of intimacy and mutual acceptance, thereby creating a negative atmosphere for resolving conflicts in their relationship. In this case, sexual dysfunction caused by nonrelationship features (e.g., biological or psychological factors in an individual) may have a detrimental effect on a couple's conflict resolution.

Past as well as more recent proposals in the clinical literature have regularly associated sexual dysfunction with interpersonal conflict (see Metz and Epstein, 2002). There are a number of empirical studies that suggest a role for relationship conflict in sexual dysfunction and point to either a possible etiological association or the importance of addressing conflict interaction patterns to achieve successful sex therapy. In a cross-sectional population survey of 789 men and 979 women conducted by Dunn, Croft, and Hackett (1999), sexual problems among men were associated with anxiety and medical problems, while for women sexual dysfunction was associated with marital difficulties. Stravynski et al. (1997) conducted a controlled study of three behavioral group approaches to treating sexually dysfunctional men and noted that sex therapy that included attention to the man's "interpersonal difficulties" resulted in significantly better outcomes overall. O'Farrell et al. (1997) found that both alcoholic and nonalcoholic maritally conflicted couples reported more sexual dissatisfaction and dysfunction than nonconflicted couples.

However, conflict may also present opportunities for couples to deepen their emotional and sexual intimacy. With a positive, respectful, affirming process of conflict resolution, partners may develop a greater sense of self-esteem in their relationship, reinforce respect and admiration for each other, develop more confidence that future conflict can be positively resolved, and create positive feelings and comfort with each other that facilitate their sexual desire for each other. The important feature is less the existence of relationship conflict than the manner in which the couple deals with conflict. Positive and constructive relationship conflict interaction may produce emotional relief or even an affirmation of the couple's intimate bond and, directly or indirectly, serve as a sexual aphrodisiac. The heightened pleasure and enjoyment that some couples report when they have sex after "making up" offers further evidence of the emotional link between conflict resolution and sexual feelings.

For couples seeking help for sexual problems, therapy should usually include significant attention to the couple's conflict management patterns and skills. Even sex therapy with individuals should attend to the person's relationship conflict history and current dynamics, because the individual may be reacting to interactions from the past in his or her current or former relationships or anticipating conflict in the future. Every sexual problem, to some extent, embodies an actual or anticipated unresolved relationship conflict that is sufficiently distressing to bring the individual or couple to therapy. Whether the sexual dysfunction is caused by unsettled relationship conflict, or the sexual problem complicates one's ability to resolve disagreements, conflict resolution patterns warrant direct therapeutic attention.

4. Physiological: Relaxation and Sensual Training for the Individual Appropriate physiological relaxation facilitates satisfactory sexual functioning. Although for many patients it seems counterintuitive, for sexual arousal and function, relaxation—the antithesis of anxiety—establishes the foundation for the body to sexually function. Successful sex therapy teaches positive body image and relaxation procedures as the foundation for other methods of treatment. A number of simple and easily learned relaxation techniques that focus on the body are useful in sex therapy. Ten to twenty minutes daily of quiet focusing on breathing, awareness of body tension, and muscle relaxation is encouraged. The purpose is to concentrate on physical sensations and to ease bodily tensions.

In sensual awareness training, the individual focuses on visual and tactile exploration of one's own body. The purpose is to become more familiar with one's body visually and tactilely and to become more conscious of one's own bodily responses to touch. In sensual entrancement arousal, the individual is trained to become aroused by entrancement rather than partner interaction in order to provide him or her with the foundation for improved, more relaxed sexual arousal skill. Here one learns to focus more carefully upon one's own physical sensations (awareness) and then how to cognitively and behaviorally orchestrate his sexual arousal (management). This necessary focus upon one's own body is an aide to relaxation, overcomes the dissociation or distraction techniques that are common with individuals with sexual dysfunction, and provides the foundation for consciously working with one's body for better performance. For example, the man with premature ejaculation does well to learn to focus upon the pleasurable sensations in his penis rather than on his partner's breasts, sexual fantasy, or distractions such as sports images.

5. Kegel/Pelvic Muscle (PM) Relaxation Training for the Individual Effective treatment also teaches the conscious capacity to relax the pelvic muscle, which provides both a simple focus for monitoring the level of physical relaxation and a physiological technique that aids orgasm control. Pelvic muscle (PM) training or the Kegel technique, often taught to women in child birth classes, teaches the individual to relax the pubococcygeal muscles (bulbocavernosus and ischiocavernosus muscles) while experiencing sexual arousal. It is an effective technique to assist women to obtain orgasm more easily by constricting and relaxing these muscles when close to orgasm, and for men to establish better ejaculatory control by learning to fully relax the PM muscle prior to and during intromission (Greiner and Byers, 1997). This technique capitalizes on the natural involvement of this muscle system is orgasm and ejaculation.

6. Sensual Entrancement Arousal for the Individual: Genital Focus   Learning that sexual arousal occurs and is more easily regulated when the body is physically relaxed and focused on pleasure is learned in this exercise. For example, the man with ED begins by taking time to physically relax his body, then soothingly touches his genital area calmly, focusing his attention simply on the physical pleasure (no fantasy) and keeping his PM relaxed. After five minutes, he calmly welcomes an erection, allowing this to happen without pursuing it. He is seeking his "calm, easy erection." The objective is to blend maximal physical relaxation with the minimal amount of physical stimulation for an erection to slowly occur only by focusing on the simple physical pleasure (sensual self-entrancement arousal). When erection occurs, he calmly enjoys the simple pleasure for a few minutes, then allows the erection to subside by slowing the touch, and then increases the touch to regain an erection. This waxing and waning based on general physical relaxation, relaxed PM, calm and slow touch, and sensual self-entrancement brings sexual confidence and comfort. To learn that erections are "easy" and more reliable and long-lasting based on relaxation and the focus on pleasure is an important lesson for many men. Women benefit by using the same principles to facilitate their arousal and enjoyment.

7. Cognitive Pacing Techniques for the Individual   Arousal continuum techniques are cognitive or thought "pacing" techniques to inhibit or accelerate (regulate) arousal by focusing specifically on varying levels of sexually arousing activities or themes. With the arousal continuum technique, the man or woman systematically observes, considers, and distinguishes those detailed thoughts (fantasy), actions, feelings, scenarios, and sequences that characterize his or her individual arousal pattern. By carefully identifying or "mapping" which items are more or less arousing in relation to each other, he or she is able to rank-order them with an understanding of their incremental arousal—the "map" or "arousal continuum." During lovemaking, then, one is able to better "orchestrate" or manage the level of sexual arousal by judicious concentration on items in order to increase or decrease the level of arousal depending on the concern, such as premature ejaculation or inhibited orgasm. Even as other actual behaviors may be occurring with the partner, disciplined concentration may be used to regulate the level of stimulation.

8. Couple "Sensual Entrancement" Relaxation (Sensate Focus)   The hallmark of traditional sex therapy is the employment of behavioral "homework exercises" designed to facilitate sexual growth and satisfaction. Such behavioral interventions, prescribed by the sexual therapist and often labeled as "sensate focus exercises," are a series of gradual steps of specific sexual behaviors to be privately performed by the patients in their own home. These traditional exercises involve a series of guided light massaging or pleasuring to relax and explore the sensations in one's body, increase pleasure, and overcome whatever barriers may impede the natural physiological response of healthy sexual func-tioning. They are utilized to promote the focus on entrancement arousal established in the individual phase of treatment. Heightened concentration is required to stay focused on entrancement arousal because each will likely seek to employ "partner involvement" arousal with the presence of the lover. Homework sessions begin with the couple relax-ing and gently taking turns to pleasure each other to invite physiological relaxation and comfort. Typically intercourse and other sexually arousing touch are initially prohibited, and the partners sensually massage each other's bodies while learning to physically relax in a sexualized situation together. Such interaction allows the couples to enjoy kissing, hugging, body massage, and other sensual pleasures without the disruption that would occur if they anticipated that these activities would be followed by intercourse or other behaviors that had not been pleasurable in the past. The couple's sexual relationship is then rebuilt in a graduated series of successive approximations eventually leading to full sexual intercourse. At each step, skill training, anxiety reduction, elimination of perfor-mance demands, and the other stresses that negatively affect healthy sexual functioning are addressed.

9. Couple Genital Exploration Relaxation Training   In this home exercise, the partners (fol-lowing a predetermined protocol) take turns leading the other in a discussion of their bodies and genitals in order to provide a sensual exploration of the body's erotic parts while relaxing one's body. The purpose is to practice sexual leadership with one's own body, to become more comfortable with looking at each other's genitals, and to have one's genitals touched and looked at by one's partner in a relaxing and non-arousing way. Current forms of this exercise for the couple privately are variations that have developed to replace the "sexological exams" originally conducted by a medical doctor with a cou-ple in the doctor's office to educate partners about sexual physiology. Books, informa-tion sheets, and audiovisuals about sexual physiology are commonly used in conjunction with the partner's private exploration of their bodies.

10. Couple Arousal Pacing Training   This and other variations of cognitive-behavioral pacing techniques are effective, especially when used in conjunction with other strate-gies to manage the level of excitement. This pacing technique may be used to estab-lish greater confidence in one's ability to achieve sexual arousal, such as teaching a woman to gain confidence in her ability to lubricate and achieve vaginal engorgement or teaching a man to develop greater confidence in his ability to gain an erection, then allow it to subside, and regain erection. Such confidence with arousal is also commonly used as a platform to achieve other sexual performance goals, such as better ejacula-tory control for men or easier orgasm for women. "Stop-Start" (Semans' technique, 1956) and its many adaptations includes progressive manual stimulation exercises to familiarize a man or woman with sensual awareness, and self-regulation during sexual arousal by slowing or building arousal. Graduated steps in this technique commonly include sexual arousal by sensual entrancement focus, then partner interaction arousal focus, and then intercourse (fantasy or behavior). This technique is commonly utilized in both individual and couples therapy. In couples therapy, the individual first may learn this pacing technique privately and then later integrate the technique into couple cooperative interaction.

11. The Intercourse Acclimation Technique   In the vaginal "acclimation" technique, the couple has sexual intercourse in a calm and relaxed way. This technique is useful in treating a variety of male sexual performance problems, especially premature ejaculation, but also erectile dysfunction, inhibited orgasm, and problems with low desire. The man concentrates on relaxing the PM (especially when PE is the problem) while his partner inserts his penis into her vagina. He then quietly "rests" inside, calmly expecting to reach the physical pleasure "saturation point" (a sensual dullness) in his penis during which the penis "acclimates" to the warmth and sensuousness of the vagina (or the mouth, in oral sex training). For most men this "acclimated sensation" develops after approximately ten minutes of resting inside the vagina. He is allowed to move only minimally to maintain an erection and instructed that the more he moves, the longer for the acclimation to occur—even thirty minutes. The man is advised that after this acclimation occurs, the penis can begin to tolerate and enjoy more intense pleasure while maintaining ejaculatory control. He may thereby increase not only the length of intercourse time but also the quality of pleasure by learning to manage his arousal pattern.

For the woman, prolonged and relaxed intercourse may facilitate her arousal and potential for orgasm. For the man with ejaculatory inhibition, however, the couple will postpone intercourse and pursue higher levels of arousal by other means before intercourse in order to avoid intercourse acclimation (which can contribute to ejaculation inhibition).

12. Progressive Intercourse: Alternative Scenarios   This phase of psychosexual skills training may incorporate a number of cognitive-behavioral exercises to facilitate comfort, enjoyment, playfulness, and flexibility in the couple's love-making. It is important for the couple to develop alternative or flexible scenarios for pleasure that are both arousing and satisfying. Alternative scenarios are flexible, different love-making patterns such as different positions, activities like oral sex, or experimental activities such as light and safe or playful bondage. Alternative scenarios inoculate the couple from exclusive focus on demand performance (requiring lubrication, erection, intercourse, orgasm) that create performance anxiety and often sex dysfunction. With flexible scenarios, the couple can adapt to the varying circumstances of a realistic sexual relationship. For example, moods can be accepted, difficult arousal can be shifted to relaxing touch, or oral sex can replace intercourse. When couples have several flexible patterns they can use, when sexual performance on occasion falters, it is not a problem.

13. Maintenance Plan and Agreement   To expect that a man or woman will never have another sex dysfunction experience (he ejaculates rapidly, she can't lubricate or reach orgasm) is unrealistic, setting the couple up for failure, a return to sexual avoidance, and a blame and counterblame cycle. The key to relapse prevention is to establish positive, realistic expectations and to emphasize that arousal, intercourse, and orgasm are inherently variable. Whether once every ten times, once a month, or once a year, performance issues will reoccur. The reality of the "good-enough sex" model (Metz and McCarthy, 2004) is that problems with desire, arousal, and orgasm are an occasional part of most couples' sexual experience. The key is to cooperate as an intimate team, accept an occasional episode of dysfunction as normal, to recognize that it is a lapse (a single event which is not overly significant), and to not allow it to be a relapse (a pattern perpetuated by anticipatory anxiety, tense sexual performance, and avoidance).

There are cognitive, behavioral, and emotional components of an individualized relapse prevention program. Cognitive components include reinforcing a pleasure rather than performance orientation; seeing the partner as his intimate friend; remaining receptive to stimulation and arousal; and feeling genuinely satisfied with good-enough sex, not feeling pressure to strive for perfect intercourse performance. The behavioral components of relapse prevention include maintaining a regular rhythm of sexual experiences; blending self-entrancement arousal and partner interaction arousal; pacing with use of the arousal continuum and pelvic muscle exercises; cooperating as a couple and treating a performance problem episode simply as a lapse alerting the couple to take more care to manage progressive arousal; and a return to structured arousal exercises (such as "stop-start" exercise) to reinforce the psychosexual skills. The emotional components of relapse prevention include continuing to value each other as intimate friends and reinforce a sense of acceptance and cooperation. Especially important is setting aside quality couple time to share feelings of intimacy and sexuality. The couple can individualize a relapse prevention plan (McCarthy, 2001) by choosing strategies to maintain their alternative sexual scenarios.

Adjunctive Psychological Interventions

There are a number of adjunctive interventions utilized in comprehensive sex therapy. Different individuals may respond better to alternative techniques depending upon the individual and the sexual difficulty. The variety of tools include body-image work, fantasy, hypnosis, dildo, vibrator, dilators, meditation, audiovisual modeling, dance, yoga, assertiveness training, communication workshops, cotherapy, biofeedback, acupuncture, sexological exam, surrogate sex partner, and other techniques.

Sex Therapy Treatment Outcome Studies

There are a number of studies of treatment effectiveness that have reported high success rates (Masters and Johnson, 1970), although outcome studies of the psychological treatment of sexual dysfunction are frequently flawed (Metz et al., 1997). As in other fields, uncontrolled research reports commonly infer causality that is scientifically often overstated—that is, assumptions claimed about what is "the chicken" and what is "the egg." For example, anxiety may cause sex dysfunction, but sex dysfunction may also cause anxiety; or, relationship conflict may cause sex dysfunction, and sex dysfunction may also cause relationship conflict in some couples. Treatment success appears to vary depending upon: (1) methodological limitations; (2) adequate differential diagnosis and treatment of the subtype of sexual problem, (3) the level of problem severity; (4) comorbidity with nonsexual psychological problems, and (5) clinical trial drop-out rates.

Until recently, research and clinical attention about women's sexual functioning has been neglected (Verma, Khaitan, and Singh, 1998). Research about women's sexual functioning in the United States has disproportionately focused on the effects of sexual abuse of women (Browning and Laumann, 1997; Gregoire and Dhugra, 1996). Results are mixed, even contradictory. Other studies have examined the long-term effects of childhood abuse on adult sexual functioning (Hunter, 1991). Overall, there is a strong need for integration of medical and psychological approaches, in addition to increased research in this area (see Rosen, 1996). A number of valid and reliable sexuality-related assessment measures are available for clinical and research uses in human sexuality (Davis et al., 1997).

There is a trend currently to distinguish more specifically the psychological subtypes of the various sexual disorders, to conduct more detailed differential diagnoses, and to specifically target treatment to these psychological features (e.g., Rowland and Slob, 1995; Metz and Pryor, 2000). This more refined focus holds promise for new advances in the psychological understanding of the sexual disorders.

In recent years, increasing attention has also been drawn to diagnosis and treatment of other sexual disorders such as the sexual paraphilias (notably those behaviors that are illegal—"sex offenses"), sexually compulsive behavior or "sex addiction," dystonic sexual orientation, the impact of sexually transmitted diseases, diverse gender identity issues, and sexual dysfunction among same-sex couples.

3.3.3. Treatment Modalities

Sexual therapy may be conducted utilizing several psychotherapeutic modalities formats or treatment genres. While individual therapy has been the more common format (perhaps due to tradition, practical considerations such as ease of scheduling appointments with the doctor, or privacy concerns), other treatment modalities offer unique features and often increase treatment success or outcome effectiveness.

3.3.3.1. Individual Therapy

Individual therapy has been the traditional treatment modality, evolving strongly in the Western world since the advent of nineteenth-century individualistic philosophies and psychoanalysis. The use of psychoanalysis in sexual disorders has been controversial. There are no studies that gauge the effectiveness of psychoanalysis in the treatment of specific sex problems, although psychodynamic psychotherapy may be useful in some specific cases when personality disorders or other severe psychopathologies are present. However, the length and cost of the psychoanalytic process may be a barrier to common use.

Contemporary individual therapy offers an opportunity for the sex therapy patient to experience understanding and empathy in cases where shame or anxiety are associated with sex. In most parts of the world, individual therapy may be the most common treatment modality or setting because of financial cost, traditional psychotherapeutic custom, or the difficulties of involving the sexual partner in couples sex therapy.

3.3.3.2. Group Therapy

The accomplishment of assorted general psychotherapeutic goals (such as the management of anxiety or depression) through the group format is well established. Specific group formats are also common for treating individuals with sex dysfunction, couples with sex and marital dysfunction, individuals with sexual paraphilias (sex offenders), and persons with gender dysphoria.

Recognizing the inherent strength of the traditional group therapy format primarily developed in the 1960s and 1970s to reach participants on the affective level, and the power of cognitive-behavioral processes to effect change, group formats were created in the 1970s and 1980s to integrate these influences in the treatment of sexual problems. Integrating the directive techniques of the cognitive-behavioral approach with the strong affective focus typical of classical group therapy has been shown to offer effective and comprehensive results in sex therapy. There are indications that couples and group treatment may be consistently more effective than individual therapies (Hurlbert et al., 1993; Leiblum and Rosen, 1989; Vansteenwegen, 1996).

In treating a variety of sexual problems, men-only, women-only, and couples groups have several decades of experience with varying degrees of outcome success. More recently, couples experiencing both sexual dysfunction and significant relationship distress have also been treated concomitantly. In treating persons with gender dysphoria or paraphilias, the group treatment modality offers special treatment advantages in addition to individual therapy, as these clinical problems typically involve shame and alienation, which group support may dramatically help ameliorate. In addition, in treating "sex offenders," the group format offers a powerful medium to therapeutically address the common resistance and denial because group members, who understand the disorder frequently better than therapists, can effectively confront and support other group member's resistance and defense mechanisms.

An example of a group therapy approach to treat simultaneous marital and sexual dysfunction is included in Metz and Weiss (1992). Group treatments for sexual dysfunction (Metz and Weiss, 1992) and sexual offenses (paraphilia management) appear to be moderately effective. Relapse prevention programs also appear to be valuable (Miner et al., 1990; McCarthy, 2001). The effect of group treatment for other sexual problems (e.g., sexual trauma) is not known at this time as the data are inconclusive (Reeker, Ensing, and Elliott, 1997). Increasingly, a combination of biopsychosocial treatment modalities appears to offer the highest degree of outcome effectiveness—combining biological, pharmacological, psychological, and social (group) components.

3.3.3.3. Family and Marital Therapy

The emergence of couples and family therapies from the classic tradition of individual treatment is a major development in modern psychiatry. The added complexity for the professional of understanding and working with two or more individuals simultaneously has been compensated for by the wealth of additional therapeutic data and opportunity for treatment that this modality offers. While formally emerging in Western psychology, many cultures throughout the world traditionally conceptualize interpersonal relationships as the primary focus of psychological meaning (more so than the individualism that characterizes Western thinking), so that couples or family therapy is frequently the treatment of comfort and choice.

In Western thinking, a number of theoretical schools have attempted to identify and formulate the processes that occur in relationships and families. Major schools include structural family therapy (Minuchin, et al.), Bowenian family systems theory and treatment, Italian family therapy, contextual family therapy, as well as behavioral marital therapy (BMT), cognitive family therapy (CBT), and integrative marital therapy (IMT) (Jacobson and Christensen, 1996).

Family therapy is increasingly used to address sexual difficulties of children (such as sexual precociousness, childhood gender identity, and family incest). This is because in family therapy, such difficulties are commonly conceptualized as problems that may be symptomatic of family environmental conflicts or intergenerational difficulties in the family itself, which warrant therapeutic attention in comprehensive and effective treatment. Therapies that include the couple or other members of the family increasingly are the treatment of choice, when appropriate and possible because of the interactional nature of human sexuality itself. In such cases, treating only the individual sexual problem (e.g., the effect of incest) may limit the effectiveness of the professional effort to help. In addition, enlisting the family as a supportive group to facilitate change for the child or adolescent identified as the patient offers an important source for growth in both the patient and the family.

In the treatment of adults, marital or relationship therapy is an important treatment consideration and should be preferred to individual therapy because of the interactional nature of human sexuality itself. Relationship distress (such as unresolved emotional relationship conflicts, hypersensitivity to the partner, or reactivity to infidelity) is common, and sex therapists traditionally have believed that relationship dynamics play an important etiological role in sexual dysfunction. Even in treating individuals with sexual problems, therapeutic attention to the patient's history of relationships is important, because even though the patient may not be in a current sexual relationship, he or she may be reacting to past or anticipated relationship distresses that may play an important role in the sexual difficulty. Although there is no prevailing partner interaction pattern among couples with sexual dysfunction, virtually any general relationship deficiency may undermine the mutual emotional acceptance that is important to healthy sexual functioning. Couples or relationship therapy considers three basic relationship patterns: (1) interpersonal issues may be the cause of the sexual problem; (2) interpersonal issues may maintain a sexual dysfunction caused by another source (e.g., a biological medical problem or illness); or (3) a sexual dysfunction caused by another source may have a detrimental effect on the relationship quality. When interpersonal issues are the apparent cause of or are a maintaining component of a sexual problem, standard relationship or marital therapy is required that specifically focuses upon the dysfunctional feature, such as unresolved conflict, dysfunctional communication, or inadequate empathy. When the cause or maintaining feature is alleviated, normal sexual functioning should then return. If it does not, additional causes should be pursued, especially medical or psychiatric possibilities.

The evaluation of relationship quality can be aided by such objective measures as the Dyadic Adjustment Scale (DAS, Spanier, 1976), the Marital Satisfaction Inventory (MSI, Snyder, 1997), or the Marital Adaptation Test (Locke and Wallace, 1959), which measure overall relationship satisfaction and relationship strengths and weaknesses (e.g., communication, parenting, gender roles, areas of conflict). There are a number of other assessments tools available for assessing a variety of features of sex problems (Davis, Yarber, et al., 1998).

Integrative Approaches to Care

An integrative approach to sexual therapy is essential because sexual problems are invariably multidetermined with multiple effects upon the individual and couple. Integrative sex therapy is comprehensive, and while it addresses the physical causes first because of the constitutional priority of biology, it is essential to address the psychological issues, relationship dimensions, and psychosexual skills involved in any sexual disorder. Even when an organic factor is present, it is essential to treat the principal psychological factors that can complicate the organic problem or that could have resulted from it.

Contemporary sexual therapy utilizes *all* clinical resources—medical, pharmacological, psychological, relational, and psychosexual skills—in a variety of treatment approaches. For psychogenic sex dysfunction, there are a number of clinically useful models or therapeutic approaches to treating sexual dysfunction and sexual disorders. While sex therapy treatment studies suggest that the cognitive-behavioral approach and the conjoint and group therapy modalities may be more effective in treating sex problems, integrative sex therapy incorporates features from various theoretical schools and treatment options, and in an eclectic fashion, employs techniques judiciously chosen by the professional in order to help improve the patients' sexual health and quality of life.

Comprehensive Treatment of Specific Sexual Disorders

The previous few chapters reviewed the major biological and psychological procedures commonly used to treat sexual dysfunctions and sexual disorders. In this chapter the biopsychosocial interventions for comprehensively dealing with the specific sexual problems of men and women are summarized. The more common treatment procedures for each of the sexual disorders are presented in table 3.5.1.

The specific pathogenesis of how a single biological or psychological feature (e.g., a physical illness such as diabetes or anemia, or a mental illness such as depression, psychosocial stressors, negative attitudes toward sexuality, or relationship conflicts) may produce different effects in one person versus another (e.g., low sexual desire in one but inhibited sexual arousal in another) is not well understood. It is thought that a similar psychological feature may precipitate any one of the different kinds of sexual dysfunction in different persons. For example, the pathogenesis whereby major depression or relationship conflict can apparently cause low desire in one person, erectile dysfunction in another, or inhibited orgasm in yet another individual is insufficiently understood. It has been thought this variability may reflect not only the inconsistency in causes but also individual psychological differences, effects of the sex dysfunction itself, or independent features accompanying the sexual problem. From the therapeutic perspective, whether the feature is the cause, effect, or companion of the sexual problem, it is necessary to address all features. Treating only the biological problems without attention to psychological factors and vice versa will contribute to the ineffectiveness of the therapy and destine the person and couple (and clinician) to frustration and disappointment.

Contemporary sex therapy is comprehensive and integrative and operates from a biopsychosocial approach to both assessment and treatment. Clinicians who are more biologically oriented (e.g., family physicians) must devote special attention to psychological features, while those more psychologically oriented (e.g., psychiatrist, psychologist) must devote special attention to evaluating or referring for medical evaluation and treatment (if appropriate).

Part 2 reviewed the basic biological and psychological features that may contribute to the specific sexual problems. The essential task in the treatment of the sexual disorders is to determine accurately its etiological features in order to guide treatment. Inclusive treatment follows from the biological and psychological evaluations to diag-

Table 3.5.1. BIOPSYCHOSOCIAL SEXUAL THERAPY TECHNIQUES AND INTERVENTIONS FOR SPECIFIC SEXUAL DIFFICULTIES AND DISORDERS

Sexual Problem	Sexual Therapy Techniques and Interventions			TX Modality	Comment
	Education	Biological	Psychological		
Conflict over sexual frequency	Inform couple this is a common problem. Sharing epidemiological data is often reassuring that this is common and flexibility by both partners is required. Encourage mutual conflict resolution. Basic sexual physiological knowledge. The "purposes" for sexual activity.	Treat underlying medical problem that may precipitate a frequency conflict (such as pharmacological treatment for loss of desire due to thyroid illness) as appropriate.	Relevant sexual education about partner expectations and sexual performance confusion. Mutual couple therapy to resolve conflict in a mutually satisfying way.	Couple therapy.	Very common couple issue. Rule out underlying dysfunctions requiring treatment such as inhibited sexual arousal as source of frequent conflict.
Concerns about normalcy (e.g., penis/breast size, past fantasy, behaviors, oral sex, anal sex, etc.)	Sexual education about specific concerns is the most useful and appropriate intervention. The "purposes" for sexual activity. The types of sexual arousal. Intimacy as the ultimate objective more so than sexual performance.	Corrective medical treatments if concerns are physiological.	Assess if concerns are typical worries based on lack of accurate sexual knowledge. Assess degree of obsessiveness or body dysmorphic psychiatric features if manifested.	Individual therapy. Short-term educational group therapy based on sexual education modalities may be effective to impart knowledge but also normalize common concerns.	Exceptionally common concern throughout the life cycle.

Sexual Therapy Techniques and Interventions

Sexual Problem	Education	Biological	Psychological	TX Modality	Comment
Concerns about normalcy of sexual orientation (e.g., same sex, bisexual, etc.)	Education about orientation based on comprehensive scientific information. Education programs for the family and relatives of same-sex individuals.	(No biological treatment)	Address the self-rejection, anxiety about being nonheterosexual in a heterosexual world, and the need for self-acceptance and integration.	General individual therapy. Supportive group therapy. Brief group therapy with other persons suffering from the common social rejection and alienation.	Homosexuality is no longer considered a mental problem by scientific psychiatry. However, some same-sex men or women may struggle with self-esteem problems as well as a fear of rejection, the effects of social prejudice, and the need for acceptance bring them to seek therapeutic support.
History of child/youth physical, sexual, and/or psychological abuse	Basic sexual physiological knowledge.	(No biological treatment)	Goals of acceptance of past events; address issues of broken trust, and the need for recovery and resiliency.	Individual, couple, and group therapy.	Nonsexual abuse, deprivation, and neglect may affect sexuality in adulthood by creating a disposition of mistrust, hurt, or anger.

(Continued)

Table 3.5.1. CONTINUED

Sexual Problem	Sexual Therapy Techniques and Interventions				
	Education	Biological	Psychological	TX Modality	Comment
Adjusting to sexual changes with adult aging	Adequate understanding of sexuality is important at any age, but especially for older adults. Ignorance of normal changes after age 40 may create fear of aging/disease, sexual anxiety, and a subsequent distraction or heightened effort to perform, resulting in psychogenic sexual dysfunction. Audio-visual education.	Medical treatment as appropriate for general illnesses.	If adjustment reaction is intense, psychological treatment addresses the anxiety, potential decline in self-image and self-esteem, underlying concerns and issues.	Individual counseling. Sexual enrichment programs. Group educational meetings for accurate knowledge and support.	Most sexual problems among older persons are the result of physical illness (not normal aging itself) or a psychological "self-fulfilling prophecy" of expecting sexual decline with aging.
Hypoactive sexual desire (low desire)	Basic sexual physiological knowledge. The "purposes" for sexual activity. The types of sexual arousal. Sexual enrichment. Audio-visual education.	Medical treatment for any underlying causes of the sexual problem. Hormonal replacement (testosterone; thyroid medication). Judicious use of antidepressant pharmacological agents when HSD is assessed as caused by depression.	Age and gender appropriate and realistic expectations. Address psychological features assessed to be major influences: (1) Sexual shame (2) Prior trauma (e.g., physical abuse, sexual abuse, etc.) (3) Conflict between roles (e.g., sexual partner vs. parent) (4) Deficits in marital emotional relationship (5) Marital conflict	Sexual enrichment program. Individual or group therapy is preferred for treating individual features of HSD such as sexual shame, history of trauma, obsessive-compulsive disorder, etc. Couple therapy is preferred to address relational features such as expectation differences, unresolved conflict, or deficits in emotional empathy in the relationship.	HSD is commonly multidetermined requiring multifaceted treatment features.

Sexual Therapy Techniques and Interventions

Sexual Problem	Education	Biological	Psychological	TX Modality	Comment
Sexual aversion disorder	Basic information about common associations with emotional aversiveness, about value of emotional desensitization. Audio-visual education to model positive and healthy sexuality.	Medical treatment for any underlying causes of the sexual problem. Optional pharmacological therapy for intense phobia or anxiety to lower the anxiety barrier to psychotherapy and sex therapy. (1) Sexual shame (2) Prior trauma (e.g., physical abuse, sexual abuse, etc.) (3) Obsessive-compulsive features	Address psychological features assessed to be major influences.	Individual, couple, and/or group therapy.	Because aversion to sexual interaction is often caused by multiple and severe sources, this condition is usually difficult to treat well.

(Continued)

Table 3.5.1. Continued

Sexual Problem	Sexual Therapy Techniques and Interventions			
	Education	Biological	Psychological	TX Modality	Comment
Hypersexual disorder	Basic sexual physiological knowledge. The "purposes" for sexual activity. The types of sexual arousal. Audio-visual education to model positive and healthy sexuality. Education regarding the interrelationship between sexuality and emotions.	Pharmacological treatment (notably medications approved for treatment of obsessive-compulsive disorder, or some antidepressants and anxiolytics).	Address psychological features assessed to be major influences: Goals may include: (1) Regulation of sexual behavior, but also (2) Affirming healthy sexuality (because common features of excessive sexual behavior are negative attitudes and emotional shame about sexuality), and (3) How to integrate healthy sexual behavior into one's lifestyle.	Individual, couple, and group therapies.	Individual therapy is employed to explore the intrapsychic features that may facilitate the sexual compulsivity. Conjoint therapy is utilized to address potential relationship issues, and to heal any relationship damage from the patient having acted out. Group therapy is used to address the social features (e.g., shame) and to offer supportive confrontation for appropriate behavioral change and management. Basic work integrating general emotions with sexual emotions is commonly required as some repress or dissociate from general feelings (e.g., depression, anxiety) and "sexualize" them ("act them out").

Sexual Therapy Techniques and Interventions

Sexual Problem	Education	Biological	Psychological	TX Modality	Comment
Female sexual arousal dysfunction	Basic sexual physiological knowledge. The "purposes" for sexual activity. The types of sexual arousal. Audio-visual education to demonstrate psychosexual skills for positive sexuality and arousal.	Pharmacologic therapy. Eros-CVD device. Vaginal supplemental lubricants (e.g., Lubrim, K-Y jelly, etc.).	Address psychological features assessed to be major influences. Goals may include the following: Learning basic physiological relaxation techniques, cognitive management of distracting thoughts such as performance pressures and "spectatoring," sensual touch at first without sexual arousal, genital exploration, and progressive introduction of sexual stimulation. Women are taught how to induce arousal (lubrication) by balancing the level of relaxation with the level of sexual stimulation, and how to obtain progressive arousal and then choose to let it subside before regaining arousal. Such steps are designed to assist the woman and couple to regain confidence with sexual performance, increase the pleasure, and overcome the sexual performance anxiety.	Combined individual and couple therapy supplemented with women's sexual enrichment group.	

(Continued)

Table 3.5.1. CONTINUED

	Sexual Therapy Techniques and Interventions				
Sexual Problem	Education	Biological	Psychological	TX Modality	Comment
Male sexual arousal disorder (erectile dysfunction)	Basic sexual physiological knowledge. The "purposes" for sexual activity. The types of sexual arousal. Audio-visual education to model positive sexuality and arousal.	Pharmacological therapy: (1) Oral therapies (e.g., PDE inhibitors, apomorphine) (2) Intracavernosal injection of vasoactive (papaverine, E1-prostaglandin insidomine). (3) Intraurethral therapies (e.g., MUSE [Medicated Urethral System for Erection]). (4) Vacuum devices. (5) Penile prosthetic implants (e.g., malleable prosthesis, hydraulic or inflatable prosthesis). (6) Hormonal replacement therapy. 7) Arterial and venous vascular surgery (still considered experimental).	Address psychological features assessed to be major influences. Goals may include the following: Learning basic physiological relaxation techniques, cognitive management of distracting thoughts such as performance pressures and "spectatoring," sensual touch at first without sexual arousal, genital exploration, and progressive introduction of sexual stimulation. Men are taught by self-pleasuring or couple-pleasuring exercises how to induce an erection by balancing the level of relaxation with the level of sexual stimulation, and how to obtain an erection and then choose to let it subside before regaining an erection. Such steps are designed to assist the man and couple to regain confidence with sexual performance, increase the pleasure, and overcome the sexual performance anxiety.	Couple therapy is preferred. Men's sex therapy. Group and individual therapy may also be useful.	

Sexual Therapy Techniques and Interventions

Sexual Problem	Education	Biological	Psychological	TX Modality	Comment
Female orgasmic disorder (inhibited orgasm)	Basic sexual physiological knowledge. The "purposes" for sexual activity. The types of sexual arousal. Audio-visual education (e.g., educational films of women self-pleasuring to orgasm to model healthy arousal and orgasm).	Pharmacological therapy such as "off-label" sympathomimetic agents.	Address psychological features assessed to be major influences. Goals may include the following: Learning basic physiological relaxation techniques, cognitive management of distracting thoughts such as performance pressures and "spectatoring," sensual touch at first without sexual arousal, genital exploration, and progressive introduction of sexual stimulation. Particularly important in treatment is therapeutic facilitation of the person to use both sensual entrancement and partner involvement types of sexual arousal. Also important to aid orgasm is the training in the specialized use of the pubococcygeal muscles (Kegel exercise) to facilitate orgasm.	Women's sexual therapy group. When the woman has a supportive sexual partner, couple therapy may be the preferred treatment modality.	

(Continued)

Table 3.5.1. Continued

	Sexual Therapy Techniques and Interventions			
Sexual Problem	Education	Biological	Psychological	TX Modality	Comment
Male orgasm disorder (inhibited or "retarded" ejaculation)	Basic sexual physiological knowledge. The "purposes" for sexual activity. The types of sexual arousal. Audio-visual education.	Pharmacological therapy (sympathomimetic agents, e.g., pseudo-epinephrine hydrochloride).	Address psychological features assessed to be major influences. Goals may include the following: Learning basic physiological relaxation techniques, cognitive management of distracting thoughts such as performance pressures and "spectatoring," sensual touch at first without sexual arousal, genital exploration, and progressive introduction of sexual stimulation. Particularly important is to teach the person to blend both sensual entrancement and partner involvement and types of sexual arousal. Also important to facilitate orgasm is training in the specialized use of progressive arousal and the pubococcygeal muscles (PM) to facilitate orgasm.	Men's sexual therapy group. When the man has a supportive sexual partner, couple therapy may be the preferred treatment modality.	This disorder is thought to be more common among men than was believed to be the case in the past, and is thought to increase in frequency with aging. A common cause among men who can ejaculate by masturbation but not with intercourse is an overexposure to pornography and dependence on a ritualized masturbation pattern.

Sexual Therapy Techniques and Interventions

Sexual Problem	Education	Biological	Psychological	TX Modality	Comment
Premature or rapid ejaculation	Basic sexual physiological knowledge. The "purposes" for sexual activity. The types of sexual arousal. Audio-visual education.	Pharmacological therapy: Antidepressants, especially the SSRIs; also some tricyclics, monoamine oxidase inhibitors. Anxiolytics may offer some ejaculatory delay. Antipsychotics delay but have significant risks (use with caution). Anesthetic creams (e.g., benzocaine, lidocaine). Testicular restraint devices.	Address psychological and skills deficit features assessed to be major influences. Teach psychosexual skills: Physiological relaxation training. Sensual awareness training—"entrancement arousal." The pelvic muscle (PM) relaxation. Behavioral "stop-start" technique (Semans [1956] technique). Behavioral "squeeze technique" (Masters and Johnson, 1970). Cognitive "arousal continuum" technique. Couples "sensate focus" exercises for "entrancement arousal." The partner genital exploration relaxation exercise. Couple use of the behavioral pacing method: "stop-start" technique. The intercourse acclimation technique.	Couple therapy preferred. Individual or men's group.	PE is the most common male sexual dysfunction. Contrary to previously published material, PE is often difficult to treat effectively.

(Continued)

Table 3.5.1. CONTINUED

Sexual Problem	Education	Sexual Therapy Techniques and Interventions			
		Biological	Psychological	TX Modality	Comment
Dyspareunia					
Female	Basic sexual physiological knowledge. Audio-visual education.	Address physical cause determined by comprehensive medical evaluation. If common post-menopausal feature, use of a brand-name lubricant such as K-Y, Venus, or Astroglide.	Address psychological features assessed to be major influences.	Couple therapy.	Dyspareunia in women is thought to be caused predominantly by gynecologic problems, often undetected by general medical examination (such as chlamydia, vaginitis, etc.). Be attentive that dyspareunia may be secondary to female arousal dysfunction.
Male	Basic sexual physiological knowledge. Audio-visual education.	Address physical cause determined by comprehensive medical evaluation.			Dyspareunia in men is commonly caused by insufficient arousal, excessive masturbation or intercourse, insufficient lubrication of the partner, or injury.

Sexual Therapy Techniques and Interventions

Sexual Problem	Education	Biological	Psychological	TX Modality	Comment
Vaginismus	Basic sexual physiological knowledge.	Assess and treat potential physical cause (e.g., dyspareunia) that could cause reflexive vaginismus. Gradual dilator (device) therapy.	Address psychological features assessed to be major influences.	Individual, couple, and/or group therapy.	Vaginismus and dyspareunia commonly co-occur.
Substance-induced dysfunction	Basic physiological knowledge about the influence of various chemicals on sexual functioning.	Removal of substance when appropriate. If health benefit requires medication that has negative sexual side effect, change to other medication that meets the same health need but may not have sexual side effect.	Address psychological features assessed to be major influences.	Individual consultation. Couple therapy in cases where the substance-induced dysfunction is complicated.	The substances that most frequently have a negative effect on sexual functioning are alcohol and recreational drugs. Medications to treat illnesses commonly have detrimental sexual side effects. For example, hypertension increases dramatically with age, and sexual dysfunction is a common side effect of the drugs employed to control it in as much as 25% of treated hypertensives.

(Continued)

Table 3.5.1. Continued

Sexual Problem	Sexual Therapy Techniques and Interventions				
	Education	Biological	Psychological	TX Modality	Comment
Paraphilia	Basic sexual physiological knowledge. The "purposes" for sexual activity. The types of sexual arousal.	Medical treatment to address findings of comprehensive medical evaluation (e.g., neurologic disease). Pharmacologic therapy to address any medical cause or to help manage detrimental sexual behavior.	Address psychological features assessed to be major influences when the paraphilia is behaviorally enacted in a criminal way (e.g., pedophilia). Specialized sex offender therapy is required.	Individual, couple, group, and family therapy when relevant to the issue.	Incarceration may be protective of the public, but is not "treatment."
Gender identity disorder	Basic sexual physiological knowledge.	Medical treatment regarding genetic, endocrinology, etc., findings. When psychologically appropriate, two-stage physical sex change: (1) Hormonal sex reassignment (SHR). (2) Surgical sex reassignment (SRS).	Address psychological features assessed to be major influences from the psychiatric, psychological, and social evaluations. International standards of care require treatment that includes a minimum of 6 months psychotherapy; 2 years of satisfactory living in the assigned role; professional team consensus of the appropriateness of reassignment.	Individual therapy. Marital and family therapy to address family changes and adaptation to SRS. Group therapy for support and "coaching" in the new gender role.	

nose the specific type of sex dysfunction, develop a careful formulation, and chart a comprehensive treatment plan that addresses all of the physiological and psychological causes and effects. Comprehensive treatment addresses the multiple features of individual cases. For example, while medically treating a case of premature ejaculation caused by a urinary tract infection with antibiotics, the clinician also ameliorates any detrimental impact of PE on the individual's psychological well-being and intimate relationship, even if these features are the result rather than cause of the PE.

Sexual Desire Disorders

Lack or Loss of Sexual Desire (ICD-10: F52.0)

Hypoactive Sexual Desire Disorder (DSM-IV: 302.71)

The more common biological causes of a lack or loss of sexual desire are endocrinology problems including hormonal deficiencies, diabetes, and other major illness that may stress the body. The more common psychological causes are negative attitudes about sexuality, unrealistic sexual expectations, depression, fatigue, relationship alienation, and reaction to other sex dysfunctions (e.g., ED, inhibited orgasm). Treatment that corrects hormonal deficits (e.g., low levels of testosterone in either men or women treated with hormone replacement therapy) and other medical problems are fundamental in a biopsychosocial treatment approach. The more common features warranting therapeutic attention are various physical sources of fatigue, psychosocial stressors (such as family life, over-work, and poverty), loneliness in marriage, depression, and a sense of inadequacy. Psychological and relationship features are treated with standard psychotherapy, relationship therapy, and sexual enrichment. For example, negative attitudes toward sexuality are addressed by sexual enrichment such as educational workshops, bibliotherapy, or body image work. Relationship alienation may be addressed by marital therapy including such features as empathy skills work or conflict resolution and cooperation training.

Sexual Aversion and Lack of Sexual Enjoyment (ICD-10: F52.1)

Sexual Aversion Disorder (DSM-IV: 302.72)

As described in part 2, sexual aversion is thought to arise from a history of childhood physical or sexual trauma wherein the trauma results in overprotection in the sexual area to prevent future victimization. It may also develop out of a more generalized anxiety disorder or obsessive/compulsive disorder with a specific manifestation in the sexual area. When the sexual aversion disorder includes depressive, anxious, shame, phobic, and/or obsessive or paranoid features that are overwhelming and subsequently prevent the patient from following traditional sexual therapy and enrichment, then use of psychotropic medications may be appropriate to relieve the detrimental symptoms. Usually, individual and group therapy to address the psychological distress and the traumatic roots of the sexual aversion are required modalities of treatment prior to traditional sexual therapy that endeavors not only to overcome sexual dysfunctions that are commonly associated with a sexual aversion (inhibited sexual desire, arousal, and inhibited orgasm) but also to provide basic sexual enrichment. Such enrichment may be required to assist the traditional sensate-focus exercises. Sensual enrichment may involve detailed attention to enhancing sensual awareness through massage, relaxation training, positive cognitive visualization training, and other such procedures.

Sexual Arousal Disorders

Failure of Genital Response (ICD-10: F52.2)

Female, Male, Sexual Arousal Disorder (DSM-IV: 302.73)

Female failure of genital response or sexual arousal disorder may result from a number of causes. In cases of clear and exclusive organicity (e.g., thyroidism), the medical or surgical corrective treatment may be singular and targeted to the physical problem. In other cases with multiple causal features, mixed therapies are considered, combining medical therapy, individual psychotherapy, individual or couples sexual therapies, pharmacological therapy, or use of external devices. While currently less is known about female inhibited sexual arousal than about male arousal disorder, a wave of research is underway internationally that may offer not only new understanding but also new treatment options for women. It is likely that treatments and devices (such as the EROS-CTD) will eventually present as many options for women suffering inhibited arousal as there are now for men.

Male failure of genital response (sexual arousal disorder or erectile dysfunction) is the treatment that is most understood and developed, with a variety of biological and psychological treatment options. The biological, pharmacological, surgical, and device treatment options are outlined in the earlier section on biological treatment. In the psychological treatment of both female and male failure of genital response, the common features of general sexual therapy are employed (as outlined previously) for the individual and couple. Steps include learning basic physiological relaxation techniques, cognitive management of distracting thoughts such as performance pressures and "spectatoring," sensual touch at first without sexual arousal, genital exploration, and progressive introduction of sexual stimulation. Women with arousal disorder are taught how to induce arousal by balancing the level of relaxation with the level of sexual stimulation. Men with ED are taught how to facilitate an erection by balancing the level of relaxation with the level of sexual stimulation, and then to let it subside, before regaining an erection in a relaxed mode. Such steps are designed to assist the individual and couple to regain confidence with sexual performance, increase pleasure, and overcome the sexual performance anxiety.

Orgasmic Dysfunctions

Orgasmic Dysfunction (ICD-10: F52.3)

Female, Male Inhibited Orgasm (DSM-IV: 302.74)

Among the more common sexual complaints of women is having difficulty achieving orgasm consistently or not having experienced orgasm previously at all. Treatment commonly includes positive sexual attitudes work, self-pleasuring exercises, fantasy enhancement, positive body-image work, as well as Kegel (pelvic) muscle exercises to facilitate easier orgasms. Like ED among men, a number of treatment approaches to treating orgasmic dysfunction among women have been developed and evaluated for their treatment effectiveness. Male orgasmic dysfunction or inhibited ejaculation is a difficulty that had been thought to manifest rarely in younger men and to increase in frequency with aging. More recent studies have suggested that it is more common than previously thought, affecting as many as 10% of men. For some men, when the problem develops in a long-term relationship with the same partner, the typical male reliance upon "partner involvement arousal" may slow the excitement and subsequent ejaculation and orgasm as the sexual relationship becomes familiar and routine. Helping the man learn that sensual entrancement arousal is an alternative can supplement partner involvement arousal, often with good effect. For some men, an idiosyncratic masturbation practice may impede ejaculation with a partner (Perelman, 2004). It is also known that a good number of men with increasing age do not feel the urge to ejaculate each time they have intercourse and may not perceive it as a problem at all. Training the man in effective pacing techniques such as the arousal continuum technique, the use of the pelvic muscles (similar to the Kegel exercises for women with orgasm disorder), and supplemental pharmacological sympathomimetic agents are sometimes helpful treatments to improve orgasmic response.

Premature Ejaculation (ICD-10: F52.4; DSM-IV: 302.75)

While in the past, premature ejaculation was often considered to be an innocuous sexual problem that was easily treated, current awareness is that this dysfunction, the most common male sex dysfunction, in fact has an often profound effect upon the marital relationship and is quite difficult to treat successfully. Sometimes PE is caused by a physical illness (e.g., prostatitis) and a general medical evaluation is important. PE can lead to a crisis as the woman repeatedly experiences emotional as well as sexual abandonment, and an important relationship conflict may emerge. PE also may be the cause of other dysfunctions. For example, for some men, the frustration of PE may cause a level of anxiety that then causes erectile dysfunction by deterring arousal in order to avert premature ejaculation. Such repeated failures may also create, in one or both members of the couple, a pattern of avoidance of sexual behavior.

Treatment in the past relied strongly upon the "squeeze technique" advocated by Masters and Johnson (1970), although this technique alone has not been shown to be effective long-term by several treatment outcome studies. Contemporary sex therapy employs a more intricate approach to diagnosing the subtypes of PE (Metz and McCarthy, 2004; Metz and Pryor, 2000), and then integrates several techniques simultaneously to address the etiological features. For example, PE determined to be caused by the man's neurological constitution is usually treated by either or both pharmacological agents or psychosexual skills training. A number of psychotropic medications possess as a side effect the ability to inhibit orgasm or ejaculation and can be used as an aide to slowing ejaculation. These medications must be evaluated carefully as some may have a detrimental effect on the overall psychological health of the individual and may not be appropriate in spite of their sexual effect. Among the medications utilized to slow ejaculation are a number of antidepressants (e.g., paroxetine hydrochloride, clomipramine), anxiolytics (e.g., benzodiazepines), and neuroleptics (trifluoperazine) (see table 3.2.2).

When clinical use is required and secondary negative sexual effects are to be treated, the use of cholinergic agents (e.g., betanecol) and antiserotonergic drugs (e.g., cyproheptadine) is recommended, which may revert the negative sexual effects of tricyclics. Direct negative effects on sexuality may include sexual desire disorders; erectile difficulties; orgasmic abnormalities, notably inhibition or quantitative decrease of orgasms; galactorrhea; or gynecomastia. Such medications may also be used by psychiatrists for the treatment of hypersexuality and sexual phobias. In addition, a number of anesthetic creams have been utilized although effectiveness has not been verified consistently in studies to date. While some men with PE may feel desperate for help, surgeries such as severance of the penile dorsal nerve are to be discouraged because they result in irreversable diminution of physical sexual pleasure. The existence of less intrusive yet effective treatment options may render such surgeries unwarranted.

Sexual Pain Disorders

Nonorganic Vaginismus (ICD-10: F52.5)

Vaginismus (DSM-IV: 30xx)

Vaginismus is ordinarily very amenable to psychological and behavioral treatment. In one group of patients studied for four years, sexual functioning was achieved and maintained in 95% of the cases. Successful outcomes were associated with a desire for childbearing, a husband-initiated consultation, and a couple's perception that the problem was psychogenic. Unsuccessful outcomes were associated with a perception that the problem was organic, previous experience with an anatomic problem, abundant sexual misinformation, extensive sexual knowledge deficiency, a negative attitude toward genitalia, fear of sexually transmitted disease, and negative parental attitudes toward sex. Treatment includes graduated desensitization of the vagina to accommodate sized "dilators" (progressively sized devices, or one's own or partner's finger(s), inserted into the vagina and left in for several minutes to overcome the reflexive spasm of the vaginal muscles). When vaginismus is a reflexive reaction to past trauma or fear of dyspareunia, medical and psychological assessment and treatment address these sources.

Nonorganic Dyspareunia (ICD-10: F52.6)

Dyspareunia (DSM-IV: 3xx)

The prognosis for dyspareunia varies considerably, depending on the nature of any associated organic problems and the success of medical or surgical management. In those cases with a purely psychogenic cause, success rates reportedly may be as high as 90% or 95% of cases. It is thought that the majority of cases of sexual pain are caused by biological or medical illnesses. Psychological sexual pain is thought to commonly manifest from the effects of sexual trauma (e.g., incest, rape, gynecological injuries such as traumatic birthing), or poor sexual interaction skill (e.g., clumsy or rough sexual partner). Dyspareunia is common with mild to moderate cases of vaginismus, and infrequently, dyspareunia may be a symptom of serious psychopathology. Dyspareunia has been a neglected area in sex therapy, probably because it infrequently is the major presenting concern in clinical practice. However, more recent surveys (Laumann et al., 1999) suggest a prevalence of 14% among women and 3% of men, apparently caused by medical problems, sexual practices, or difficulties of the partner (e.g., vaginismus).

Other Sexual Disorders

Excessive Sexual Drive (ICD-10: F52.7)

Just as some people become obsessed and compulsive about other behaviors, some can become exceptionally focused upon sexual thoughts, feelings, and behaviors. Excessive sexual drive and behavior has been called compulsive sexual behavior, hypersexuality, hyperphilia, hypereroticism, hyperlibidity, hyperaesthesia, erotomania, perversion, nymphomania, Don Juanism, satyriasis, and more recently sexual addiction. This feature is commonly formulated as a behavior driven by anxiety-reduction mechanisms rather than by sexual desire that creates a self-perpetuating cycle, often manifesting as personal suffering as it puts the person at risk of sexually transmitted diseases, injuries, or moral, social, and legal sanctions. From the biopsychosocial, psychiatric perspective, formulation and treatment of the problem as a compulsion demands consideration of the complex interplay of biological, social, and psychological factors that may cause the problem and warrant therapeutic attention. In the biopsychosocial model, comprehensive professional sex therapy addresses the sexual behavioral as a compulsivity. Possible biological and psychiatric causes should be assessed (bipolar mood disorder, endocrine and neurological disorders) that may manifest with hypersexuality. Treatment may include pharmacological treatment (notably medications approved for treatment of mood disorders, obsessive compulsive disorder, or some antidepressants) and individual, marital, and group therapies. Treatment goals from this perspective include not only regulation of sexual behavior but affirmation of healthy sexuality (because common features of excessive sexual behavior are negative attitudes and emotional shame about sexuality) and education about how to integrate healthy sexual behavior into one's lifestyle. When formulated as a sexual addiction, treatment is commonly modeled on alcohol and chemical dependency treatment such as the Alcoholics Anonymous program's well-known twelve-step format.

There is considerable professional debate between the theoretical perspectives regarding compulsivity and addiction, with implications for treatment approaches. An important issue is distinguishing between what is considered a "normal" or common sexual behavior and what is seriously detrimental or destructive to the person, relationship, or community. Pharmacological treatment, individual, marital, and group therapies are common in the treatment protocol.

Gender Identity Disorder

Transsexualism (ICD-10: F64.0)

Gender Identity Disorder (DSM-IV: 285.5)

Gender identity clinics utilize a high degree of consistency of policies and criteria for approving hormonal and surgical sex reassignment for transsexual patients (Petersen and Dickey, 1995). Diagnostic care is required in evaluating this sexual problem as there are a number of psychiatric and sexual problems for which gender confusion and cross-dressing may be a symptom. Psychotherapy at the different clinics is less consistent. The Harry Benjamin International Gender Dysphoria Association's Standards of Care have established the professional protocol for sex reassignment internationally. Treatment should include medical (genetic, endocrinology, etc.), psychiatric, psychological, and social evaluation in order to treat any disorders in these areas; a minimum of six months of psychotherapy to understand and clarify the motivation for sex reassignment; two years of satisfactory living in the assigned role where the patient attends to the activities of daily living; and a consensus by the treating professional team of the appropriateness of reassignment.

The biological treatment for reassignment involves two major phases: hormonal reassignment and surgical reassignment. Typically, hormonal assignment is initiated when the person begins living full-time in the gender role to which one is moving. Hormonal reassignment precipitates many of the secondary sex characteristics (e.g., breast development for male-to-female, or beard growth for female to male), which often helps the person appear to the public more like the gender to which the patient is changing. Progesterone is commonly administered to male-to-females and testosterone injections to female-to-male transsexuals. Surgery commonly involves castration and vaginal construction for male-to-female patients and mastectomy and phalloplasty for the female-to-male patients. Some female-to-male patients forego constructive phalloplasty, relying instead on the clitoral enlargement induced by the androgen therapy. Most treatment programs also now provide medical and psychotherapeutic after-care services to offer continual support in the long transsexual transition.

Some gender identity treatment programs report positive results with sex reassignment while a number of sex reassignment programs have stopped reassignment, citing a lack of significant improvement in the lives of these patients (Green and Fleming, 1990; Rehman et al., 1999; Carroll, 1999; Snaith, Tarsh, and Reid, 1993). For adolescents with gender dysphoria, especially prior to age eighteen, psychotherapy rather than premature sex reassignment is encouraged (Meyenburg, 1999). Psychotherapy appears to help determine the need for sex reassignment and to assist patients to accept their given gender role.

Disorders of Sexual Preference (ICD-10: F65)

Sexual Paraphilia (DSM-IV: 302.90)

Disorders of sexual preference (ICD-10), or paraphilia (DSM-IV), are sexual arousal patterns that are distressing to the person or detrimental and unwelcome to others. Treatment for sexual preference disorders sometimes occurs subsequent to legal arrest for having behaviorally enacted a legally prohibited paraphilic arousal in a public way. Not all individuals with paraphilia are sex offenders and not all sex offenders have paraphilia (they may have bipolar or antisocial personality disorder). Some persons with paraphilia may voluntarily seek help for their distress, or their partner's distress, surrounding the arousal pattern (e.g., fetish, pedophilia, sado-masochism). It is important in this area of sexuality to consider the legal jurisdiction in which the behavior is at issue, because there is considerable variance in legal positions toward acceptable/unacceptable behaviors in communities around the world. The prevalence of sexual preference disorders (estimates: <.5%–2%) is not adequately known because of the heterogeneous definitions of this disorder. The sex offender field is diverse in approaches and depth. There is an emerging trend toward evaluating treatment and effectiveness (Maletzky, 1998), and standards of care are being formulized by international associations of professionals who treat sex offenders (Coleman et al., 2000).

Psychiatric comorbidity and interpersonal skills deficits appear to be moderately high among some paraphilias. For example, mood and anxiety disorders were found in more than 60% of pedophilic sex offenders (Raymond et al., 1999), as well as negative relationship conflict styles (Metz and Dwyer, 1993).

There appears to be effective treatment for nonviolent sex offenders; prison is neither an effective treatment nor a deterrent. Treatment appears more effective for pedophilia and exhibitionism than for rape (Marshall et al., 1991; Fordham, 1993). Effective treatment is comprehensive, is cognitive-behaviorally based, and includes a relapse prevention component (Marshall and Pithers, 1994). However, there are opposing data and opinion. For example, McConaghy (1999a) demonstrates a consistent finding that treatment is less effective than placebo psychological therapies. Treatment for more dangerous sex offenders is being evaluated (Barbaree and Marshall, 1998). In one meta-analysis of sexual offender treatment studies, a small but robust overall effect size was found for treatment versus comparison conditions. Also, cognitive-behavioral and hormonal treatments were significantly more effective than behavioral treatments alone (Hall, 1995; Hernandez and Eher, 1998).

The treatment of paraphilia, when it is particularly distressing to the individual or the community, has advanced considerably with the use of pharmacological agents as well as psychotherapy. Pharmacological agents (e.g., mood disorder and obsessive-compulsive medications) may alleviate some sexual obsessions, particularly for those who experience seemingly overwhelming sexual fantasies and urges to act on such fantasies. With pharmacotherapy the need for chemical castration (anti-androgens) has lessened, although it may still be employed in extreme cases. At the same time, scientific research and professional opinion has suggested that surgical castration is not directly effective as well as ethically questionable. Lowering testosterone may inhibit sexual desire but does not appear to directly influence the fantasy or arousal pattern of persons with paraphilia. Psychotropic medications, notably antidepressants and anti-obsessive/compulsive agents, may offer some relief by diminishing some sexual fantasy and sexual impulses although no effective treatment is universal.

The psychological treatment of paraphilia appears to be more effective when it incorporates group therapy, and marital and family therapy when feasible, which focuses upon development of support persons. Having nonrejecting support persons in the offender's life is particularly important. Therapy focuses on developing congruent thinking and problem-solving abilities, as well as cognitive restructuring. "Hesitation prevention" is commonly advocated as an innovative manner of relapse prevention. Therapy also focuses on increasing acceptance of the patient's concealed depressive features (sadness, loneliness, emotional suffering, etc.). Different versions of empathy treatment are being utilized in order to treat these patients more humanely (partly built upon clinical experience and post-prison observation that more punitive approaches [like prison] do not appear to prevent recidivism and may actually promote reoffending behavior).

Psychotherapy promotes patient acknowledgement of the detrimental behavior and its effects upon others, promotes insight into the emotional foundations that may promote the paraphilic behavior, and enhances the patient's self-esteem, which may help the patient to accept and address the disorder more effectively. In addition, for some offenders with concomitant sex dysfunction (e.g., ED) unless he employs the paraphilic behavior or fantasy with a normative partner, cognitive-behavioral therapy may help improve his quality of life and lower the risk of reoffense when the man can adequately sexually perform with an appropriate partner (Metz and Sawyer, 2003). Cognitive-behavioral and hormonal treatments were significantly more effective than behavioral treatments alone (Hall, 1995; Hernandez, Eher, et al., 1998). Outpatient sex offender treatment program dropouts appear to be at higher risk for reoffending (Miner and Dwyer, 1995). Outcome research suggests a reduction in recidivism of 30% over seven years with comparable effectiveness for hormonal and cognitive behavioral treatments (Grossman, Martis, and Fichtner, 1999). Outpatient treatment has better outcome than institutional (prison) programs. Criminal records appear to be an important prognostic factor.

Psychological and Behavioral Disorders Associated with Sexual Development and Orientation (ICD-10: F66)

According to ICD-10 and DSM-IV, sexual orientation by itself is not to be regarded as a disorder. However, there is a considerable community and professional disagreement about the significance, causes, and variation of sexual orientation, and whether orientation is amenable to change through medical or psychiatric therapeutic processes. Scientifically, sexual orientation is known to be a complex phenomenon with a wide range of arousal and behavioral patterns. Increasingly, scientific evidence supports the notion of biological determinants of sexual orientation in both animal studies as well as human genetic studies. As with other sexual concerns, the manifestations of sexual attraction or orientation may present in a number of subtypes that are not yet well understood or distinguished. The task of the sexual professional is to address clinical problems arising from sexual orientation (heterosexual, homosexual, bisexual, or asexual) as defined by the patient and to conduct a comprehensive and detailed assessment and differential diagnosis. Current scientific evidence indicates that there is no scientific evidence that sexual orientation as a fundamental erotic cognitive/affective domain can be significantly changed.

Comprehensive Treatment of Complex and Special Situations

In addition to the common sexual dysfunctions that draw the predominant attention of most psychiatrists or sexual therapists, certain groups of people with sexual disorders or difficulties warrant special attention and call to mind the vastness and variety of sexual concerns that invite the professional's empathetic and skillful therapeutic care.

Other Sexual Difficulties or Common Sexual Concerns

In addition to sexual dysfunctions and sexual disorders, there are a number of concerns that are often expressed as concerns by patients either as a primary concern or as a feature of sexual dysfunction or disorder. Data suggest that while sexual dysfunction, for example, is common, difficulties with sexual intimacy are even more common, perhaps affecting virtually every human person at one time or another. These difficulties usually are not of such severity or intensity that they are conceptualized as sexual dysfunctions (problems that prevent the satisfactory performance of sexual intercourse) or sexual disorders (sexual problems that significantly interfere with sexual performance or well-being), but nevertheless are disturbing or distracting to sexual well-being. Among these are a variety of concerns about one's sexual "normalcy" or health (e.g., the role of sexual fantasy in one's life, worries about the normalcy of one's body such as penis or breast size, or behaviors such as anal intercourse, oral sex, use of erotica); couple conflicts over sexual frequency or sexual practices; distresses arising from sexual arousal orientation; the sexual manifestations from body dysmorphic concerns; physical disabilities; common distresses arising from developmental stages in life such as normalcy of sexuality in childhood or aging; concerns about HIV/AIDS; and couples experiencing infertility.

A number of surveys on the prevalence of sexual problems conducted around the world have suggested that virtually every human being at one point or another in life has personal concerns about one's sexual thoughts, feelings, or behaviors. Most common are worries about the normalcy of one's sexual fantasies (e.g., desire for persons other than one's spouse), disturbing sexual dreams, the normalcy of one's sexual body parts (penis, breasts, vaginal "lips" or labia); the desire for unconventional objects or situations; and the normalcy of certain behaviors (masturbation, wet dreams, a woman's experiencing pleasurable feelings while nursing the infant, or speed of ejaculation). While these concerns are not considered sexual disorders, they can nevertheless create considerable anxiety in the person and thus may contribute to sexual disorders. Sometimes they are the result of the cultural discomfort about openly discussing sexual matters and the subsequent lack of accurate and age-appropriate information about normal sexual physiology and psychology. These concerns frequently can be ameliorated by the professional giving helpful information. Below is a brief summary of the several groups of persons with special sexual difficulties and contemporary therapeutic formulation and treatment.

Individuals with Physical and Developmental Disabilities

Often in the past, discussions of human sexuality about individuals with disabilities have been excluded or at best limited from the usual educational channels such as the home, school, or church. Health care providers have also denied, avoided, or inappropriately handled the sociosexual needs of recipients of health care. Kempton (1975) reported in her book *Sex Education for Persons with Disabilities That Hinder Learning* that our society has always had difficulty coping with the sexuality of its members, particularly those with some kind of disability. It is only in the last few decades that the recognition of all humans as sexual beings with rights and responsibilities to sexual expression, regardless of their physical and mental capabilities, has been more widely acknowledged and accepted. This has occurred through the efforts of such organizations as the Sex Information and Education Council of the United States (SIECUS) and pioneers in this field such as Drs. Mary Calderone, Kirkendall, Ted and Sandra Cole, Winifred Kempton, and Sol Gordon, to name a few. This has also been motivated by the philosophical commitment to the normalization principle and statements mandating sex education and counseling in schools and health care facilities. Wolfenberger (1972), who publicized the concept of normalization in the United States, defined it as the "utilization of means which are as culturally normative as possible, in order to establish or maintain personal behaviors and characteristics which are as culturally normative as possible" (p. 28). This requires that human services programs do all that they can to integrate persons with mental retardation and other developmental special needs into everyday community life, viewing the recipient of services in a holistic manner and attending to a range of his or her human needs, including their sexuality.

The United Nations passage of the Bill of Rights for Retarded Individuals (1970) furthered this position by affirming both the need for and the right to sex education for this population. It also resolved that persons with retardation and disabilities should have the right to cohabit and marry, which increases their need for access to sex education and counseling from their health providers.

It is imperative that facilities that service people with physical and mental disabilities have effective sex education programs available, supported by policy and staff training. Otherwise, this population will be left to the demise of prejudice and myths, thwarting their self-esteem and healthy sexual development and expression.

Effective programs for sex education among people with developmental disabilities focus on learning pathways for hygiene, social interaction, and sexual experience (McDermott et al., 1999). Persons with such developmental disabilities may benefit from appropriate educational programs to enrich their sexual lives. Sexual behavior problems can be effectively managed with long-term comprehensive and individualized psychological and social treatment (Lund, 1992).

Persons with HIV/AIDS and Other Sexually Transmitted Diseases (STDs)

Undoubtedly fear of AIDS and other sexually transmitted diseases (STDs) has contributed to campaigns that promote sexual abstinence, epidemiological chains, and promotions of isolated strategies. This has not been able to reduce the incidence of new cases in the pandemic that affects the world before the almost insensitive eyes of the communities and governments. It seems that we are getting used to living with this situation. Certain STDs are literally a threat to one's life. Too often advances in treatment are limited to those few who can financially afford them. This generates an unacceptable discrimination. Consequently, the use of condoms and safe sex must be openly promoted, without fear.

Other STDs, while not as life-threatening as HIV/AIDS, often bring significant health threats (e.g., long-term effects of dementia from untreated syphilis) and distress to the individual and a couple. STDs involve not only the medical problem requiring treatment (e.g., genital herpes) but also anxiety and disruption to the sexual relationship, which itself may cause sexual dysfunction. While treating the medical aspects of STDs is essential, addressing the psychological and relational aspects of STDs is also vital.

Couples with Reproductive Problems

Sexual problems may arise surrounding a couple's effort to have children, prevent pregnancy, adjust to pregnancy, or adjust to the early stages of establishing a family. The decision to have children is increasingly a conscious decision among peoples of the world, and contraception is a common issue among couples: whether or not to use contraception, what form to use, the appropriateness of abortion as a contraceptive technique, and the role of religion in contraceptive decisions. Often such conflicts are part of larger relationship issues concerning cooperation and problem-solving.

Struggling with infertility may present a significant emotional and relationship problem for some couples. Working with their physician, they may employ techniques that maximize the possibility of impregnation but cause serious sexual problems and sexual dysfunctions. For example, often the physician may encourage the couple to have sexual intercourse at a specific time (during ovulation), and this "demand" may create performance anxiety and erectile dysfunction. Some estimates suggest that such dysfunctions may affect as many as 80% of couples undergoing prescribed techniques to maximize impregnation. Infertility experts, as a result, frequently include a sex therapist to their team to address such iatrogenic difficulties.

Sex during pregnancy, while usually not a medical concern, may create confusion or conflict within some couples when they may erroneously believe it unsafe or dishonorable. There are different norms around the world regarding the value or appropriateness of sexual intercourse during pregnancy. Sometimes couples worry that sexual intercourse during pregnancy may harm the fetus or induce miscarriage, although these are unwarranted concerns unless there is a specific medical difficulty with the pregnancy. Many couples experience sexual interest fluctuations at times during the nine-month pregnancy that are usually related to hormonal fluctuations in the woman's endocrine system.

The early years of establishing a family, when children are very young, also presents a challenge to the sexual relationship of many couples. The demands and needs of the child or children commonly create emotional and physical fatigue as well as intrude upon the couple's privacy and opportunities to be sexual. Unless a couple consciously decides that their sexual relationship is a marital priority, this time in a couple's lives may see a decline in sexual intimacy and other problems.

Sexual Disorders in Older Adults

Adequate understanding of sexuality is important at any age but especially for older adults. Ignorance of normal changes after age forty may create fear of aging or disease, sexual anxiety, and a subsequent distraction or heightened effort to perform, resulting in psychogenic sexual dysfunction. No adequate representative studies exist on the overall sexual functioning of older adults. But studies utilizing availability samples of older adults indicate that there are considerable individual differences (see Schiavi, 1990; Schiavi and Rehman, 1995). Unfortunately, a number of studies have methodological flaws (e.g., not controlled for physical illness and medications), and studies of women's adjustment to aging are less extensive that those for men. Diokno, Brown, and Herzog (1990) reported that 74% of married men older than sixty remain sexually active, while Bretschneider and McCoy (1988) found that 63% between ages eighty and one hundred and two continued to be active. In regard to sexual desire, 80%–90% of men reportedly retained sexual interest well into their seventies or beyond (Pfeiffer, Verwoerdt, and Davis, 1971). Some researchers, however, have recorded progressive declines in male sexual interest, activity, and performance with age (McKinlay and Feldman, 1994). Mallett and Badlan (1987) reported the prevalence of ED to be 20% for men sixty years old, 27% among seventy years old, and 75% among men eighty years old. Krane and colleagues (1989) reported a 1.9% prevalence among forty-year-olds and 25% among sixty-year-olds. In the Baltimore Longitudinal Study of Aging, Martin (1981) noted 7% incidence of ED among men twenty to thirty years old and 57% at ages seventy to seventy-nine; he concluded that physical health and well-being contributed to the maintaining of sexual activity. Other studies (Starr and Weiner, 1981; Bretschneider and McCoy, 1988) have suggested that positive attitudes toward sexuality are important influences on sexuality among older adults. Persson (1980) studied seventy-year-old men and found that 46% continued to have intercourse, which was associated with global ratings of mental health and quality of life, positive sex attitudes, and the individual's reported strength of sexual desire in younger years. The Starr and Weiner (1981) survey noted that 80% of the sixty- to ninety-one-year-olds sampled were sexually active, 50% having sex on a regular basis, and of these, 50% having sex once a week or more often.

The predictors of sexual interest and activity in older adults are (1) their overall physical health, (2) their characteristic level of sexual activity in youth (Persson, 1980; Berman and Lief, 1976), and (3) the health and sexual interest of the sexual partner (Weiss and Mellinger, 1990). The association of sexual problems with aging appears to be more related to illness than normal aging itself. For example, researchers at the Mayo Clinic (Panser et al., 1995) examined sexual function among 2,115 randomly sampled men ages forty to seventy-nine and noted that sexual function was an important component of the quality of life of men and that more men were satisfied than dissatisfied at every age. Sexual satisfaction decreased with increasing age, but dissatisfaction was not predicted by age but rather by "age-related declines in physiological function (illness, erectile dysfunction and diminished libido) and the potential failure to compensate psychologically for that loss" (p. 1110). Others conclude that there is no evidence to suggest that sexual problems are inevitable among aging men who are physiologically and psychologically healthy (see Meston, 1997; McKinlay and Feldman, 1994). Sexual dysfunction has been associated with a number of organic features such as diminished testosterone, elevated luteinizing hormone, and abnormal pituitary function. Korenman, Morley, and Mooradian (1990) noted that after adjustment for age and body mass index (bmi = weight/height squared), there was no difference in bioavailable testosterone levels in potent versus impotent older men, suggesting that hypogonadism and impotence are independent and that impotence in aging men is more likely due to neurological or vascular changes than hypogonadism. Subsequently, testosterone replacement therapy is questionable unless the individual is frankly hypogonadal (Meston, 1997). Accurately distinguishing between and adapting to the normal sexual "mellowing" common with healthy aging from physical illness that has negative effects on sexual function is an important challenge among older persons.

Health Promotion

Health promotion is emerging as an important consideration and activity in health care (Herrman, Saxena, and Moodie, 2005). This is associated with the broadening of the concept of health to include not only disease and problems but also positive aspects of health, such as functioning, supports, and quality of life as outlined in the WPA International Guidelines for Diagnostic Assessment (Mezzich, Berganza, et al., 2003). Health promotion involves a number of creative steps to enhance the status of health. This is true for general health as well as sexual health. Primary prevention is a related concept but is focused on avoidance or preemption of disease risk factors, while health promotion promotes the stimulation of the person and his social context to explore and to achieve higher levels of health.

The Sexuality Information and Education Council of the United States (SIECUS) has developed a comprehensive sexuality education program to promote sexual health. This program includes sections on information; attitudes, values and insights; relationships and interpersonal skills; and responsibility. SIECUS described the following goals and values for comprehensive sex education: Sexuality education is a lifelong process of acquiring information and forming attitudes, beliefs, and values about identity, relationships and intimacy. It encompasses sexual development, reproductive health, interpersonal relationships, affection, intimacy, body image, and gender roles. Sexuality education addresses the biological, sociocultural, psychological, and spiritual dimensions of sexuality from (1) the cognitive domain, (2) the affective domain, and (3) the behavioral domain, including the skills to communicate effectively and make responsible decisions.

The primary goal of sexuality education is the promotion of sexual health. In 1975, the World Health Organization defined sexual health as "the integration of the physical, emotional intellectual, and social aspects of sexual being in ways that are positively enriching, and that enhance personality, communication, and love. . . . Every person has a right to receive sexual information and to consider accepting sexual relationships for pleasure as well as for procreation."

Sex education can assist people in gaining a positive view of sexuality, provide them with information and skills about taking care of their sexual health, and help them acquire skills to make decisions now and in the future. The desired outcomes of a sex education program are based on the following four primary goals for sex education:

1. *Information:* to provide accurate information about human sexuality, including growth and development, human reproduction, anatomy, physiology, masturbation, family life, pregnancy, childbirth, parenthood, sexual response, sexual orientation, contraception, abortion, sexual abuse, and HIV/AIDS and other STIs.
2. *Attitudes, values, and insights:* to provide an opportunity for young people to question, explore, and assess their sexual attitudes in order to understand their family's values, develop their own values, increase self-esteem, develop insights concerning relationships with families and members of both genders, and understand their obligations and responsibilities to their families and others.
3. *Relationships and interpersonal skills:* to help young people develop interpersonal skills, including communication, decision-making, assertiveness, and peer refusal skills, as well as the ability to create satisfying relationships; to prepare students to understand their sexuality effectively and creatively in adult roles; and to help young people develop the capacity for caring, supportive, noncoercive, and mutually pleasurable intimate and sexual relationships.
4. *Responsibility:* to help young people exercise responsibility regarding sexual relationships, including addressing abstinence, how to resist pressures to become prematurely involved in sexual intercourse, and encouraging the use of contraception and other sexual health measures; and to reduce the prevalence of sexually related medical problems, including teenage pregnancy, STIs, and sexual abuse.

SIECUS also identifies life behaviors of a sexually healthy adult classified into the following six areas: human development, relationships, personal skills, sexual behavior, sexual health, and society and culture. The program structure and goals are presented in figure 3.7.1.

Human development includes appreciation of one's own body and that of others. It affirms that human development includes sexual development and that information about sexuality and reproduction should be freely available. A key concept is that interaction with both genders should be appropriate and respectful.

It emphasizes that meaningful relationships are important to develop and maintain, and love and intimacy should be appropriately expressed. Cultural heritage affects ideas about interpersonal relationships, ethics, and family. Choices about relationships and family options should be informed, and exploitative and manipulative relationships avoided. Personal skills to this effect involve good communication with peers, family, and partners; identification of personal values; responsibility for personal behavior; and effective decision-making.

Sexual behavior can be pleasurable and expressed throughout life in ways congruent with personal and cultural values. Sexual feelings can be enjoyed without necessarily acting out on them, and the expression of one's sexuality should include respect for the rights of others. This includes engaging in sexual relationships that are consensual, not exploitative, abusive, or irresponsible.

Sexual health includes practicing health-promoting behavior, such as the effective use of contraceptives and the avoidance of STIs.

Figure 3.7.1. The SIECUS sexual health curriculum: life behaviors of a sexually healthy adult.

The SIECUS Sexual Health Curriculum:
Life Behaviors of a Sexually Healthy Adult

- Affirm that human development includes sexual development, which may or may not include reproduction or genital sexual experience.
- Interact with both genders in respectful and appropriate ways.
- Affirm one's own sexual orientation and respect the sexual orientation of others.
- View family as a powerful source of support.

The goal of a comprehensive sexuality education program is to facilitate sexual health. After learning the six key concepts and associated topics, subconcepts, and developmental messages, at an appropriate age the student will demonstrate certain life behaviors.

A sexually healthy adult will do the following:

Human Development
Appreciate one's own body.
Seek further information about reproduction as needed.
Express love and intimacy in appropriate ways.
Develop and maintain meaningful relationships.
Avoid exploitative or manipulative relationships.
Make informed choices about family options and lifestyles.
Exhibit skills that enhance personal relationships.
Understand how cultural heritage affects ideas about family, interpersonal relationships, and ethics.

Personal Skills
Identify and live according to one's values.
Take responsibility for one's own behavior.
Practice effective decision making.
Communicate effectively with family, peers, and partners.

Sexual Behavior
Enjoy and express one's sexuality throughout life.
Express one's sexuality in ways congruent with one's values.
Enjoy sexual feelings without necessarily acting on them.
Discriminate between life-enhancing sexual behaviors and those that are harmful to self and/or others.
Express one's sexuality while respecting the rights of others.
Seek new information to enhance one's sexuality.
Engage in sexual relationships that are characterized by honesty, equity, and responsibility.

Sexual Health
Use contraception effectively to avoid unintended pregnancy.
Prevent sexual abuse.
Act in a way consistent with one's own values in dealing with an unintended pregnancy.
Seek early prenatal care.
Avoid contracting or transmitting a sexually transmitted disease, including HIV.
Practice health-promoting behaviors, such as regular checkups, breast and testicular self-exam, and early identification of potential problems.

(Continued)

Society and Culture
Demonstrate respect for people with different sexual values and lifestyles.
Recognize that usual intergenerational stress and value conflicts between family
    members are compounded by different rates of acculturation.
Exercise democratic responsibility to influence legislation dealing with sexual issues.
Assess the impact of family, cultural, religious, media, and societal messages on one's
    thoughts, feelings, values, and behaviors related to sexuality.
Promote the rights of all people to accurate information about sexuality.
Avoid behaviors that exhibit prejudice and bigotry.
Reject stereotypes about the sexuality of diverse populations.
Educate others about sexuality.

Social and cultural issues include respecting people with different sexual values and avoiding behaviors that exhibit prejudice, bigotry, and stereotypes. Family, cultural, religious, media, and societal messages impact on sexual thoughts, feelings, values, and behaviors. The rights of all people to accurate sexual information, and legislation to deal appropriately with sexual issues, should be promoted.

As it has been presented throughout this volume, health, both general and sexual, are complex and encompassing concepts. Accordingly, health care must be aimed at both dealing with the problems people present as well as taking advantage of clinical encounters for advancing the status of health in a creative, empowering, and responsible manner and engaging all the resources of the individual, the couple and their social contexts.

Illustrative Clinical Case with Comprehensive Diagnostic Formulation and Treatment Plan

Clinical Vignette

A thirty-six-year-old computer programmer, sought treatment for "impotence." He is married to a thirty-two-year-old housewife and is very much worried about work. He was an employee of an Italian branch of a French corporation. Over the last two years, the Italian staff was reduced from ten to four persons and now he is unemployed, receiving 80% of his usual salary as a form of unemployment compensation. In the south of Italy, where he lives, there are few alternative employment opportunities and his wife does not want to move to the north where it would be easier for him to find a job. The couple would like to have a child but it is impossible, at this time, for their precarious economic situation. No organic factors for his sexual difficulties were found. The erectile dysfunction (ED) began just a few weeks after he was placed on temporary unemployment compensation. During the clinical interview, the patient underlined the overwhelming sense of responsibility (connected to cultural traditions) toward his family's destiny and the emerging anxiety deriving from that and the diminishing status he has in his community. In line with this, he does not feel "masculine enough," and it reminds him of an early experience, when he was a child, and his doctor discovered he had just one testicle.

Figure A.1.1. COMPREHENSIVE DIAGNOSTIC FORMULATION FORM FOR PERSONS WITH SEXUAL DISORDERS (SAMPLE).

Comprehensive Diagnostic Formulation Form for Persons with Sexual Disorders

Based on the WPA International Guidelines for Diagnostic Assessment (Mezzich, Berganza, et al., 2003)

Name: *JE Berguelic* Code: ______________

Date: *17/9/2000*

Age: *36* Sex: (M) F Marital Status: *Married*

Occupation: *Computer Programmer*

First Component: Standardized Multiaxial Formulation (*Sexual Health Version*)

Axis I. Clinical disorders (as classified in ICD-10)

A. Sexual disorders (sexual dysfunctions, paraphilias, and gender identity disorders)

Disorders	Codes
Failure of genital response (erectile dysfunction)	F52.2

B. Comorbidities (coexisting mental and general medical disorders)

Disorders	Codes
Adjustment disorder with a mixed reaction of anxiety and depression	F43.22
Undescended testicle (cryptorchidism)	

Axis II: Disabilities

	Disability Scale*						
Areas of Functioning	0	1	2	3	4	5	U
A Personal care	X						
B Occupational (wage earner, student, etc.)	X						
C With spouse or partner				X			
D With other relatives							X
E Social in general				X			

0 = None; 1 = Minimal; 2 = Moderate; 3 = Substantial; 4 = Severe; 5 = Massive; U = Unknown; according to the intensity and frequency of the recent presence of the different types of disabilities

Axis III: Contextual factors (psychosocial problems pertinent to the presentation, course, or treatment of the patient's disorders or relevant to clinical care, as well as personal problems that do not amount to a standard disorder)

Problem Areas (to be specified)	Codes Z
1. Family/house:	
2. Education/work:	
3. Economic/legal: *Lack of secure financial situation, partial unemployment, threat of unemployment*	
4. Cultural/environmental:	
5. Personal:	

Figure A.1.1. CONTINUED

Comprehensive Diagnostic Formulation Form
for Persons with Sexual Disorders
*Based on the WPA International Guidelines for Diagnostic Assessment
(Mezzich, Berganza, et al., 2003)*

Axis IV: Quality of life (indicates the perceived level of quality of life by the patient, from poor to excellent, by marking one of the 10 points in the line bellow; this level can be determined through an appropriate multidimensional instrument or by direct global rating)

Poor										Excellent
0	1	2	3	4	5	6	7	8	9	10

Second Component: Idiographic Formulation

I: Clinical problems and their contextualization (Include disorders and problems, extracted from the Standardized Multiaxial Formulation, and formulated in language shared by the clinician, patient, partner, and family, as well as complementary key information, mechanisms, and explanations from biological, psychological, social, and cultural perspectives.)

JEB is experiencing failure of genital response (erectile dysfunction, impotence) that followed a
stressful period of underemployment, with loss of self-esteem, and earning capacity, which threat-
ened his sense of masculinity and of responsibility to his family, as well as the possibility of produc-
ing offspring.

II: Positive factors of the patient (Include resources pertinent to treatment and health promotion, e.g., maturity of personality, abilities and talents, self-awareness, motivation for change, capacity for sexual fantasies and playfulness, social supports and resources, personal and spiritual aspirations.)

JEB is a skilled computer technician. He is personally well motivated to deal with his sexual prob-
lem. Wife is substantially supportive. Couple looks forward to enriched family life.

III: Expectations on restoration and promotion of health (Include specific expectations on types of treatment and outcome as well as aspirations on health status and quality of life in the foreseeable future.)

He requested comprehensive individual and couples assessment and resolution of his sexual prob-
lem. He also expects a more fulfilling and creative sexual life within the framework of his family.

(Continued)

Figure A.1.1. Continued

Treatment Plan Format

(Based on the WPA International Guidelines For Diagnostic Assessment)

Name: _JE Berguelic_ _____ Record N°: _____

Date: _17/9/2000_ _____

Age: __36__ _____ Sex: (M) F Marital Status: _Married_ _____

Occupation: _Computer Programmer_ _____

Clinicians involved: _____

Setting: _____

Instructions:

Under **Clinical Problems** list as targets for care key clinical disorders, disabilities, and contextual problems presented in the Multiaxial Diagnostic Formulation, as well as problems noted in the Idiographic Formulation. Keep the list as simple and short as possible. Consolidate into one encompassing term all those problems that share the same intervention.

Interventions should list diagnostic studies as well as treatment and health promotion activities pertinent to each clinical problem. Be as specific as possible in identifying modalities planned, doses and schedules, amounts and time frames, as well as the corresponding responsible clinicians.

The space for **Observations** may be used in a flexible way as needed. Illustratively, it could include target dates for problem resolution, dates of scheduled reassessments, and notes that a problem has been resolved or has become inactive.

Clinical Problems	Interventions	Observations
1. Erectile dysfunction	*Diagnostic:* 1. *Complete clinical evaluation: history, mental status examination, and sexual history.* 2. *Lab: routine tests.* *Therapeutic:* 1. *Individual sessions of supportive psychotherapy.* 2. *Consider in due course the use of vasoactive medication.*	1. *Reassess patient in 1 month.*
2. Mixed anxiety and depression	*Diagnostic:* 1. *Interviewing Mr. B's wife.* *Therapeutic* 1. *Individual sessions of supportive psychotherapy.* 2. *Physical training to alleviate tension.* 3. *Relaxation techniques.*	1. *Obtain Mr. B's consent.* 2. *Write reference to the behavior modification therapist.*

Figure A.1.1. CONTINUED

Clinical Problems	Interventions	Observations
3. Cultural identity conflict	*Diagnostic:* 1. Complete a DSM-IV cultural formulation. *Therapeutic:* 1. Raise the issue of his concepts of masculinity and reframe his understanding of his difficulties during therapy sessions. 2. Sexual education program involving couple.	1. Ask Mr. B's permission to involve his wife in this educational program. 2. Reassess patient in 1 month
4. Marital conflict	*Diagnostic:* 1. Assess sources of conflict and own contributions during therapy sessions with Mr. B. 2. Consider involving his wife in order to complete understanding of the marital situation. *Therapeutic:* 1. Supportive psychotherapy sessions.	1. Reassess in a month.
5. Underemployment	*Diagnostic:* 1. Ask social services to find out if unemployment compensation includes medical and/or psychiatric insurance. *Therapeutic:* 1. Discuss alternative employments during supportive psychotherapy sessions. 2. Involve social security services in providing counseling on work-related issues.	1. Reassess in 2 months.
6. Cryptorchidism	*Diagnostic:* 1. Explore previous records concerning previous assessment of his undescended testicle and the procedures applied if any. 2. Endocrinology consultation. *Therapeutic:* 1. Bring up issue during psychotherapy sessions.	1. Reassess in 3 months.

World Health Organization's Statement on Sexual Health (2002)

Introduction

Sexual health is influenced by a complex web of factors ranging from sexual behaviour and attitudes and societal factors, to biological risk and genetic predisposition. It encompasses the problems of HIV and STIs/RTIs, unintended pregnancy and abortion, infertility and cancer resulting from STIs, and sexual dysfunction. Sexual health can also be influenced by mental health, acute and chronic illnesses, and violence. Addressing sexual health at the individual, family, community or health system level requires integrated interventions by trained health providers and a functioning referral system. It also requires a legal, policy and regulatory environment where the sexual rights of all people are upheld.

Addressing sexual health also requires understanding and appreciation of sexuality, gender roles and power in designing and providing services. Understanding sexuality and its impact on practices, partners, reproduction and pleasure presents a number of challenges as well as opportunities for improving sexual and reproductive health care services and interventions. Validity of data collection, given researcher bias and difficulties in discussing such a private issue, also remains a problem in some settings that must be overcome if a greater understanding of sexuality in various settings is to be achieved. Sexuality research must go beyond concerns related to behaviour, numbers of partners and practices, to the underlying social, cultural and economic factors that make individuals vulnerable to risks and affect the ways in which sex is sought, desired or refused by women, men and young people. Investigating sexuality in this way entails going beyond reproductive health by looking at sexual health holistically and comprehensively. To do this requires adding to the knowledge base gained from the field of STI/HIV prevention and care, gender studies, and family planning, among others.

Sexual health represents a new thematic area of work for the Department of Reproductive Health and Research. While sexual health has been implicitly understood to be part of the reproductive health agenda, the emergence of HIV/AIDS, of sexual and gender-based violence and of the extent of sexual dysfunction (to name just some of the

186

developments over the past two decades), have highlighted the need for the Department to now focus more explicitly on sexuality and the promotion of sexual health.

Working Definitions

Sex

Sex refers to the biological characteristics which define humans as female or male. [These sets of biological characteristics are not mutually exclusive as there are individuals who possess both, but these characteristics tend to differentiate humans as males and females. In general use in many languages, the term "sex" is often used to mean "sexual activity," but for technical purposes in the context of sexuality and sexual health discussions, the above definition is preferred.]

Sexuality

Sexuality is a central aspect of being human throughout life and encompasses sex, gender identities and roles, sexual orientation, eroticism, pleasure, intimacy and reproduction. Sexuality is experienced and expressed in thoughts, fantasies, desires, beliefs, attitudes, values, behaviours, practices, roles and relationships. While sexuality can include all of these dimensions, not all of them are always experienced or expressed. Sexuality is influenced by the interaction of biological, psychological, social, economic, political, cultural, ethical, legal, historical and religious and spiritual factors.

Sexual Health

Sexual health is a state of physical, emotional, mental and social well-being related to sexuality; it is not merely the absence of disease, dysfunction or infirmity. Sexual health requires a positive and respectful approach to sexuality and sexual relationships, as well as the possibility of having pleasurable and safe sexual experiences, free of coercion, discrimination and violence. For sexual health to be attained and maintained, the sexual rights of all persons must be respected, protected and fulfilled.

Sexual Rights

Sexual rights embrace human rights that are already recognized in national laws, international human rights documents and other consensus documents. These include the right of all persons, free of coercion, discrimination and violence, to:

- the highest attainable standard of health in relation to sexuality, including access to sexual and reproductive health care services;
- seek, receive and impart information in relation to sexuality;
- sexuality education;

- respect for bodily integrity;
- choice of partner;
- decide to be sexually active or not;
- consensual sexual relations;
- consensual marriage;
- decide whether or not, and when to have children; and
- pursue a satisfying, safe and pleasurable sexual life.

The responsible exercise of human rights requires that all persons respect the rights of others.

World Association for Sexology's Declaration of Sexual Rights (1997/1999)

Declaration of the 13th World Congress of Sexology, 1997, Valencia, Spain. Revised and approved by the General Assembly of the World Association for Sexology (WAS) on August 26, 1999, during the 14th World Congress of Sexology, Hong Kong, People's Republic of China.

Sexuality is an integral part of the personality of every human being. Its full development depends upon the satisfaction of basic human needs such as the desire for contact, intimacy, emotional expression, pleasure, tenderness and love.

Sexuality is constructed through the interaction between the individual and social structures. Full development of sexuality is essential for individual, interpersonal, and societal well being.

Sexual rights are universal human rights based on the inherent freedom, dignity, and equality of all human beings. Since health is a fundamental human right, so must Sexual Health be a basic human right. In order to assure that human beings and societies develop healthy sexuality, the following sexual rights must be recognized, promoted, respected, and defended by all societies through all means. Sexual health is the result of an environment that recognizes, respects and exercises these sexual rights.

1. *The right to sexual freedom.* Sexual freedom encompasses the possibility for individuals to express their full sexual potential. However, this excludes all forms of sexual coercion, exploitation and abuse at any time and situations in life.
2. *The right to sexual autonomy, sexual integrity, and safety of the sexual body.* This right involves the ability to make autonomous decisions about one's sexual life within a context of one's own personal and social ethics. It also encompasses control and enjoyment of our own bodies free from torture, mutilation and violence of any sort.
3. *The right to sexual privacy.* This involves the right for individual decisions and behaviors about intimacy as long as they do not intrude on the sexual rights of others.

4. *The right to sexual equity.* This refers to freedom from all forms of discrimination regardless of sex, gender, sexual orientation, age, race, social class, religion, or physical or emotional disability.

5. *The right to sexual pleasure.* Sexual pleasure, including autoeroticism, is a source of physical, psychological, intellectual and spiritual well being.

6. *The right to emotional sexual expression.* Sexual expression is more than erotic pleasure or sexual acts. Individuals have a right to express their sexuality through communication, touch, emotional expression and love.

7. *The right to sexually associate freely.* This means the possibility to marry or not, to divorce, and to establish other types of responsible sexual associations.

8. *The right to make free and responsible reproductive choices.* This encompasses the right to decide whether or not to have children, the number and spacing of children, and the right to full access to the means of fertility regulation.

9. *The right to sexual information based on scientific inquiry.* This right implies that sexual information should be generated through the process of unencumbered and yet scientifically ethical inquiry, and disseminated in appropriate ways at all societal levels.

10. *The right to comprehensive sexual education.* This is a lifelong process from birth throughout the lifecycle and should involve all social institutions.

11. *The right to sexual health care.* Sexual health care should be available for prevention and treatment of all sexual concerns, problems and disorders.

World Association for Sexual Health Montreal Declaration
Sexual Health for the Millennium

17th World Congress of Sexology, Montreal 2005

We, the participants of the 17th World Congress of Sexology, assert our commitment to the Mission of the World Association for Sexual Health (WAS), to promote sexual health throughout the lifespan. We also reaffirm the 1999 WAS Declaration on Sexual Rights; the recommendations from the Pan-American Health Organization/WAS 2000 report "Promotion of Sexual Health: Recommendations for Action"; and the 2002 World Health Organization's Working Definitions of Sexual Health and Sexual Rights. Considering the urgent need for collective action to attain sustainable health and development goals and milestones stated in international agreements, including the Millennium Declaration,

We declare that:

The promotion of sexual health is central to the attainment of wellness and well-being and to the achievement of sustainable development and more specifically to the implementation of the Millennium Development Goals.

Individuals and communities who experience well-being are better positioned to contribute to the eradication of individual and societal poverty. By nurturing individual and social responsibilities and equitable social interactions, promotion of sexual health fosters quality of life and the realization of peace. Therefore, we urge all governments, international agencies, private sectors, academic institutions and society at large, and particularly, all member organizations of the World Association for Sexual Health to:

1. *Recognize, promote, ensure and protect sexual rights for all.* Sexual rights are an integral component of basic human rights and therefore, are inalienable and universal. Sexual health cannot be obtained or maintained without sexual rights for all.

2. *Advance toward gender equity.* Sexual health requires gender equity and respect. Gender-related inequities and imbalances of power deter constructive and harmonic human interactions and therefore the attainment of sexual health.

3. *Eliminate all forms of sexual violence and abuse.* Sexual health cannot be attained until people are free of stigma, discrimination, sexual abuse, coercion and violence.

4. *Provide universal access to comprehensive sexuality information and education.* To achieve sexual health, all individuals, including youth, must have access to comprehensive sexuality education, and sexual health information and services throughout the life cycle.

5. *Ensure that reproductive health programs recognize the centrality of sexual health.* Reproduction is one of the critical dimensions of human sexuality and may contribute to strengthening relationships and personal fulfillment when desired and planned. Sexual health is a more encompassing concept than reproductive health. Current reproductive health programs must be broadened to address the various dimensions of sexual health in a comprehensive manner.

6. *Halt and reverse the spread of HIV/AIDS and other sexually transmitted infections (STIs).* Universal access to prevention, voluntary counseling and testing, comprehensive care and treatment of HIV/AIDS and other STIs are equally essential to sexual health. Programs that assure universal access must be scaled up immediately.

7. *Identify, address and treat sexual concerns, dysfunctions and disorders.* Since sexual fulfillment has the capacity of enhancing quality of life, it is critical to recognize, prevent and treat sexual concerns, dysfunctions and disorders.

8. *Achieve recognition of sexual pleasure as component of well-being.* Sexual health is more than the absence of disease. Sexual pleasure and satisfaction are integral components of well-being and require universal recognition and promotion.

It is essential that international, regional and local plans of action for sustainable development prioritize sexual health interventions, allocate sufficient resources, address systemic, structural and community barriers and monitor progress.

International Survey on Human Sexuality and Sexual Disorders
Synoptic Report
JUAN E. MEZZICH AND RUBEN HERNÁNDEZ-SERRANO

The Program Committee of the World Psychiatric Association (WPA) Educational Program on Sexual Health (SHEP) conducted in 1999 an International Survey on Human Sexuality and Sexual Disorders aimed at ascertaining the prevalent views on sexual health among leading psychiatrists and sexologists across the world.

To this effect, a questionnaire was designed to facilitate responses by the participants in the following content areas: a) respondent's professional profile, b) communications with patients about sexual functioning, c) training received on sexual issues, d) factors contributing to sexual problems, e) perceived prevalence and comorbidities of sexual disorders, f) competence evaluating and treating sexual problems, g) clinical specialities relevant to treatment of sexual problems, h) treatment modalities, and i) additional comments.

The questionnaire was distributed to 260 leading psychiatrists and sexologists as follows: (1) 200 psychiatrists connected to the various components of the World Psychiatric Association (Member Societies, Scientific Sections, and various leadership standing and operational committees), and (2) 60 leaders of associations belonging to the World Association for Sexology (WAS).

The project obtained 238 completed questionnaires, 187 from psychiatrists and 51 from sexologists. They included 79% men and 21% women. Agewise, 32% were between ages 45-54. Concerning geographic distribution, 42% were from Europe, 30% from the Americas, 22% from Asia and the South Pacific and 6% from Africa and the Middle East. Regarding their professional activities, 52% reported that they dedicated significant time to clinical care, teaching and research. More information on respondents is presented in table A.1.

Concerning frequency with which patients were asked about their sexual functioning, it was found that 28% of the psychiatrists and 8% of the sexologists only "sometimes" or "rarely" ask about sexual functioning as part of a regular clinical evaluation. Table A.2 presents detailed information on this topic.

With regard to frequency with which patients ask about sexual issues, it was found that 86% of patients only "sometimes" or "rarely" asked their psychiatrists, and 29% of patients asked their sexologists. More intensive information is presented in table A.3.

With respect to the extent of training in human sexuality in medical school and residency, only 38% of psychiatrists and 45% of sexologists reported extensive or moderate training. See table A.4 for further details.

Regarding extent of training in human sexuality during continuing medical education (also termed professional development), only 40% of psychiatrists and 76% of sexologists reported moderate to extensive training (see table A.5).

Concerning the most frequent sexual problems encountered, both psychiatrists and sexologists reported erectile dysfunction and premature ejaculation among men, and loss of sexual desire and anorgasmia in women. Similarity in psychiatrists' and sexologists' reports were also seen for other sexual disorders as shown in table A.6.

With regard to perceived contributors to sexual problems, both psychiatrists and sexologists identified, in order, as most important anxiety/stress, relationship problems and ignorance/faulty expectations (see table A.7).

About confidence in making evaluations and diagnoses of sexual problems, only 30% of psychiatrists and 74% of sexologists reported themselves as quite confident (see table A.8).

With regard to confidence in treating sexual problems, only 19% of psychiatrists and 71% of sexologists indicated they felt quite confident (see table A.9).

Concerning perceived relevance of various specialities for the treatment of sexual disorders, the results were similar. Both psychiatrists and sexologists identified sexology and psychiatry as most relevant (see table A.10).

Regarding importance of multi-disciplinary teams for treatment of sexual disorders, 48% of psychiatrists and 71% of sexologists considered arranging treatment of sexual disorders with a multi-disciplinary team (see table A.11).

About the most important treatment modalities for sexual disorders, both psychiatrists and sexologists identified, in order, sex therapy, cognitive behavioral therapy, and couples/family therapy (see table A.12).

With regard to comorbidities of sexual disorders, the most frequently identified by psychiatrists and sexologists were depression, other mental disorders and diabetes (see table A.13).

Finally, concerning other important factors for dealing with sexual health, psychiatrists listed, in order, most frequently professional training, cultural, social and environmental factors and patient and public education. Sexologists listed professional training, patient and public education, cultural, social and environmental factors, and relationship and marital issues (see table A.14).

In conclusion, this survey documented first an enormous need for communication on sexual issues between patients and health professionals. Limited professional training in human sexuality throughout medical school, residency and continuing medical education was also noted. The survey also yielded interesting information on the frequency, perceived causation, and comorbidities of sexual disorders; and on treatment patterns and requirements to help people experiencing sexual disorders. All these findings make compelling the development of an educational program on sexual health for psychiatrists and other health professionals, which could, in due course, be extended to the general public.

References

Mezzich JE: International Surveys on the Use of ICD-10 and Related Diagnostic Systems. *Psychopathology* 35: 72-75, 2002.

Parra-Colmenárez A, and Hernández-Serrano R (Editors): *10th International Symposium on Sexual Education*, World Association for Sexology, Caracas, 1995.

SIECUS: *Guidelines for Comprehensive Sexual Education*. Author, New York, 1991.

Table A.1. RESPONDENTS' DEMOGRAPHIC AND PROFESSIONAL IDENTIFICATION

Items	Respondents (N = 238)	
	n	%
Gender		
Male	188	79.0
Female	50	21.0
Age		
Younger than 35	23	9.7
35–44	45	18.9
45–54	76	31.9
55–64	61	25.6
65 or older	20	8.4
Unspecified	13	5.5
Region		
Americas	72	30.3
Europe	101	42.4
Africa and Middle East	13	5.5
Asia and South Pacific	52	21.8
Types of practice		
Clinical care	39	16.4
Teaching	10	4.2
Research	6	2.5
Clinical, teaching	33	13.9
Clinical, research	10	4.2
Teaching, research	7	2.9
Clinical, teaching, research	123	51.7
Other and unspecified	10	4.2
Professional identification		
Qualified psychiatrists	187	78.6
Qualified sexologists	51	21.4

Table A.2. Frequency with Which Patients Are Asked about Their Sexual Functioning

How frequently do you ask patients about their sexual functioning as part of a clinical evaluation?	Qualified Psychiatrists (n)	Qualified Psychiatrists (%)	Qualified Sexologists (n)	Qualified Sexologists (%)
Always	51	37.3	43	84.4
Usually	83	44.4	4	7.8
Sometimes	40	21.4	4	7.8
Rarely	12	6.4	0	0
Unspecified	1	0.5	0	0
Total	**187**	**100**	**51**	**100**

Table A.3. Frequency with Which Patients Ask about Sexual Issues

How frequently do your patients spontaneously ask about sexual issues?	Qualified Psychiatrists (n)	Qualified Psychiatrists (%)	Qualified Sexologists (n)	Qualified Sexologists (%)
Always	4	2.1	19	37.3
Usually	22	11.8	17	33.3
Sometimes	131	70.1	11	21.6
Rarely	30	16.0	4	7.8
Unspecified	0	0	0	0
Total	**187**	**100**	**51**	**100**

Table A.4. Extent of Training in Human Sexuality during Medical School and Residency

How extensive was your training in human sexuality during medical school and residency?	Qualified Psychiatrists (n)	Qualified Psychiatrists (%)	Qualified Sexologists (n)	Qualified Sexologists (%)
Extensive	10	5.3	16	31.4
Moderate	62	33.2	7	13.7
Minimal	98	52.4	16	31.4
None	17	9.1	12	23.5
Unspecified	0	0	0	0
Total	**187**	**100**	**51**	**100**

Table A.5. EXTENT OF TRAINING IN HUMAN SEXUALITY DURING CME

How extensive was your training in human sexuality as part of recent continuing medical education?	Qualified Psychiatrists (n)	Qualified Psychiatrists (%)	Qualified Sexologists (n)	Qualified Sexologists (%)
Extensive	16	8.6	34	66.7
Moderate	59	31.6	5	9.8
Minimal	79	42.2	6	11.8
None	32	17.1	4	7.8
Unspecified	1	0.5	2	3.9
Total	**187**	**100**	**51**	**100**

Table A.6. MOST FREQUENT SEXUAL PROBLEMS

Rank for men and women of the most frequent sexual problems from 1 (most frequent) to 8 (least frequent).	Qualified Psychiatrists (average rank) (N = 187)	Qualified Sexologists (average rank) (N = 51)
Men		
Loss of sexual desire	3.1	3.8
Sexual desire incompatibility	4.8	4.3
Erectile dysfunction	2.2	1.6
Selective orgasmic dysfunction	5.0	5.6
Premature ejaculation	3.0	2.6
Ejaculatory incompetence	4.9	5.5
Paraphilias	6.9	6.5
Gender-related problems	6.1	6.5
Women		
Loss of sexual desire	2.2	2.2
Sexual desire incompatibility	4.1	3.8
Anorgasmia	2.8	2.4
Dyspareunia	4.5	4.6
Sexual aversion or phobia	4.6	4.8
Sexual arousal problems	4.1	4.0
Paraphilias	7.3	7.4
Gender-related problems	6.4	6.7

Table A.7. Contributors to Sexual Problems

Rank from 1 (most important) to 11 (least important) the following contributors to sexual problems.	Qualified Psychiatrists (average rank) (N = 187)	Qualified Sexologists (average rank) (N = 51)
Ignorance/faulty expectations	4.5	3.1
Fears (pregnancy, STDs, rejection from partner)	4.9	4.9
Anxiety/stress	2.9	2.4
Traumatic experiences	5.0	6.0
Relationship problems	3.1	2.6
Alcohol and drugs	5.3	6.8
General medical problems	6.3	6.2
Surgery sequelae	8.9	9.2
Aging	6.6	7.7
Side effects from medication	5.3	6.9
Other	9.1	8.9

**Other contributors
to sexual problems**

Gender dysphoria problem	Childhood psychogenetic disorders
Religion and guilt	Smoking
No love	Self-image troubles
Work problems	Low self-esteem
Urogenitalis problems, sexual information	False beliefs
Depressive state	Indulgence in masturbation
Paraphilias	Multiple wives and age difference
Alone	Misleading cultural factors
Expectation fear	Upbringing
Sexual torture in war or dictatorship	Lack of knowledge
Chat chewing	Macho social stereotype
Religious convictions	Another partner
Social and cultural problems	Depressive disorders

Table A.8. Confidence in Evaluation and Diagnosis of Sexual Problems

How confident do you feel in making an evaluation and diagnosis of sexual problems?	Qualified Psychiatrists (n)	Qualified Psychiatrists (%)	Qualified Sexologists (n)	Qualified Sexologists (%)
Quite confident	57	30.5	38	74.5
Moderately confident	97	51.9	11	21.6
Marginally confident	26	13.9	0	0
Not confident	6	3.2	0	0
Unspecified	1	0.5	2	3.9
Total	**187**	**100**	**51**	**100**

Table A.9. Confidence in Treatment of Sexual Problems

How confident do you feel in treating sexual problems?	Qualified Psychiatrists (n)	Qualified Psychiatrists (%)	Qualified Sexologists (n)	Qualified Sexologists (%)
Quite confident	36	19.2	36	70.6
Moderately confident	87	46.5	10	19.6
Marginally confident	57	30.5	3	5.9
Not confident	5	2.7	0	0
Unspecified	2	1.1	2	3.9
Total	**187**	**100**	**51**	**100**

Table A.10. Relevance of Various Specialties to the Treatment of Sexual Problems

Indicate with a number (1, 2, or 3) which of the following specialties you consider of high relevance (1), moderate relevance (2), or low relevance (3) for the treatment of sexual problems.	Qualified Psychiatrists (average rank) (N = 187)	Qualified Sexologists (average rank) (N = 51)
Clinical psychology	1.6	1.7
Endocrinology	2.0	2.1
Geriatrics	2.4	2.4
Gynecology	1.8	1.9
Neurology	2.5	2.6
Psychiatry	1.3	1.7
Sexology	1.2	1.7
Urology	1.8	2.0
Dermatology and venereology	2.6	2.8
Other	2.4	2.5

Other specialties considered for the treatment of sexual problems

Religion/philosophy

Education problems

Family medicine

Couples therapy

Culture

General medicine

Psychotherapy

Infectious diseases

Sex education

Psychodynamics

Vascular surgery

Sociology

Andrology

Clinical pharmacology

Traditional medicine

General practitioners and nurses

Table A.11. Importance of Multidisciplinary Team for the Treatment of Sexual Disorders

How frequently do you consider it important to arrange treatment of sexual disorders through a multidisciplinary team?	Qualified Psychiatrists (n)	Qualified Psychiatrists (%)	Qualified Sexologists (n)	Qualified Sexologists (%)
Always	20	10.8	15	29.4
Usually	70	37.4	21	41.2
Sometimes	67	35.8	12	23.5
Rarely	27	14.4	2	3.9
Unspecified	3	1.6	1	2.0
Total	**187**	**100**	**51**	**100**

Table A.12. Treatment Modalities for Sexual Problems

Rank from 1 (most important) to 8 (least important) the following treatment modalities for sexual problems.	Qualified Psychiatrists (average rank) (N = 187)	Qualified Sexologists (average rank) (N = 51)
Behavioral/cognitive therapy	2.7	2.4
Psychodynamic therapy	4.7	5.1
Sex therapy	2.6	1.6
Couples/family therapy	2.8	3.0
Group therapy	5.7	6.2
Vasoactive drug (oral or intracavernous) therapy	4.8	4.5
Psychotropic medication	5.1	5.5
Hormonal treatment	5.9	6.6

Table A.13. COMORBIDITIES OF SEXUAL DISORDERS

Rank from 1 (most frequent) to 10 (least frequent) the following comorbidities of sexual disorders.	Qualified Psychiatrists (average rank) (N = 187)	Qualified Sexologists (average rank) (N = 51)
Depression	1.4	1.7
Other mental disorders	3.2	3.3
Diabetes	3.1	3.2
Other endocrine and hypogonadal conditions	4.6	5.2
Neurological disorders	4.8	5.6
Cardiovascular disorders	4.7	4.3
Cancer	6.6	7.5
Liver disorders	7.2	7.3
Arthritis	7.9	8.1
Other	8.7	8.5

Other comorbidities of sexual disorders

Anxiety/PTST disorders

Hysteria

Neurosis, phobias, sociopsychological problems

Mesenquimopatias

Vascular diseases

Incest victims

Gynecology

Infidelity

Limited experience

Pharmacology and side effects

General debility, renal disorders

Urological disorders (prostatitis, fimosis)

Gynecological problems

Gynecological and urological surgery

Couple dysfunction

Genetic disorders

Table A.14. Other Factors in Dealing with Sexual Health

What factors other than those previously mentioned do you consider important for health practitioners in dealing with the sexual health of their patients?	Qualified Psychiatrists (n)	Qualified Psychiatrists (%)	Qualified Sexologists (n)	Qualified Sexologists (%)
Comorbidity of sexual disorders	15	6.6	4	4.8
General medical issues	22	9.7	4	4.8
Professional training	60	26.5	25	29.7
Patient and public education	32	14.2	16	19.0
Ethical concerns and issues	9	4.0	4	4.8
Cultural, social, and environmental factors	35	15.5	8	9.5
Prejudice and other problematic beliefs and attitudes about sex	25	11.1	5	5.9
Relationship and marital issues	15	6.6	8	9.5
Media and public opinion factors	6	2.7	4	4.8
Traumatic experiences	4	1.8	3	3.6
Gender-related factors	2	0.9	3	3.6
Other issues	1	0.4	0	0
Total	**226**	**100**	**84**	**100**

References

Aaronson, N. (1988). Quality of life: What is it? How should it be measured? *Oncology* 2: 69–74.

Academia Internacional de Sexología Médica. (2004). *Consenso sobre eyaculación rápida*. Caracas: Fondo Editorial El Colega.

Acierno, R., Resnick, H., Kilpatrick, D. G., Saunders, B., and Best, C. L. (1999). Risk factors for rape, physical assault, and posttraumatic stress disorder in women: Examination of differential multivariate relationships. *J Anxiety Disord* 13(6): 541–63.

Agger, I., and Mimica, J. (1996). *European community humanitarian office: Psychosocial assistance to victims of war in Bosnia-Herzegovina and Croatia*. Zagreb: European Community Task Force.

Alarcon, R., Mazzoti, G., and Nicolini, H. (2005). *Psiquiatria. Manual moderno/OPS*.

Albornoz, O. (1995). Amor y sexo en la família y escuela venezolana. In Parra, A., and Hernández-Serrano, R. (eds.), X Simposium Internacional de Educación Sexual. WAS. FNUAP. Caracas.

Alexander, P. C., and Lupfer, S. L. (1987). Family characteristics and long-term consequences associated with sexual abuse. *Arch Sexual Behav* 16: 235–245.

Allers, C.T., and Benjack, K. J. (1991). Connections between childhood abuse and HIV infection. *Journal of Counseling and Development* 70: 309–313.

Allers, C. T., Benjack, K. J., White, J., and Rousey, J. T. (1993). HIV vulnerability and the adult survivor of childhood sexual abuse. *Child Abuse and Neglect* 17: 291–298.

Althof, S. (2000). Erectile dysfunction, psychotherapy with men and couples. In Leiblum S., and Rosen, R. (eds.), *Principles and practice of sex therapy* (3rd ed.). New York: Guilford.

American Psychiatric Association. (1952). *Diagnostic and statistical manual of mental disorders* (DSM-I) (1st ed.). Washington, DC: American Psychiatric Association.

American Psychiatric Association. (1968). *Diagnostic and statistical manual of mental disorders* (DSM-II) (2nd ed.). Washington, DC: American Psychiatric Association.

American Psychiatric Association. (1980). *Diagnostic and statistical manual of mental disorders* (DSM-III) (3rd ed.). Washington, DC: American Psychiatric Association.

American Psychiatric Association. (1987). *Diagnostic and statistical manual of mental disorders* (DSM-III-R) (3rd ed., revised). Washington, DC: American Psychiatric Association.

American Psychiatric Association. (1993). Practice guideline for eating disorders. *Am J Psychiatry* 150(2): 207–228.

American Psychiatric Association. (1994). *Diagnostic and statistical manual of mental disorders* (DSM-IV) (4th ed.). Washington, DC: American Psychiatric Association.

American Psychiatric Association. (2000). *Diagnostic and statistical manual of mental disorders* (DSM-IV-TR) (4th ed., revised). Washington, DC: American Psychiatric Association.

Anastasi, A. (ed.). (1982). *Psychological testing* (5th ed.). New York: Macmillan.

Anderson, A., and Lynch, T. (1988). *Listening: Language teaching: A scheme for teacher education*. Oxford, UK: Oxford University Press.

Anderson, A., and Lynch, T. (1996). *Listening*. Oxford, UK: Oxford University Press.

Annon, J. S. (1974). The Behavioral Treatment of Sexual Problems: Intensive Therapy. Honolulu, Hawaii: Enabling Systems.

Apt, C., Hurlbert, D. F., and Clark, K. J. (1994). Neglected subjects in sex research: A survey of sexologists. *Journal of Sex and Marital Therapy* 20(3): 237–243.

Arujo, A. B., Durnate, R., Feldman, H. A., Goldstein, I., and McKinlay, J. B. (1998). The relationship between depressive symptoms and male erectile dysfunction: cross-sectional results from the Massachusetts Male Aging Study. *Psychosom Med* 60: 458-465.

Arujo, A. B., Johannes, C. B., Feldman, H. A., Derby, C. A., and McKinlay, J, B. (2000). Relation between psychosocial risk factors and incident erectile dysfunction: Prospective results from the Massachusetts male aging study. *Am J Epidemiol* 152: 533–541.

Asencio, M. W. (1999). Machos and sluts: Gender, sexuality, and violence among a cohort of Puerto Rican adolescents. *Medical Anthropology Quarterly* 13(1):107–126.

Bailey, J. M., et al. (1993). Heritable factors influence sexual orientation in women. *Archives of General Psychiatry* 50: 217–223.

Balon, R., and Segraves, R. T. (2003). *Basic facts: Sexual pharmacology.*

Bancroft. J. (1999a). Sexual science in the 21st century. *Journal of Sex Research* 36(3): 226–229.

Bancroft, J. (1999b). *The role of theory in sex research.* Bloomington: Indiana University Press.

Bancroft, J. (1999c). Sexual science in the 21st century. *Journal of Sex Research* 36: 226-229.

Bancroft, J. (1989). *Human sexuality and its problems* (2nd ed.). Edinburgh, UK: Churchill Livingstone.

Barbaree, H. E., and Marshall, W. L. (1998). *Treatment of the sexual offender.* New York: Guilford.

Barlow, D. H. (1986). Causes of sexual dysfunctions: The role of anxiety and cognitive interference. *Journal of Consulting and Clinical Psychology* 54: 140–148.

Barlow, D. H. (1988). *Anxiety and its disorders: The nature and treatment of anxiety and panic.* New York: Guilford.

Bartlik, B., and Goldberg, J. (2000). Female sexual arousal disorder. In Leiblum, S., and Rosen, R. (eds.), *Principles and practice of sex therapy* (3rd ed.) (pp. 85–117). New York: Guilford.

Bartlik, B., and Goldstein, M. Z. (2000). Maintaining sexual health after menopause. *Psychiatric Services* 51(6): 751–753.

Bartlik, B., and Kaplan, P. (1999). Testosterone treatment for women. *The Harvard Mental Health Letter* December: 4–6.

Bartlik, B., Kaplan, P., Kaminetsky, J., Roentsch, G., and Goldberg, J. (1999). Medications with the potential to enhance sexual responsivity in women. *Psychiatric Annals* 28(1): 46–52.

Bartlik, B., Kaplan, P., and Kocsis, J. (1995). Letter to the editor Re: Balon, R. Effects of antidepressants on sexuality. *Primary Psychiatry* 2(10): 13.

Basson, R. (2000). The female sexual response: A different model. *J Sex and Marital Therapy* 26: 51-65.

Basson, R. (2002). A model of women's sexual arousal. *Journal of Sex and Marital Therapy* 28(1):1–10.

Basson, R., Berman, J., Burnett, A., Derogatis, L., Fourcroy, J., Goldstein, I., Graziottin, Heiman, J., Laan, E., Leiblum, S., Padma-Nathan, H., Rosen, R., Segraves, K., Segraves, R.T., Shabsigh, R., Sipski, M., Wagner, G., and Whipple, B. (2000). Report of the international consensus development conference on female sexual dysfunction: Definitions and classifications. *Journal of Urology* 163(3): 888–893.

Beaglehole, R., Bonita, R., and Kjellström, T. (1993). *Basic epidemiology.* Geneva: World Health Organization.

Becher, E., and Gueglio, G. (eds.). (1999). 1er. consenso Argentino sobre disfunción eréctil. Sociedad Argentina de Urología.

Belsey, M. A. (1993). Child abuse: Measuring a global problem. *World Health Statistics Quarterly* 46(1): 69–77.

Berg, P. and Snyder, D. K. (1981). Differential diagnosis of marital and sexual distress: A multidimensional approach. *Journal of Sex and Marital Therapy* 7(4): 290–295.

Berganza, C., Mezzich, J. E., Otero, A., Hernández-Serrano, R., Rojas, M. C., et al. (2004). La guía latinoamericana de diagnóstico psiquiátrico (GLADP). Asociación Psiquiátrica de América Latina, Editorial de la Universidad de Guadalapia, México.

Berman, J., Goldstein, I., Werbin, T., Wong, J., Jacobs, S., and Chai, T. (1999). Double-blind placebo controlled study with crossover to assess effect of sildenafil on physiological parameters of the female sexual response. *Journal of Urology* 4(2): 161.

Berman, J., Jolin, J., Raz, S., and Chaudhuri, G. (2001). Immunohistochemical analysis of androgen receptors in human vagina: Effects of age and menopausal status on androgen receptor expression in women. *Female Sexual Function Forum* (p. 102).

Berman, E. M., and Lief, H. I. (1976). Sex and the aging process. In Oaks, W. W., Melchide, G. A., and Fisher, I., *Sex and the life cycle* (pp. 125–134). New York: Grune & Stratton, Inc.

Bhuga, D., and de Silva, P. (1995). Sexual dysfunction and sex therapy: A historical perspective. *International Review of Psychiatry* 7(2): 159–167.

Bianco, F. (1976). *Sexología clínica*. Caracas: CIPPSV.

Bianco, F. (1998). *La teoría de la variante sexual*. Caracas: CIPPSV.

Bianco, F., and Hernández-Serrano, R. (1990). *Sexology. An independent field*. Elsevier.

Bianco, F., and Hernández-Serrano, R. (1992). *Manual de diagnóstico de las enfermedades en sexología*. Velo Horizonte, Brazil: FLASSES.

Bianco, F., and Hernández-Serrano, R. (1999). *Book I*. WAS. Caracas.

Bianco, F., and Hernández-Serrano, R. (1993). *Book II*. WAS. Rio de Janeiro.

Bieber, I. (1967). Sexual deviations. In Freedman, A. M., and Kaplan, H. I. (eds.), *Comprehensive textbook of psychiatry* (pp. 959–962). Baltimore, MD: Lippincott Williams & Wilkins.

Billy, J. O., Tanfer, K., Grady, W. R., and Kleppinger, D. H. (1993). The sexual behavior of men in the United States. *Family Planning Perspective* 25: 52–60.

Bisset, A. F., and Hunter, D. (1992). Child sexual abuse in general practice in northeast Scotland. *Health Bulletin (Edinburg)* 50(3): 237–247.

Blacker, D., and Endicott, J. (2000). Psychometric properties: Concepts of reliability and validity. In *American Psychiatric Association handbook of psychiatric measures* (pp. 7–13). Washington, DC: American Psychiatric Association.

Bland, L., and Doan, L. (1998). *Sexology uncensored*. Cambridge, UK: Polity Press.

Bodkin, J., Lasser, R., Wine, J., Gardner, D., and Baldessarini, R. (1998): Combining serotonin reuptake inhibitors and bupropion in partial responders to antidepressant monotherapy. *Clinical Psychiatry* 58(4): 137–145.

Bolin, A., and Whelehan, P. (1999). *Anthropological perspectives on human sexuality*. Albany: State University of New York Press.

Bortz, W. M., and Wallace, D. H. (1999). Physical fitness, aging, and sexuality. *West J Med* 170(3): 167–169.

Bortz, W. M., Wallace, D. H., and Wiley, D. (1999). Sexual function in 1,202 aging males: Differentiating aspects. *Journal of Gerontology and Biologic Sci Medicine Science* 54(5): 237–241.

Brady, K. T., Killeen, T. K., Brewerton, T., and Lucerini, S. (2000). Comorbidity of psychiatric disorders and posttraumatic stress disorder. *J Clin Psychiatry* 61(7): 22–32.

Bretschneider, J. G., and McCoy, N. L. (1988). Sexual interest and behavior in healthy 80–102 year olds. *Arch Sexual Behav* 17: 109–129.

Briere, J., and Runtz, M. (1987). Post sexual abuse trauma: Data and implications for clinical practice. *Journal of Interpersonal Violence* 2: 367–379.

Broderick, G. A., and Foreman, M. M. (1999). Iatrogenic erectile dysfunction: Pharmacological therapies that alter male sexual behavior and erectile performance. In Carson, C. C., Kirby, R. S., and Goldstein, I. (eds.), *Textbook of erectile dysfunction* (pp. 149–170). Oxford, UK: Oxford ISIS.

Brookman, R. (1990). Adolescent sexual behavior. In Holmes, K. K., Mardh, P. A., Sparling, P. F., et al. (eds), *Sexually transmitted diseases* (2nd ed) (pp. 77–84). New York: McGraw-Hill.

Browning, D. R., and Laumann E. O. (1997). Sexual contact between children and adults: A life course perspective. *American Sociological Review* 62(4): 540–560.

Brundtland, G. H. (1999). *Reproductive health: A health priority report*. ICDP+5 Forum, February 1999. Geneva: World Health Organization.

Bullough, V. (1976). *Sexual variance in society and history*. Chicago: University of Chicago Press.

Butler, L., Banfield, V., Sveinson, T., and Allen, K. (1998). Conceptualizing sexual health in cancer care. *West J Nurs Res* 20(6): 683–99.

Butler, R. N., and Lewis, M. (1990). Sexuality. In Abrams, W. B., and Fletcher, A. J. (eds.), *The Merck manual of geriatrics* (pp. 631–644). Rahway, NJ: Merck, Sharp and Dohme Research Laboratories.

Carnes, P. J. (1983). *Out of the shadows: Understanding sexual addiction*. Minneapolis, MN: CompCare Publications.

Carnes, P. J. (1989). *Contrary to love: Helping the sexual addict*. Minneapolis, MN: CompCare Publications.

Carnes, P. J. (1991). *Don't call it love*. New York: Bantam Books.

Carrier, S. (2003). Pharmacology of phosphodiesterase 5 inhibitors. *Can J Urol* 10(1): 12–6.

Carroll, R. A. (1999). Outcomes of treatment for gender dysphoria. *Journal of Sex Education and Therapy* 24(3): 128–136.

Carter, J. E. (1998) Surgical treatment for chronic pelvic pain. *Soc Laparoendosc Surg* April 2(2): 129–139.

Casper, R. C., Redmond, E., Katz, M. M., Schafer, C. B., Davis, J. M., and Kaslow. S. H. (1985). Somatic symptoms in primary affective disorder. *Arch Gen Psychiatry* 42: 1098–1104.

Casson, P. R., Straughn, A. B., Urnstot, E. S., Abraham, G. E., Carson, S. A., and Buster, J. E. (1996). Delivery of dehydroepiandrosterone to premenopausal women: Effects of micronization and non oral administration. *American Journal of Obstetrics and Gynecology* 174(2): 649–653.

Cavagna, N., Rajtman, M., and Resnicoff, D. (2000). Sexual harassment in the psychiatric psychological and sexological environments. SHEP. WPA.

Cavagna, N., Rajtman, M., and Resnicoff, D. (2000). *Sexualidad en el climaterio*. SHEP. WPA.

Cavagna, N., and Sapetti, A. (2000). *The partner of the patient treated with Sildenafil*. SHEP. WPA.

Chivers, M., and Blanchard, R. (1996). Prostitution advertisements suggest association of transvestitism and masochism. *Journal of Sex and Marital Therapy* 22(2): 97–102.

Choquet, M., Darves-Bornoz, J. M., Ledoux, S., Manfredi, R., and Hassler, C. (1997). Self-reported health and behavioral problems among adolescent victims of rape in France: Results of a cross-sectional survey. *Child Abuse and Neglect* 21(9): 823–32.

Coates, S., and Person, E. S. (1985). Extreme boyhood femininity: Isolated behavior or pervasive disorder. *Journal of the American Academy of Child and Adolescent Psychiatry*. 24: 702–709.

Cohen, M. A., and Alfonso, C. A. (1997). A comprehensive approach to sexual history-taking using the biopsychosocial model. *International Journal of Mental Health* 26: 3–14.

Coleman, E. (1991). Compulsive sexual behavior: New concepts and treatments. *Journal of Psychology and Human Sexuality* 4(2): 35–37.

Coleman, E., Dwyer, M., Abel, G., Berner, W., Breiling, J., Eher, R., Hindman, J., Langevin, R., Langfeldt, T., Miner, M., Pfafflin, F., and Weiss, P. (2000). Standards of care for the treatment of adult sex offenders. *Journal of Psychology and Human Sexuality* 11(3): 11–17.

College of American Pathologists. (1977). *Systematized nomenclature of medicine (SNOMED)*. Skokie, IL: College of American Pathologists.

Connell, R., and Dowsett, G. (1992). *Rethinking sex: Social theory and sexuality research*. Philadelphia: Temple University Press.

Coomaraswamy, R. (2002). *Integration of the human rights of women and the gender perspective: Violence against women*. Report to United Nations Economic and Social Council GE.02–1048 (E) 130202.

Cooper, A., Morahan-Martin, J., Mathy, R., Maheu, M. (2002). Toward an increased understanding of user demographics in online sexual activities. *Journal of Sex and Marital Therapy* 28(2): 105–106, 112–113, 117.

Cooper, A., Scherer, C., Boies, S., and Gordon. B. (1999). Sexuality on the Internet: From sexual exploration to pathological expression. *Professional Psychology: Research and Practice* 30: 154–164.

Cox, M. (1980). *Personal reflections upon 3000 hours in therapeutic groups with sex offenders*. Cambridge, UK.

Crenshaw, T. L., and Goldberg, J. P. (1996). *Sexual pharmacology: Drugs that affect sexual function*. New York: W. W. Norton & Co.

Crenshaw, T. L., Goldberg, J. P., and Stem, W. C. (1987): Pharmacologic modification of psychosexual dysfunction. *Journal of Sex and Marital Therapy* 13: 239–252.

Creti, L., Fichten, C. S., Amsel, R., Brender, W., Schover, L. R., Kalogeropoulos, D., and Libman. E. (1998). Global sexual functioning: A single summary score for Nowinski and LoPiccolo's Sexual History Form (SHF). In Davis, C. M., Yarber, W. L., Bauserman, R., Scheer, G., and Davis, S. L. (eds.), *Handbook of sexuality-related measures* (pp. 261–267). Thousand Oaks, CA: Sage Publications.

Creti, L., Fichten, C. S., Libman, E., Kalogeropoulos, D., and Brender, W. (1987). *A global score for the Sexual History Form and its effectiveness*. Paper presented at the 21st annual convention of the Association for Advancement of Behavior Therapy. Boston.

Cutler, W. (1998). Pheremonal influences on sociosexual behavior in men. *Arch Sexual Behav* 27(1): 1–13.

D'Augelli, A. R., Hershberger, S. L., and Pilkington, N. W. (1998). Lesbian, gay, and bisexual youth and their families: Disclosure of sexual orientation and its consequences. *American Journal of Orthopsychiatry* 68(3): 361–371, 372–375.

Davey-Smith, G., Frankel, S., Yarnell, J. (1997). Sex and death: Are they related? Findings from the Caerphilly Cohort Study. *British Medical Journal* 315(7123): 1641–1644.

Davis, C. M., Yarber, W. L., Bauserman, R., Scheer, G., and Davis, S. L. (eds.). (1998). *Handbook of sexuality-related measures*. Thousand Oaks, CA: Sage Publications.

Davis, D. (1998). The sexual and gender identity disorders. *Transcultural Psychiatry* 35(3): 401–412.

Davis, D., and Herdt, G. (1996). *Cultural sensitivity and the sexual disorders*. In Widiger, T. A., Francisa, A. J., Pincus, H. A., Ross, R., First, M. B., and Davis, W. (eds.), *DSM-IV sourcebook*. Washington, DC: American Psychiatric Association.

Davis, D., and Whitten, R. (1987). The cross-cultural study of human sexuality. *Annual Review of Anthropology* 16: 69–98.

De Buono, B. A., Zinner, S. H., Daamen, M., et al. (1990). Sexual behavior of college women in 1975, 1986, and 1989. *N Eng J Med* 322: 821–825.

Desjarlais, R., Eisemberg, L., Good, B., and Kleinman, A. (1995). *World Mental Health: Problems and priorities in low-income countries*. Oxford, UK: Oxford University Press.

De Souza, A. I., Cecatti, J. G., Ferreira, L. O., and Santos, L. C. (1999). Reasons for hospitalization due to abortion and pregnancy termination. *Journal of Tropical Pediatrics* 45(1): 31–36.

Devries, P., and Hernández-Serrano, R. (2000). *Sexuality and quality of life*. FLASSES. X Congreso Latinoamericano de Sexologia y Educacion Sexual [X Latin American Congress of Sexology and Sexual Education]. Cuzco.

Diokno, A. C., Brown, M. B., and Herzog, A. R. (1990). Sexual function in the elderly. *Arch Intern Med* 150: 197–200.

Duffy, L. M. (1998). Lovers, loners, and lifers: Sexuality and the older adult. *Geriatrics* 53(1): S66–69.

Dunn, K. M. (2000). Satisfaction in the sex life of a general population sample. *Journal of Sex and Marital Therapy* 26: 141–151.

Dunn, K. M., Croft, P. R., and Hackett G. I. (1998). Sexual problems: A study of the prevalence and need for health care in the general population. *Family Practice* 15(6): 519–524.

Dunn, K. M., Croft, P. R., and Hackett G. I. (1999). Association of sexual problems with social, psychological, and physical problems in men and women: A cross sectional population survey. *Journal of Epidemiology and Community Health* 53(3): 144–148.

Dunn, K., Jordan, K., Croft, P., and Assendelft, W. J. J. Systematic review of sexual problems: Epidemiology and methodology. *Journal of Sex and Marital Therapy* 28(5): 399–422.

Ehhardt, A. A., and Wasserheit, J. N. (1991). Age, gender and sexual risk behaviors for sexually transmitted diseases in the United States. In Wasserheit, J. N., Aral, S. O., and Holmes, K. K. (eds.), *Research issues in human behavior and sexually transmitted diseases in the AIDS era* (pp. 97–12). Washington, DC: American Society for Microbiology.

Engel, G. L. (1977). The need for a new medical model: A challenge for biomedicine. *Science* 196: 129–136.

Farquhar, J. (2002). *Appetites: Food and sex in post-socialist China*. Durham, NC: Duke University Press.

Fava, M., et al. (1998). An open trial of oral sildenafil in antidepressant-induced sexual dysfunction. *Psychother Psychosom* 67: 328–331.

Feldman, H. A., Goldstein, I., Hatzichristou, D. G., Krane, R. J., and McKinlay, J. B. (1994). Impotence and its medical and psychological correlates: Results of the Massachusetts Male Aging Study. *Journal of Urology* 151(1): 54–61.

Ferrans, C. E., and Power, M. J. (1992). Psychometric assessment of the quality of life index. *Research in Nursing and Health* 75: 29–38.

Ferraro, G. P. (2000). *Cultural anthropology: An applied perspective*. Belmont, CA: Wadsworth Publishing.

Ferreira, J. L., Pérez, L., De Moya, E. A., De La Rosa, J., Hernán, M., and Marsh, J. C. (1999). El debate sobre la educación de la sexualidad en las escuelas dominicanas. *Investigación para el Desarrollo* 5(3): 89–102.

Fishbein, D. (1985). Biofeedback applications to psychiatric disorders. *Psychological Record* 35(1): 3–21.

Fishbein, M. (1998). Changing behavior to prevent STDs/AIDS. *Int J Gynaecol Obstet* 63(1): S175–181.

Fleming, J. M. (1997). Prevalence of childhood sexual abuse in a community sample of Australian women. *Medical Journal of Australia* 166(2): 65–68.

Flores-Colombino, A. (1999). Advances on the causes of paraphilias. Paper presented at the 14th World Congress of Sexology. Revista Argentina de Sexualidad Humana. Hong Kong.

Fogel, G. I., and Mayers. W. A. (1991). *Perversions and near-perversions in clinical practice: New psychoanalytic perspective*. New Haven, CT: Yale University Press.

Ford, C. S., and Beach, F. (1951). *Patterns of sexual behavior*. New York: Harper & Row.

Fordham, A. S. (1993). An evaluation of sex offender treatment programmes. *Issues in Criminological and Legal Psychology* 19: 60–65.

Fordney, D. S. (1978). Dyspareunia and vaginismus. *Clinical Obstetrics and Gynecology* 21(1): 205–221.

Francis, S. H., and Corbin, J. D. (2003). Molecular mechanisms and pharmacokinetics of phosphodi-esterase-5 antagonists. *Curr Urol Rep* 4(6): 457–465.

Frank, M. W., Bauer, H. M., Arican, N., Fincanci, S. K., and Iacopino, V. (1999). Virginity examinations in Turkey: Role of forensic physicians in controlling female sexuality. *JAMA* 282(5): 485–490.

Frayser, S. (1999). Human sexuality. In Suggs, D., and Miracle, A. (eds.), *Culture, biology and sexuality* (pp. 1–16). Athens: University of Georgia.

Freedman, L. P., and Isaacs, S. L. (1993). Human rights and reproductive choice. *Studies in Family Planning* 24(1): 18–30.

Freud, S. (1974). Three essays on the theory of sexuality (1905). In Strachey, J. (ed.), *The Standard Edition of the Complete Psychological Works of Sigmund Freud* (Vol. 7) (pp. 123–243). London: Hogarth Press.

Gagnon, J. H. (1989). Sexuality across the life course in the United States. In Turner, C. F., Miller, H. G., and Moses, L. E. (eds.), *DS, sexual behavior and intravenous drug use* (pp. 73–258). Washington, DC: National Academy Press.

Garofalo, R., Wolf, R. C., Wissow, L. S., Woods, E. R., and Goodman, E. (1999). Sexual orientation and risk of suicide attempts among a representative sample of youth. *Archives of Pediatric and Adolescent Medicine* 153(5): 487–493.

Gartrell, N. (1986). Increased libido in women receiving trazodone. *Am J Psychiatry* 143: 781–782.

Geada, E. (1987). Sexualidade e creatividade—Cinema. In *Sexologia em Portugal* (II Vol.). Lisbon: Texto Editora.

Giuliano, F., Rampin, O., and Allard, J. (2002). Neurophysiology and pharmacology of female genital sexual response. *Journal of Sex and Marital Therapy* 28(1): 101–115. *Journal of Sex and Marital Therapy* 28(2):139–164.

Gleaves, D. H., Eberenz, K. P., and May, M. C. (1998). Scope and significance of posttraumatic symptomatology among women hospitalized for an eating disorder. *Int J Eat Disord* 24(2): 147–156.

Gold, E. R. (1986). Long-term effects of sexual victimization in childhood: An attributional approach. *Journal of Consulting and Clinical Psychology* 54: 471–475.

Gonçalves, J. (1987). Comunicação em Sexologia. In *Sexologia em Portugal* (I Vol.). Lisbon: Texto Editora.

Goodman, L. A., and Fallot. R. D. (1998). HIV risk-behaviors in poor urban women with serious mental disorders: Association with childhood physical and sexual abuse. *American Journal of Orthopsychiatry* 68: 73–83.

Goy, R. W., Bercovitch, F. B., and McBrair, M. C. (1988). Behavioral masculinization is independent of genital masculinization in prenatally androgenized female rhesus macaques. *Hormones and Behavior* 22: 552–571.

Graham, C., and Bancroft, J. H. (1997). A comparison of retrospective interview assessment versus daily ratings of sexual interest and activities in women. In Barncoft, J. H. (ed.), *Researching sexual behavior* (pp. 227–236). Bloomington: University of Indiana Press.

Green. R. (1987). *The "Sissy Boy Syndrome" and the development of homosexuality*. New Haven, CT:Yale University Press.

Green, R., and Fleming, D. T. (1990). Transsexual surgery follow-up: Status in the 1990s. *Annual Review of Sex Research* 1: 163–174.

Green, R., and Money, J. (1960). Incongruous gender role: Nongenital manifestations in prepubertal boys. *Journal of Nervous and Mental Diseases* 131: 160–168.

Gregersen, E. (1994). *The world of human sexuality*. New York: Irvington.

Gregoire, A., and Dhugra, D. (1996). Outcome studies of psychological interventions: Lessons from sex therapy research. *Sexual and Marital Therapy* 11(4): 407–418.

Grenier, G., and Byers, E. S. (1997). The relationship among ejaculatory control, ejaculatory latency, and attempts to prolong heterosexual intercourse. *Arch Sexual Behav* 26(1): 27–47.

Gresser, U., and Gleiter, C. H. (2002). Erectile dysfunction: Comparison of efficacy and side effects of the PDE-5 inhibitors sildenafil, vardenafil and tadalafil—Review of the literature. *Eur J Med Res* 7(10): 435–446.

Grossman, L. S., Martis, B., and Fichtner, C. G. (1999). Are sex offenders treatable? A research overview. *Psychiatric Services* 50(3): 349–361.

Guamaccia, P. J. (1996). Anthropological perspectives: The importance of culture in the assessment of quality of life. In Spilker, B. (ed.), *Quality of life and pharmacoeconomics in clinical trials* (2nd ed.). Philadelphia: Lippincott-Raven Publishers.

Habach, E. (1995). Empleo de la TV comercial en la educación sexual. In Parra, A., and Hernández-Serrano, R. (eds.), X Simposium Internacional de Educación Sexual. WAS. FNUAP. Caracas.

Hall, G. C. N. (1995). Sexual offender recidivism revisited: A meta-analysis of recent treatment studies. *Journal of Consulting and Clinical Psychology* 63(5): 802–809.

Hall, L. A., Sachs. B., Rayens, M. K., and Lutenbacher, M. (1993). Childhood physical and sexual abuse: Their relationship with depressive symptoms in adulthood. *Image Journal Nursing School* 25(4): 317–323.

Halvorsen, J., Mommsen, C., Metz, M. E., Moriarty, J., Hunter, D., and Lange, P. (1988). Male sexual impotence: A case study in evaluation and treatment. *The Journal of Family Practice* 27(6): 583–594.

Hamer, D. H., et al. (1993). A linkage between DNA markers on the X chromosome and male sexual orientation. *Science* 261: 321–327.

Heaberle, E. (1983). *The birth of sexology*. Washington DC: World Congress of Sexology.

Heiman, J. (2000). Orgasmic disorders in women. In Leiblum, S., and Rosen, R. (eds.), *Principles and practice of sex therapy* (3rd ed.). New York: Guilford.

Heiman, J. R., and Verhulst, J. (1990). Sexual dysfunction and marriage. In Fincham, F. D., and Bradbury, R. N. (eds.), *The psychology of marriage: Basic issues and applications* (pp. 299–322). New York: Guilford.

Herdt, G. (1997). *Sexual cultures and migration in the era of AIDS: Anthropological and demographic perspectives (International Studies in Demography)*. Oxford, UK: Clarendon Press.

Herdt, G. (1999). Sexing anthropology. In Suggs, D., and Maracle, A. (eds.), *Culture, biology and sexuality* (pp. 17–32). Athens: University of Georgia Press.

Hernandez, R., and Eher, R. (1998). *Violence and sexual health*. Proceedings of the World Congress of Sexology, Caracas.

Hernández-Serrano, R. (2000a). Advances in the treatment of sexual disorders. *Forum Psychiatry and Human Sexuality. Current Opinion in Psychiatry* 13: 271–273.

Hernández-Serrano, R. (2000b). Paraphilias: A phenomenological classification. In the Proceedings of the II Conference on Sexual Perversion. Instituto di Sessuologia Clinica. Rome.

Hernández-Serrano, R. (2000c). Parafilie: Una classificazione fenomenologica. In Simonelli, C., Petruccelli, F. e Vizzari, V. (a cura di), *Le perversioni sessuali. Aspetti clinici e giuridici del comportamento sessuale deviante* (pp. 70–77). Milano: Franco Angeli.

Hernández-Serrano, R. (2001). *Lo bueno del sexo*. Conferencia Magistral. X Congreso Colombiano de Sexología. Cartagena de Indias.

Hernández-Serrano, R. (2002). Avances en el tratamiento de los trastornos sexuales. *Acta Portuguesa de Sexología* IV(1).

Hernández-Serrano, R., and Bianco, F. (1994). Transexualism in Venezuela. Cleveland: ICTSO.

Hernández-Serrano, R., and Parra, A. (1980). III Symposium Internacional Sexualidad Masculina. UCV, SAS, CMEM. Caracas.

Hernández-Serrano, R., and Parra, A. (1981). IV Symposium Internacional de Sexualidad en el Impedido. UCV. SAS. CMEM. Caracas.

Hernández-Serrano, R., and Parra, A. (1982). V Symposium Internacional Ley, Sexualidad y Violencia. UCV, SAS, CMEM. Caracas.

Hernández-Serrano, R., and Parra, A. (1983). VI Symposium Internacional Cultura, Sexualidad y Antropologia. UCV, SAS. CMEM. Caracas.

Hernández-Serrano, R., and Parra, A. (1984). VII Symposium Internacional Sexualidad: Infidelidad. I Congreso Venezolano de Sexologia. Caracas.

Hernández-Serrano, R., and Parra, A. (1995). X Symposium Internacional: Educación Sexual. FNUAP, WAS, UCV, SVSM. Caracas.

Hernández-Serrano, R., and Parra, A. (1998). *Violence*. Proceedings, World Congress on Violence. ICPMS. IATSO, WPA, WAS. UCV. SVSM. Caracas.

Hernández-Serrano, R., and Parra, A. (2000). *Clasificación de las disfunciones sexuales*. I International Congress of Sexology. Rome.

Hernández-Serrano, R., Parra, A., and Castro, J. (1978). I Symposium Internacional de Sexualidad Femenina. UCV, SAS, CMEM. Caracas.

Hernández-Serrano, R., Parra, A., and Castro, R. (1979). II Symposium Internacional Sexualidad Infantil. UCV, SAS, CMEM. Caracas.

Hernández-Serrano, R., Parra, A., and De Vries, R. (1996). *Sexualidad y vida. Perspectivas hacia el siglo XXI*. Congreso Latinoamericano de Sexología. Montevideo, Uruguay.

Hernández-Serrano, R., Parra, A., and De Vries, R. (1999). *Educación sexual: Una estrategia para combatir la violencia*. IX Congreso Colombiano de Sexología. Bogota.

Hernández-Serrano, R., Parra, A., Flores, C. A., et al. (2005). *Sexología y trastornos sexuales. UTES historia clínica sexual*. In Alarcón, R., Mazzoti, G., and Nicolini, H. (eds.), *Psiquiatría* (2nd ed.). Buenos Aires: Editorial Panamericana.

Herrman, H., Saxena, S., and Moodie, R. (eds.). (2005). *Health promotion*. Geneva: World Health Organization.

Hidalgo, R. B., and Davidson, J. R. (2000). Posttraumatic stress disorder: Epidemiology and health-related considerations. *J Clin Psychiatry* 61(7): 5–13.

Hines, A. M., Snowden, L. R., and Graves, K. L. (1998). Acculturation, alcohol consumption and AIDS related risky sexual behavior among African American women. *Women Health* 27(3): 17–35.

Hitt, J. (2000): Better loving through chemistry. *The New York Times Magazine* (February 20).

Hoffman, J. A., Klein, H., Eber, M., and Crosby, H. (2000). Frequency and intensity of crack use as predictors of women's involvement in HIV-related sexual risk behaviors. *Drug Alcohol Depend* 58(3): 227–236.

Holzapfel, S. (1994). Aging and sexuality. *Canadian Family Physician* 40: 748–750, 753–754, 757–758.

Holzapfel, S. (1998). The physician's role in dealing with men's sexual health concerns. *Canadian Journal of Human Sexuality* 7(3): 273–286.

Hunter, J. A. (1991). A comparison of the psychosocial maladjustment of adult males and females sexually molested as children. *Journal of Interpersonal Violence* 6(2): 205–217.

Hurlbert, D. F., White, L. C., Power, R. D., and Apt, D. (1993). Orgasm consistency training in the treatment of women reporting hypoactive sexual desire: An outcome comparison of women-only groups and couples-only groups. *Journal of Behavior Therapy and Experimental Psychiatry* 24(10): 3–13.

Irvine, J. (1990). *Disorders of desire: Sex and gender in modern American sexology*. Philadelphia: Temple University Press.

Irvine, J. (1995). *Sexuality education across cultures: Working with differences*. Scarborough, Ontario: Jossey-Bass.

Jacobson, N. S., and Christensen, A. (1996). *Integrative couple therapy: Promoting acceptance and change*. New York: W. W. Norton.

James, J., and Meyerding, J. (1997). Early sexual experience and prostitution. *Am J Psychiatry* 134: 1381–1385.

Janca, A., Kastrup, M. C., Katschnig, H., Lopez-Ibor, J. J., Mezzich, J. E., and Sartorius, N. (1996a). ICD-10 Multi-axial system for use in adult psychiatry: Structure and applications. *Journal of Nervous and Mental Disease* 184: 191–192.

Janca, A., Kastrup, M. C., Katschnig, H., Lopez-Ibor, J. J., Mezzich, J. E., and Sartorius, N. (1996b). The WHO Short Disability Assessment Schedule: A tool for the assessment of difficulties in selected areas of functioning of patients with mental and physical disorders. *Social Psychiatry and Psychiatric Epidemiology* 31: 349–354.

Janca, A., Kastrup, M. C., Katschnig, H., Lopez-Ibor, J. J., Mezzich, J. E., and Sartorius, N. (1996c). Contextual aspects of mental and phsyical disorders: A proposal for Axis III of the ICD-10 multi-axial system. *Acta Psychiatrica Scandinavica* 94: 31–36.

Janca, A., Kastrup, M. C., Katschnig, H., Lopez-Ibor, J. J., Mezzich, J. E., and Sartorius, N. (1999). *Multi-axial presentation of ICD-10 for adults*. Cambridge, UK: Cambridge University Press.

Jarvis, T. J., and Copelman, J. (1997). Child sexual abuse as a predictor of psychiatric co-morbidity and its implications for drug and alcohol treatment. *Drug Alcohol Dependency* 49(1): 61–69.

Jeffreys, S. (1985). *The spinster and her enemies: Feminism and sexuality 1880–1930*. London: Pandora.

Jensen, J., Lendorf, A., Stimpel, H., Frost, J., Ibsen, H., and Rosenkilde, P. (1999). The prevalence and etiology of impotence in 101 male hypertensive outpatients. *American Journal of Hypertension* 12(3): 271–275.

Johannes, C. B., Araujo, A. B., Feldman, H. A., Derby, C. A., Kleinman, K. P., and McKinlay, J. B. (2000). Incidence of erectile dysfunction in men 40 to 69 years old: Longitudinal results from the Massachusetts male aging study. *Journal of Urology* 163: 460–463.

Jung, P., Hunt, M., and Balakrishna, R. (2001). *Good sex: Feminist perspectives from the world's religions*. New Brunswick, NJ: Rutgers University Press.

Kafka, M. P. (2000). The paraphilia-related disorders: Nonparaphilic hypersexuality and sexual compulsivity/addiction. In Leiblum, S. R., and Rosen, R. C. (eds.), *Principles and practice of sex therapy* (3rd ed). New York: Guilford.

Kaplan, H. I., and Sadock, B. J. (1994). *Kaplan and Sadock's synopsis of psychiatry: Behavioral sciences clinical psychiatry* (7th ed). Baltimore, MD: Lippincott Williams & Wilkins.

Kaplan, H. I., Sadock, B. J., and Grebb, J. A. (1994). *Synopsis of psychiatry* (7th ed). Baltimore: Williams & Wilkins.

Kaplan, H. S. (1974). *The new sex therapy*. New York: Brunner-Routledge Publishing.

Kaplan, H. S. (1983). *The disorders of sexual desire*. Simon & Schuster, Inc.

Kaplan, H. S. (1983). *The evaluation of sexual disorders: Psychological and medical aspects*. New York: Brunner-Routledge Publishing.

Kaplan, H. S. (1989). *How to overcome premature ejaculation*. New York: Brunner-Routledge Publishing.

Kaplan, H. S., et al. (1987). *Sexual aversion and sexual phobias and panic disorder*. New York: Brunner-Routledge Publishing.

Kaplan, S. A., et al. (1999): Safety and efficacy of Sildenafil in postmenopausal women with sexual dysfunction. *Urology* 50(3): 491.

Kastrup, M. (1993). Psychosocial domains in comprehensive diagnostic models. In Costa e Silva, J. A., and Nadelson, C. C. (eds.), *International review of psychiatry* (Vol. 1) (pp. 97–110). Washington, DC: American Psychiatric Press.

Kastrup, M., Skodol, A., Mezzich, J. E., and Berganza, C. E. (in preparation). *Standardized multiaxial diagnostic formulation. The international guidelines for diagnostic assessment*. Educational Program of the World Psychiatric Association.

Katschnig, H. (1997). How useful is the concept of quality of life in psychiatry? In Katschnig, H., Freeman, H., and Sartorius, N. (eds.), *Quality of life in mental disorders* (pp. 3–16). New York: Wiley & Sons.

Katschnig, H., and Angermeyer, M. C. (1997). Quality of life in depression. In Katschnig, H., Freeman, H., and Sartorius, N. (eds.), *Quality of life in mental disorders* (pp. 137–148). New York: Wiley & Sons.

Katz, J. (1995). *The invention of heterosexuality*. New York: Plume Books.

Katz, J. N., and Vidal, G. (1995). *The invention of heterosexuality*. Penguin Group (USA) Inc.

Kegel, A. H. (1948). Progressive resistance exercises in the functional restoration of the perineal muscles. *Am J Obstet Gynecol* 56: 238.

Kempton, W. (1975). *Sex education for persons with disabilities that hinder learning: A teacher's guide*. Boston: Duxbury Press.

Kennedy, G. J., Haque, M., and Zarankow, B. (1997). Human sexuality in late life. *International Journal of Mental Health* 26: 35–46.

Kingsberg, S., Althof, S., and Leiblum, S. (2002). Books helpful to patients with sexual and marital problems. *Journal of Sex and Marital Therapy* 28(3): 219.

Kivela, S. L., and Pahkala, K. (1988). Clinician rated symptoms and signs of depression in aged Finns. *Int J Soc Psychiatry* 34: 274–284.

Kivela, S. L., Pahkala, K., and Eronen, A. (1989). Depressive symptoms and signs that differentiate major and atypical depression from dysthmic disorder in elderly Finns. *Int J Ger Psychiatry* 4: 799–856.

Korenman, S. G., Morley, J. E., and Mooradian, A. D. (1990). Secondary hypogonadism in older men: Its relation to impotence. *Journal of Clinical Endocrinology and Metabolism*, 71: 963–969.

Kotloff, K. L., Tacket, C. O., Wasserman, S. S., et al. (1991). A voluntary serosurvey and behavioral risk assessment for human immunodeficiency virus infection among college students. *Sexually Transmitted Diseases* 18: 223–227.

Krane, R. J., Golstein, L., and Saenz de Tejaka, I. (1989). Impotence. *N Eng J Med* 321: 1648–1659.

Kuyken, W., and Orley, J. (1995). The World Health Organization quality of life assessment: Position paper from the World Health Organization. *Social Science Medicine* 7: 1403–1414.

Langevin, R. (1994). Genital exhibitionism and voyeurism: Theories and treatment. In Krivacska, J. J., and Money, J. (eds.), *The handbook of forensic sexology* (pp. 126–154). New York: Amherst Prometheus Books.

Laqueur, T. (1990). *Making sex: Body and gender from the Greeks to Freud.* Cambridge, MA: Harvard University Press.

Laumann, E. O., Gagnon, J. H., Michael, R. T., and Michaels. S. (1994). *The social organization of sexuality: Sexual practices in the United States.* Chicago: University of Chicago Press.

Laumann, E. O., Paik, A., and Rosen, R. C. (1999). Sexual dysfunction in the United States: Prevalence and predictors. *JAMA* 281(6): 537–544.

Laux, M., and Conrad, C. (1997). *Natural woman, natural menopause.* New York: HarperCollins Publishers.

Lavee, Y. (1991). Western and non-Western human sexuality. *Journal of Sex and Marital Therapy* 17: 203–213.

Lazarus, A., Miles, M., Niezen, P., Quintana, D., Berman, J., and Berman, L. (2001). The chicken or the egg? The role of testosterone in sexual function and stress. *Female Sexual Function Forum* (p. 69).

Lee, J. R. (1997). *Natural progesterone: The multiple roles of a remarkable hormone.* Sebasatopol, CA: BBL Publishing.

Lehmann, J. B., Lehmann, C. U., and Kelly, P. J. (1998). Development and health care needs of lesbians. *Journal of Women's Health* 7(3): 379–387.

Leiblum, S. (1998) Sex and the net: Clinical implications. *Journal of Sex Education and Therapy* 22: 21–28.

Leiblum, S. R., and Rosen, R. C. (eds.). (1989). *Principles and practice of sex therapy: Update for the 1990s* (2nd ed.). New York: Guilford.

Leiblum, S. R., and Rosen, R. C. (eds.). (2000). *Principles and practice of sex therapy* (3rd ed.). New York: Guilford.

Lief, H. I. (1982). *Handbook of sexual medicine.* Chicago: American Medical Association.

Lerer, M. L. (1999). *Sexualidad femenina y algunos de los aportes de la escuela argentina hasta.* Simposium Salud Sexual. Buenos Aires.

Lerer, M. L. (2000). *Crisis, stress, gender and intimacy.* SHEP. WPA.

Lerer, M. L. (2000). *Psychological approaches to the integrated sex therapy of sexual problems and their context.* SHEP. WPA.

Levine, S. B. (2000). Paraphilias. In Sadock, B. J., and Sadock, V. H. (eds.), *Kaplan and Sadock's comprehensive textbook of psychiatry* (7th ed.) (pp. 1631–1646). Baltimore, MD: Lippincott Williams & Wilkins.

Levitan, R. D., Parikh, S. V., Lesage, A. D., Hegadoren, K. M., Adams, M., Kennedy, S. H., and Goering, P. N. (1998). Major depression in individuals with a history of childhood physical and sexual abuse: Relationship to neurovegetative features, mania, and gender. *Am J Psychiatry* 155(12): 1746–1752.

Lieberman, R. P. (1980). *Handbook of marital therapy: A positive approach to helping troubled relationships.* New York: Plenum.

Lindal, E., and Stefansson, J. G. (1993). The lifetime prevalence of psychosocial dysfunction among 55 to 57 year olds in Iceland. *Soc Psychiatry Psychiatr Epidemiol* 28: 91–98.

Liu, D., Manlun, N., Liping, Z., and Haeberle, E. (1992). *Contemporary Chinese sexual culture: Report of the "Sex Civilization" survey on 20,000 subjects.* Shanghai, China: Sanilian Press.

Locke, H. J. and Wallace, K. M. (1959). Short marital-adjustment and prediction tests: Their reliability and validity. *Marriage and Family Living* 21: 251–255.

Lopiccolo, J., and Lopiccolo, L. (1978). *Handbook of sex therapy.* New York: Plenum.

Lorand, S., and Schneer, H. I. (1967). Sexual deviations. III. Fetishism, transvestitism, masochism, sadism, exhibitionism, voyeurism, incest, pedophilia, and bestiality. In Freedman, A. M., Kaplan, H. I. (eds.), *Comprehensive textbook of psychiatry* (pp. 977–988). Baltimore, MD: Lippincott Williams & Wilkins.

Loudon, J. B. (1998). Potential confusion between erectile dysfunction and premature ejaculation: An evaluation of men presenting with erectile difficulty at a sex therapy clinic. *Sexual and Marital Therapy* 13(4): 397–401.

Lowinson, J., Ruiz, P., Millman, R., Langrod, J. (1992). *Substance abuse: A comprehensive textbook* (2nd ed.). Baltimore, MD: Lippincott Williams & Wilkins.

Lund, C. A. (1992). Long-term treatment of sexual behavior problems in adolescent and adult developmentally disabled persons. *Annals of Sex Research* 5(1): 5–31.

Lustman, P. J., and Clouse, R. E. (1990). Relationship of psychiatric illness to impotence in men with diabetes. *Diabetes Care* 13: 893–895.

MacDonald, N. E., Wells, G. A., Fisher, W. A., et al. (1990). High risk sexual behavior among college students. *JAMA* 263: 3155–3159.

Machado, V. J. (1987). A formação em sexologia. In Gomes, F., Albuquerque, A., and Siveira Nunes, J., *Sexologia em Portugal* (II Vol.). Lisbon: Texto Editora.

Major, B., and Gramzow, R. H. (1999). Abortion as stigma: Cognitive and emotional implications of concealment. *Journal of Personality and Social Psychology* 77(4): 735–745.

Maletzky, B. M. (1998). The paraphilias: Research and treatment. In Nathan, P. E., and Gorman, J. M. (eds.), *A guide to treatments that work* (pp. 472–500). New York: Oxford University Press.

Mallett, E. C., and Badlani, G. H. (1987). Sexuality in the elderly. *Seminars in Urology* 5(2): 141–145.

Marshall, W. L., Jones, R., Ward, T., Johnson, P., et al. (1991). Treatment outcome with sex offenders. *Clinical Psychology Review* 11(4): 465–485.

Marshall, W. L., and Pithers, W. D. (1994). A reconsideration of treatment outcome with sex offenders. *Behavior Research and Therapy* 32(5): 559–564.

Martin, C. E. (1981). Factors affecting sexual functioning in 60–79 year old males. *Arch Sex Bev* 10: 399–420.

Mascia-Lees, F. E., and Black, N. J. (2000). *Gender and anthropology*. Prospect Heights, IL: Waveland Press.

Masters, W. H. (1970). *Human sexual inadequacy*. Boston: Little Brown & Co.

Masters, W. H., and Johnson, V. E. (1966). *Human sexual response*. Baltimore, MD: Lippincott Williams & Wilkins.

Masters, W. H., and Johnson, V. E. (1970; reissue 1981). *Human sexual inadequacy*. Little, Brown.

Masters, W. H., Johnson, V. E., and Kolodny, R. C. (1986). *Masters and Johnson on sex and human loving*. Boston: Little Brown & Co.

Masumori, N., Tsukamoto, T., Kumamoto, Y., Panser, L. A., Rhodes, T., Girman, C. J., Lieber, M. M., and Jacobsen, S. J. (1999). Decline of sexual function with age in Japanese men compared with American men—Results of two community-based studies. *Urology* 54(2): 335–344, 344–345.

McCabe, J. P., and Cobain, M. J. (1998). The impact of individual and relationship factors on sexual dysfunction among males and females. *Sexual and Marital Therapy* 13: 131–143.

McCarthy, B. W. (1982). Sexual dysfunctions and dissatisfactions among middle-years couples. *Journal of Sex Education and Therapy* 8: 9–12.

McCarthy, B. W. (1988). *Male sexual awareness: Increasing sexual satisfaction*. New York: Carrol & Graf.

McCarthy, B. W. (1997). Therapeutic and iatrogenic interventions with adults who were sexually abused as children. *Journal of Sex and Marital Therapy* 23: 118–125.

McCarthy, B. W. (2001). Relapse prevention strategies and techniques with erectile dysfunction. *Journal of Sex and Marital Therapy* 27: 1–8.

McConaghy, N. (1993). *Sexual behavior: Problems and management (Applied clinical psychology)*. New York: Plenum Press.

McConaghy, N. (1999a). Methodological issues concerning evaluation of treatment for sexual offenders: Randomization, treatment dropouts, untreated controls, and within-treatment studies. *Sexual Abuse: Journal of Research and Treatment* 11(3): 183–193.

McConaghy, N. (1999b). Unresolved issues on scientific sexology. *Arch Sexual Behav* 28(4): 285–318.

McCormick, N. B. (1994). *Sexual salvation: Affirming women's sexual rights and pleasures*. Westport, CT: Praeger.

McDermott, S., Martin, M., Weinrich. M., and Kelly, M., (1999). Program evaluation of a sex education curriculum for women with mental retardation. *Research in Developmental Disabilities* 20(2): 93–106.

McKinlay, J. B., and Feldman, H. A. (1994). Age related variation in sexual activity and interest in normal men: Results from the Massachusetts Male Aging Study. In Rossi, A. S. (ed.), *Sexuality across the life course* (pp. 261–285). Chicago: University of Chicago Press.

McKnight, J. T., Nagy, M. C., and Adcock, A. (1994). Adolescent sexual activity in Alabama. *Family Practice Research Development* 14(1): 59–65.

Meana, M., Binik, I., and Cohen, D. (1998). Affect and marital adjustment in women's ratings of dyspareunic pain. *Canad J Psychiatry* 43: 381–385.

Meston, C. M. (1997). Aging and sexuality. *Western Journal of Medicine* 167(4): 285–290.

Meston, C. M., and Gorzalka, B. B. (1995). The effects of sympathetic activation following acute exercise on physiological and subjective sexual arousal in women. *Behavior Research and Therapy* 33: 651–664.

Meston, C. M., and Heiman, J. R. (1998). Ephedrine and activated physiological sexual arousal in women. *Archives of General Psychiatry* 55: 652–656.

Metz, M. E., and Dwyer, S. M. (1993). Differences in conflict management styles between sex dysfunction, sex offender, and satisfied couples. *Journal of Sex and Marital Therapy* 19: 104–122.

Metz, M. E., and Epstein, N. (2002). The role of relationship conflict in sexual dysfunction. *Journal of Sex and Marital Therapy* 28: 139–164.

Metz, M. E., and McCarthy, B. W. (2004). *Coping with erectile dysfunction: How to regain confidence and enjoy great sex.* Oakland: New Harbinger Publications. (Translations in Italian, Korean, and Turkish languages.)

Metz, M. E., and Pryor, J. L. (2000). Premature ejaculation: A psychophysiological approach for assessment and management. *Journal of Sex and Marital Therapy* 26(4): 293–320.

Metz, M. E., Pryor, J. L., Abuzzahab, F., Nesvacil, L., and Koznar, J. (1997). Premature ejaculation: A psychophysiological review. *Journal of Sex and Marital Therapy* 23(1): 3–23.

Metz, M. E., and Sawyer, S.P. (2004). Treating sexual dysfunction in sex offenders: A case example. *Journal of Sex and Marital Therapy* 30: 185-197.

Metz, M., and Seifert, M. H. (1993). Differences in men's and women's sexual health needs and expectations of physicians. *The Canadian Journal of Human Sexuality* 2(2): 53–59.

Metz, M. E., and Weiss, K. E. (1992). A group therapy format for the simultaneous treatment of marital and sexual dysfunctions: A case illustration. *Journal of Sex and Marital Therapy* 18(3): 173–196.

Meyenburg, B. (1999). Gender identity disorder in adolescence: Outcomes of psychotherapy. *Adolescence* 34(134): 305–313.

Mezzich, J. E. (1979). Patterns and issues in multiaxial diagnosis. *Psychological Medicine* 9: 125–137.

Mezzich, J. E. (1991). Architecture of clinical information and prediction of service utilization and costs. *Schizophrenia Bulletin* 17: 469–474.

Mezzich, J. E., Berganza, C. E., von Cranach, M., Jorge, M. R., Kastrup, M. C., Murthy, R. S., Okasha, A., Pull, C., Sartorius, N., Skodol, A., and Zaudig, M. (2003). Essentials of the World Psychiatric Association's International Guidelines for Diagnostic Assessment (IGDA). *British Journal of Psychiatry* 182, Supplement 45: s37–s66.

Mezzich, J. E., Cohen, M. L., Ruipérez, M. A., et al. (2000). The Spanish version of the quality of life index: Presentation and validation. *Journal of Neurosis and Mental Disease* 188: 301–305.

Mezzich, J. E., Dow, J. T., and Coffman, G. A. (1981). Developing an efficient clinical information system for a comprehensive psychiatric institute. 1. Principles, design and organization. *Behavior Research Methods and Instrumentation* 7: 464–478.

Mezzich, J. E., and Hernández-Serrano, R. (1999). The International Survey on Human Sexuality. Presented at the 11th World Congress of Psychiatry. Hamburg, Germany. See also Appendix 5 of the present volume.

Mezzich, J. E., Kleinman, A., Fabrega, H., and Parron, D. L. (eds.). (1996). *Culture and psychiatric diagnosis: A DSM-IV Perspective.* Washington, DC: American Psychiatric Press.

Miner, M. H., and Dwyer, S. M. (1995). Analysis of dropouts from outpatient sex offender treatment. *Journal of Psychology and Human Sexuality* 7(3): 77–93.

Miner, M. H., Marques, J. K., Day, D. M., and Nelson, C. (1990). Impact of relapse prevention in treating sex offenders: Preliminary findings. *Annals of Sex Research* 3(1): 165–185.

Mira, J. J., Perez, M. J., Orozco, D., and Gea, J. (1992). Primary care nurses' awareness of the sexual problems of people with chronic diseases. *Sexual and Marital Therapy* 7(1): 19–28.

Money, J. (1985). *The destroying angel.* Buffalo, NY: Prometheus Books.

Money, J. (1986). *Lovemaps: Clinical concepts of sexual/erotic health and pathology, paraphilia, and gender transposition of childhood, adolescence and maturity.* New York: Irvington.

Money, J., Hanson, J. G., and Hampson, J. L. (1957). Imprinting and the establishment of gender role. *Archive of Neurology and Psychiatry* 77: 333–336.

Mosher, D. L. (1980). Three psychological dimensions of depth of involvement in human sexual response. *Journal of Sex Research* 16(1): 1–42.

Mulugeta, E., Kassaye, M., and Berhane, Y. (1998). Prevalence and outcomes of sexual violence among high school students. *Ethiopian Medical Journal* 36(3): 167–174.

Nanda, S. (2000). *Gender diversity: Crosscultural variations.* Prospect Heights, IL: Waveland.

Neal, G., Gittelman, M., Stephens, D., and Peterson, C. (2001). In-clinic evaluation of the safety of topical alprostadil for the treatment of female sexual arousal disorder. *Female Sexual Function Forum* (p. 83).

Nofzinger, E. A., Thase, M. E., Reynolds, C. F., Frank, E., Jennings, J. R., Garamoni, G. L., Fasiczka, A. L., and Kupfer, D. J. (1993). Sexual behavior in depressed men. Assessment by self-report, behavioral, and nocturnal penile tumescence measures before and after treatment with cognitive behavior therapy. *Arch Gen Psychiatry* 50: 24–30.

Normann, E. K., Tambs, K., and Magnus, P. (1992). Seksuelle overgrep mot barn—et folkehelseproblem. *Nordisk medicin* 107(12): 326–330.

Novinski, J. K., and LoPiccolo, J. (1979). Assessing sexual behaviors in couples. *Journal of Sex and Marital Therapy* 5: 225–243.

Numberg, H. G., Hensley, P. L, Lauriello, J., Parker, L. M., and Keith, S. J. (1999). Sildenafil for women patients with antidepressant-induced sexual dysfunction. *Psychiatric Services* 312: 1076-1078.

Nuñez, C. J. (2000). *Análisis histórico y actual de la sexología como disciplina científica.* SHEP. WPA.

Nuno, M. (1987). A sexualidade na adolescência e juventude. In Gomes, F., Albuquerque, A., and Siveira Nunes, J. (eds.), *Sexologia em Portugal* (I Vol.) Lisbon: Texto Editora.

Obler, M. (1973). Systematic desensitization in sexual disorders. *Journal of Behavior Therapy and Experimental Psychiatry* 4: 93–101.

O'Farrell, T. J., Choquette, K. A., Cutter, H. S., and Birchler, G. R. (1997). Sexual satisfaction and dysfunction in marriages of male alcoholics: Comparison with nonalcoholic maritally conflicted and nonconflicted couples. *Journal of Studies of Alcohol* 58(1): 91–99.

Osio, V. G. (1995). Enfermedades de transmissión sexual E.T.S. conductas preventivas en estudiantes del I.U.T.P.C. In Parra, A., and Hernández-Serrano, R. (eds.), X Simposium Internacional de Educación Sexual. WAS, FNUAP. Caracas.

Osoba, D. (1994). Lessons learned from measuring health-related quality of life in oncology. *Journal of Clinical Oncology* 72: 608–616.

Otero, A. (ed.) (1999). *Tercer glosario cubano de psiquiatría.* Havana, Cuba: Hospital Psiquiátrico de La Habana.

Pacheco Palha, A. (2000). *Conceptual basis of sexual help.* SHEP. WPA.

Padma-Nathan, H., et al. (2004). Pharamcotherapy for erectile dysfucntion. In *Sexual medicine.* Edited by Lue, T., et al. Plymouth, U.K.: Health Publications, pp 503-566.

Panser, L. A., Rhodes, T., Girman, C. J., Guess, H. A., Chute, C. G., Oesterling, J. E., Lieber, M. M., and Jacobsen, S. J. (1995). Sexual function of men ages 40 to 79 years: The Olmsted County study of urinary symptoms and health status among men. *Journal of the American Geriatric Society* 43: 1107–1111.

Paone, D., Chavkin, W., Willets, I., Friedman, P., and DesJarlais, D. (1992). The impact of sexual abuse: Implications for drug treatment. *Journal of Women's Health* 1: 149–153.

Parker, R. (1997). International perspectives in sexuality research. In Bancroft, J. (ed.), *Researching Sexual Behavior* (pp. 9–22). Bloomington: University of Indiana.

Parker, R. (1998). Sexuality, culture and the political economy: Developments in anthropological and cross-cultural research. *Annual Review of Sex Research* 9: 1–33.

Parra, C. A., DeVries, R., and Hernández-Serrano. R. (1995). *Interdependence.* XI Simposium Internacional Educación Sexual, Caracas.

Patterson, J., Nagel, J. E., and Adler, W. H. (1995). Basic and clinical considerations of HIV infection in the elderly. *Clinical Geriatrics* 3: 21.

Percy, C., van Holten, V., and Muir, C. (1990). *International classification of diseases for oncology.* World Health Organization.

Perelman, M.A. (2004). Retarded ejaculation. *Current sexual health reports,* Current Science, Inc.

Persson, G. (1980). Sexuality in a 70-year-old-urban population. *Journal of Psychosomatic Research* 24: 335–342.

Petersen, M. E., and Dickey, R. (1995). Surgical sex reassignment: A comparative survey of international centers. *Arch Sexual Behav* 24(2): 135–156.

Pfeiffer, E., Verwoerdt, A., and Davis, G. C. (1971). Sexual behavior in middle life. *Am J Psychiatry* 128: 1262–1267.

Pinto e Silva, J. L. (1998). Pregnancy during adolescence: Wanted vs. unwanted. *International Journal of Gynaecology and Obstetrics* 63(1): S151–156.

Piot, P., and O'Rourke, M. (2000). AIDS in the developing world: An interview with Peter Piot. *AIDS Clinical Care* 12: 1–5.

Pohl, R. (1983). Anorgasmia caused by MAOIs. *Am J Psychiatry* 140: 510.

Porst, H., Padma-Nathan, H., Giuliano, F., Anglin, G., Varanese, L., Rosen, R. (2003). Efficacy of tadalafil for the treatment of erectile dysfunction at 24 and 36 hours after dosing: A randomized controlled trail. *Urology* 62(1): 121–125.

Puri, J. (2002). Concerning kamasutras: Challenging narratives of history and sexuality signs. *Journal of Women in Culture and Society* 27(2): 603–639.

Raboch, J. (1984). The sexual development and life of female schizophrenic patients. *Arch Sexual Behav* 13: 341–349.

Raboch, J., and Faltus, F. (1991). Sexuality of women with anorexia nervosa. *Acta Psychiat Scand* 84: 9–11.

Raine, T. R., Jenkins, R., Aarons, S. J., Woodward, K., Fairfax, J. L., El-Khoratzaty, M. N., and Herman, A. (1999). Sociodemographic correlates of virginity in seventh-grade black and Latino students. *Journal of Adolescent Health* 24(5): 304–312.

Rako, S. (1996). *The hormone of desire: The truth about sexuality, menopause, and testosterone.* New York: Harmony Books.

Randeva, H. S., Davidson, R. M., and Bouloux, P. M. G. (1999). Endocrinology. In Carson, C. C., Kirby, R. S., and Goldstein, I. (eds.), *Textbook of erectile dysfunction.* (pp. 89–104). Oxford, UK: Oxford ISIS.

Raymond, N. C., Coleman, E., Ohlerking, F., Christenson, G. A., and Miner, M. H. (1999). Psychiatric comorbidity in pedophilic sex offenders. *Am J Psychiatry* 156(5): 786–788.

Read, S., King, M., and Watson. J. (1997). Sexual dysfunction in primary medical care: Prevalence, characteristics and detection by the general practitioner. *Journal of Public Health Medicine* 19(43): 387–391.

Redmond, G. P. (1999). Hormones and sexual function. *Int J Fertil Womens Med* 44:193–197.

Reeker, J., Ensing, D., and Elliott. R. (1997). A meta-analytic investigation of group treatment outcomes for sexually abused children. *Child Abuse and Neglect* 21(7): 669–680.

Regehr, C., and Marziali. E. (1999). Response to sexual assault: A relational perspective. *J Nerv Ment Dis* 187(10): 618–623.

Rehman, J., Lazer, S., Benet, A. E., Schaefer, L. C., and Melman, A. (1999). The reported sex and surgery satisfactions of 28 postoperative male-to-female transsexual patients. *Arch Sexual Behav* 28(1): 71–89.

Reiter, R. C. (1998). Evidence-based management of chronic pelvic pain. *Clin Obstet Gynecol* 41(2): 422–435.

Resnick, M. D., and Blum, R.W. (1994). The association of consensual sexual intercourse during childhood with adolescent health risk and behaviors. *Pediatrics* 94(6Pt1): 907–13.

Riley, A. J., and Riley, E. J. (1986). The effect of single dose diazepam on female sexual response induced by masturbation. *Journal of Sex and Marital Therapy* 1: 49–53.

Rohsenow, D., Corbett, R., and Devine, D. (1988). Molested as children: A hidden contribution to substance abuse? *Substance Abuse Treatment* 5: 13–18.

Rosen, R. C. (1996). Erectile dysfunction: The medicalization of male sexuality. *Clinical Psychology Review* 16(6): 497–519.

Rosen, R. C. (2000). Sexual pharmacology in the 21st century. *J Gend Specif Med* 3(5): 45–52.

Rosen, R. C., Brown, C., Heiman, J., Leiblum, S., Meston, C., Shabsigh, R., Ferguson, D., and D'Agostino, R. Jr. (2000). The Female Sexual Function Index (FSFI): A multidimensional self-report instrument for the assessment of female sexual function. *Journal of Sex and Marital Therapy* 26(2): 191–208.

Rosen, R. C., Lane, R. M., and Menza, M. (1999). Effects of SSRIs on sexual function: A critical review. *J Clin Psychiatry* 19: 67–85.

Rosen, R. C., and Leiblum, S. R. (1989). Assessment and treatment of desire disorders. In Leiblum, S. R., and Rosen, R. C. (eds), *Principles and practice of sex therapy: Update for the 1990s* (pp. 19–47). New York: Guilford.

Rosen, R. C., and Leiblum, S. R. (1995). Treatment of sexual disorders in the 1990s: An integrated approach. *Journal of Consulting and Clinical Psychology* 63(6): 877–890.

Rosen, R. C., and McKenna, K. E. (2002). PDE-5 inhibition and sexual response: Pharmacological mechanisms and clinical outcomes. *Annu Rev Sex Res* 13: 36–88.

Rosen, R. C., Riley, A., Wagner, G., Osterloh, I. H., Kirpatrick, J., and Mishra, A. (1997). The international index of erectile function (IIEF): A multidimensional scale for assessment of erectile dysfunction. *Urology* 49(6): 822–830.

Rousseau, P. C. (1986). Sexual changes and impotence in elderly men. *American Family Physician* 10: 131.

Rowland, D. L., and Slob, A. K. (1995). Understanding and diagnosing sexual dysfunction: Recent progress through psychophysiological and psychophysical methods. *Neuroscience and Biobehavioral Reviews* 19(2): 201–209.

Rubio-Stipeck, M., Hicks, M. H., and Tsuang, M. T. (2000). Cultural factors influencing the selection, use, and interpretation of psychiatric measures. In *American Psychiatric Association: Handbook of psychiatric measures* (pp. 33–41). Washington, DC: American Psychiatric Association.

Ruiz, M. A., and Baca, E. (1993). Design and validation of the "Quality of Life Questionnaire" (CCV): A generic health-related perceived quality of life instrument. *European Journal of Psychological Assessment* 9: 19–32.

Rust, J., and Golombok, S. (1986a). *The Golombok Rust inventory of sexual satisfaction*. Windsor, UK: NFER-Nelson.

Rust, J., and Golombok, S. (1986b). The GRISS: A psychometric instrument for the assessment of sexual dysfunction. *Arch Sexual Behav* 15: 153–165.

Rutter, M., Shaffer, D., and Shepherd, M. (1975). A multiaxial classification of child psychiatric disorders. World Health Organization.

Sadock, B. J., and Sadock, V. A. (2000). *Kaplan and Sadock's comprehensive textbook of psychiatry* (CD-ROM for Windows and Macintosh, Single Seat Multi-User) (7th ed.). Baltimore, MD: Lippincott Williams & Wilkins.

Sadock, V. A. (1995). Normal human sexuality and sexual dysfunctions. In Kaplan, H. I., and Sadock, B. J. (eds.), *Comprehensive textbook of psychiatry* (6th ed.) (pp.1295–1321). Baltimore, MD: Lippincott Williams & Wilkins.

Sadock, V. A. (2000). Normal human sexuality and sexual dysfunctions. In Sadock, B. J., and Sadock, V. A. (eds.), *Kaplan and Sadock's comprehensive textbook of psychiatry* (7th ed.) (Vol. 1) (pp. 1577–1608). Baltimore, MD: Lippincott Williams & Wilkins.

Saenz de Tejada, I., Anglin, G., Knight, J. R., and Emmick, J. T. (2002). Effects of tadalafil on erectile dysfunction in men with diabetes. *Diabetes Care* 25(12): 2159–2164.

Santos, B. O. F., Vieira, A. L. D., and Fischer, R. (1999). *Neurotomy: A new technique to treat premature ejaculation*. (Unpublished manuscript.)

Sarrell, P., Dobay, B., and Wiita, B. (1998). Estrogen and androgen replacement in postmenopausal women dissatisfied with estrogen only treatment. *J Reproduct Med* 43: 847–856.

Sarrel, P. M. (2001). Sex after sixty. *Female Sexual Function Forum* (p. 61).

Sbrocco, T., Weisberg, B., Barlow, D. H., and Carter, M. M. (1997). The conceptual relationship between panic disorder and male erectile dysfunction. *Journal of Sex and Marital Therapy* 23: 212–220.

Schapiro, B. (1943): Premature ejaculation: A review of 1130 cases. *Journal of Urology* 50: 374-379.

Schiavi, R. C. (1990). Sexuality and aging in men. *Amer J Psychiatry* 147: 766–771.

Schiavi, R. (2000). Psychiatrist role in the management of sexual disorders. Forum psychiatry and human sexuality. *Current Opinion in Psychiatry* 12: 267–269.

Schiavi, R. C., and Rehman, J. (1995). Sexuality and aging. *Urologic Clinics of North America* 22(4): 711–726.

Schiavi, R., and Segraves, R. (1995). The biology of sexual function. *Psychosomatic Clinics of North America* 18: 7–23.

Schmidt, Jr., C. W., Schiavi, R. C., Schover, L. R., Segraves, R. T., and Wise, T. N. (1996). Introduction to Section VI. Sexual Disorders. In Widiger, T. A., Frances, A. J., Pincus, H. A., Ross, R., First, M. B., and Davis, W. (eds.). *DSM-IV sourcebook*. Volume 2, pp. 1081-1089. Washington, DC: American Psychiatric Association.

Schnarch, D. (1997). *Passionate marriage: Love, sex, and intimacy in emotionally committed relationships*. New York: W. W. Norton & Company.

Schnarch, D. (2000). Desire problems: A systemic perspective. In Lieblum, S., and Rosen, R. C. (eds), *Principles and practice of sex therapy* (3rd ed.) (pp. 17–56). New York: Guilford.

Schneider, J. P. (1988). *Back from betrayal: Recovering from his affairs*. San Francisco: Harper & Row Publishers.

Schover, L. R., Novick, A. C., Steinmuller, D. R., and Goormastic, M. (1990). Sexuality, fertility, and renal transplantation: a study of survivors. *Journal of Sex and Marital Therapy* 16: 3–14.

Schover, L. R., Yetman, R. J., Tuason, L. J., Meisler, E., Esselstyn, C. B., Hermann, R. E., Grundfest-Broniatowski, S., and Dowden, R. V. (1995). Comparison of partial mastectomy with breast reconstruction on psychosocial adjustment, body image, and sexuality. *Cancer* 75: 54–64.

Secades, C. (2000). *La mujer y el SIDA*. SHEP. WPA.

Seglin, C. A. (2000). *Respuesta sexual humana*. Buenos Aires. SHEP. WPA.

Seglin, C. A. (2000). *Evolución psicosexual, infancia, pubertad y adolescencia*. SHEP. WPA.

Segraves, K. B., and Segraves, R. T. (1991a). Hypoactive sexual desire disorder: Prevalence and co-morbidity in 906 subjects. *Journal of Sex and Marital Therapy* 17: 1–9.

Segraves, K. B., and Segraves, R. T. (1991b). Multiple phase dysfunction. *Journal of Sex Education and Therapy* 17: 153–156.

Segraves, R. T. (1985). Female orgasm and psychiatric drugs. *Journal of Sex Education and Therapy* 11: 69–71.

Segraves, R. T. (1995). Psychopharmacological influences on human sexual behavior. In Oldham, J. M., and Riba, M. B. (eds.), *Review Psychiatry* 14: 697–717. Washington, DC: American Psychiatric Association.

Segraves, R. T. (1998). Antidepressant induced sexual dysfunction. *J Clin Psychiatry* 59: 48–54.

Segraves, R. T., and Balon, R. (2003). *Sexual pharmocology fast facts*. New York: Norton.

Segraves R. T., Clayton, A., Wolf, A., Warnock, J., and Croft. H. (at press). Bupropion sustained release in the treatment of female hypoactive sexual desire disorder. *Journal of Clinical Psychopharmacology*.

Segraves, R. T., and Segraves, K. B. (1991). Diagnosis of female arousal disorder. *Journal of Sex and Marital Therapy (UK)* 6: 9–13.

Segraves, R. T., and Segraves, K. B. (1995). Human sexuality and aging. *Journal of Sex Education and Therapy* 21(2): 88–92.

Segraves R. T., Kavoussi, R., Hughes, A., Batey, S. R., Johnston, A., Donahue, R., Ascher, J. (2000). Evaluation of sexual functioning in depressed outpatients: A double blind comparison of sustained release bupropion and sertraline treatment. *Journal of Clinical Psychopharmacology* 122-128.

Seidman, S. N., and Rieder, R. O. (1994). A review of sexual behavior in the United States. *Am J Psychiatry* 151(3): 330–341.

Seilhamer, R. A., and Jacob, T. (1990). Family factors and adjustment of children of alcoholics. In Windle, M., and Searles, J. S. (eds.), *Children of alcoholics: Critical perspectives* (pp. 168–186). New York: Guilford.

Semans, J. H. (1956). Premature ejaculation: A new approach. *South Medical Journal* 49: 353–358.

Shabsigh, R., Klein, L., Seidman, S., Kaplan, S. A., Lehrhoff, B. J., and Ritter, J. S. (1998). Increased incidence of depressive symptoms in men with erectile dysfunction. *Urology* 52: 848–852.

Shea, S. C. (1998). *Psychiatric interviewing: The art of understanding*. Philadelphia: Saunders.

Sherwin, B. B., and Gelfand, M. M. (1985). Differential symptom response to parenteral estrogen and/or androgen administration in the surgical menopause. *Am Journal of Obstetrics Gynecology* 151(2): 153–160.

SIECUS. (1995). *Guía para una educación sexual integral para la juventud hispano-latina. Kindergarten–12th grade*. X Simposium Internacional de Educación Sexual. WAS. FNUAP. Caracas.

Simon, P. A., Thometz, E., Bunch, J. G., Sorvillo, F., Detels, R., and Kerndt, P.R. (1999). Prevalence of unprotected sex among men with AIDS in Los Angeles County, California 1995–1997. *AIDS* 13(8): 987–990.

Sira, M. (2000). *Evaluación clínica del piso pélvico*. SHEP. WPA.

Skodol, A. E., Shaffer, D., and Gurland, B. (1997). Psychopathology across the life cycle. In Tasman, A., Kay, J., and Lieberman, J. A. (eds.), *Psychiatry* (Vol. 1) (pp. 449–476). Philadelphia: Saunders.

Skodol, A. E., and Bender, D. S. (2000). Diagnostic interviews for adults. In *American Psychiatric Association handbook of psychiatric measures* (pp. 45–49). Washington, DC: American Psychiatric Association.

Smith, L. B., Adler, N. E., and Tschann, J. M. (1999). Underreporting sensitive behaviors: The case of young women's willingness to report abortion. *Health Psychology* 18(1): 37–43.

Snaith, P., Tarsh, M. J., and Reid, R. W. (1993). Sex reassignment surgery: A study of 141 Dutch transsexuals. *British Journal of Psychiatry* 162: 681–685.

Snyder, D. K. (1997). *Marital satisfaction inventory, revised: Manual.* Los Angeles: Western Psychological Services.

Spanier, G. B. (1976). Measuring dyadic adjustment: New scales for assessing the quality of marriage and similar dyads. *Journal of Marriage and the Family* 38: 15–28.

Spilker, B. (ed.). (1990). *Quality of life assessments in clinical trials.* New York: Raven.

Stanton, B., Romer, D., Ricardo, I., Black, M., Feigelman, S., and Galbraith, J. (1993). Early initiation of sex and its lack of association with risk behavior among adolescent African-Americans. *Pediatrics* 92(1): 13–19.

Starr, B. D., and Weiner, M. B. (1981). *The Starr-Weiner report on sex and sexuality in the mature years.* New York: McGraw-Hill.

Steiger, A., Holsboer, Z. F., and Benkert, O. (1993). Studies of NPT and sleep EEG in patients with major depression and in normal controls. *Acta Psychiat Scand* 87: 358–363.

Stiffman, A.R .(1989). Physical and sexual abuse in runaway youths. *Child Abuse and Neglect* 13: 417–426.

Stoller, R. J. (1964). The hermaphroditic identity of hermaphrodites. *Journal of Nervous and Mental Diseases* 139: 453–457.

Stoller, R. J. (1985). *Presentations of gender.* New Haven, CT: Yale University Press.

Stravynski, A., Gaudette, G., Lesage, A., Arbel, H., Petit, Clerc, Fabian, Lamontagne, Langlois, Lipp, and Sidoun. (1997). The treatment of sexually dysfunctional men without partners: A controlled study of three behavioral group approaches. *British Journal of Psychiatry* 170(4):338–344.

Stroberg, P., Murphy, A., and Costigan, T. (2003). Switching patients with erectile dysfunction from sildenafil citrate to tadalafil: Results of a European multicenter, open-label study of patient preference. *Clin Ther* 25(11): 2724–2737.

Talmadge, L. D., and Wallace, S. C. (1991). Reclaiming sexuality in female incest survivors. *Journal of Sex and Marital Therapy* 17: 163–182.

Thase, M., Reynolds, C. III, Glanz, L., et al. (1987). Nocturnal penile tumescence in depressed men. *Am J Psychiatry* 184: 89–92.

Thase, M. E., Reynolds, C. F., Glanz, L. M., Jennings, J. R., Sewitch, D. E., Kupfer, D. J., and Frank, E. (1987). Nocturnal penile tumescence in depressed men. *Am J Psychiatry* 144: 89–92.

Thase, M. E., Reynolds, C. F., Jennings, J. R., Berman, S. R., Houch, P. R., Howell, J. R., Frank, E., and Kupfer, D. J. (1988). Diagnostic performance of nocturnal penile tumescence studies in health, dysfunctional (impotent) and depressed men. *Psychiatry Research* 26: 79–87.

Thase, M. E., Reynolds, C. F., Jennings, J. R., Frank, E., Howell, J. R., Houck, P. R., and Kupfer, D. J. (1988). Nocturnal penile tumescence is diminished in depressed men. *Biol Psychiatry* 24: 33–46.

Thompson, N. J., Potter, J. S., Sanderson, C. A., and Maibach, E. W. (1997). The relationship of sexual abuse and HIV risk behaviors among heterosexual adult female STI patients. *Child Abuse and Neglect* 21: 149–156.

Tiefer, L. (1995). *Sex is not a natural act and other essays (Psychology, gender, and theory).* Westview Press.

Tiefer, L. (2002). The emerging global discourse of sexual rights. *Journal of Sex and Marital Therapy* 28(5):439.

Tiefer, L., Hall, M., and Tavris, C. (2002). Beyond dysfunction: A new view of women's sexual problems. *Journal of Sex and Marital Therapy* 28(1): 225.

Tolman, D., and Diamond, L. (2001). Desegregating sexuality research: Cultural and biological perspectives on gender and desire. *Annual Review of Sex Research* 12: 33–74.

Toro Fernandez, T. (1995). Las telenovelas venezolanas y la sexualidad de los adolescentes del 7° grado de la unidad educativa "Delta Amacuro." In Parra, A., and Hernández-Serrano, R. (eds.), X Simposium Internacional de Educación Sexual. WAS. FNUAP. Caracas.

Travis, C., White, J. (2000). *Sexuality, society, and feminism.* Washington, DC: American Psychological Association.

Trudel, G. (2002). Sexuality and marital life: Results of a survey. *Journal of Sex and Marital Therapy* 28(3): 229–249.

Tullii, R. E., Guillaux, C. H., Vaccari, R., and Ferreira, R. (1994). Premature ejaculation selective neuroanatomy: A new therapeutic technique. Basis, indication and results. *International Journal of Impotence Research* 6, Suppl. 1P, 109-104-103.

United Nations (1994a). Female Circumcision. DOC HRI\GEN\1\REV.1 AT 79.

United Nations (1994b). Avoidance of the discrimination against Women in National Strategies for the Prevention and Control of Acquired Immunodeficiency Syndrome (AIDS) (6). DOC.HRI/GEN/1/RE.1 AT 81.

United Nations Development Program. (1999). *Human development report*. New York: Oxford University Press.

United Nations Population Program. (1997). *POP-647 press-release: Denial of reproductive rights kills or harms millions of women.*

Vachete, P. (1932). L'homosexualité. In *Connaissance de la vie sexuelle*. Paris: Edition de Vivre.

Valle Salazar, C. (1995). Planificación estratégica de la educación sexual en la educación superior. In Parra, A., and Hernández-Serrano, R. (eds.), X Simposium Internacional de Educación Sexual. WAS. FNUAP. Caracas.

Valois, R. F., Kammermann, S. K., and Wanzer Drane, J. (1997). Number of sexual intercourse partners and associated risk behaviors among public high school adolescents. *Journal of Sex Education and Therapy* 22(2): 5–13.

Vance, C. (1991). Anthropology rediscovers sexuality: A theoretical comment. *Social Science and Medicine* 33(8): 875–874.

Van De Velde, T. H. (1930). *The ideal marriage: Its physiology and techniques*. New York: Random House.

Vansteenwegen, A. (1996). Who benefits from couple therapy? A comparison of successful and failed couples. *Journal of Sex and Marital Therapy* 22(1): 63–67.

Verdier, V. M. (2000). *Pleasant sexuality. The challenge of the family planning*. SHEP. WPA.

Ventura Filipe, E. M., and Newman, S. P. (1998). Influence of HIV positive status on sexual behavior among males. *Rev Saude Publica* 32(6): 503–513.

Verma, K. K., Khaitan, B. K., and Singh, O. P. (1998). The frequency of sexual dysfunctions in patients attending a sex therapy clinic in North India. *Arch Sexual Behav* 27(3): 309–314.

Virag, R. (1992). Intracavernous injection of papaverine for erectile failure. *Lancet* 11: 938.

Vliet, L. W., and Meyer, J. K. (1982). Erectile dysfunction: Progress in evaluation and treatment. *Johns Hopkins Medical Journal* 151(5): 246–258.

Vroege, J. A., Gijs, L., and Hengeveld, M. W. (1998). Classification of sexual dysfunctions: Towards DSM-V and ICD-11. *Compr Psychiatry* 39(6): 333–337.

Waldhauser, M., and Schramek, R. (1988). Efficiency and side effects of prostaglandin E1 in the treatment of erectile dysfunction. *Journal of Urology* 140: 525.

Walker, E., Katon, W., Hansom, J., et al. (1992). Medical and psychiatric symptoms in women with childhood sexual abuse. *Psychosomatic Medicine* 54: 658–664.

Ware, J. E., Snow, K. K., Kosinski, M., and Gandek, B. (1993). *SF-36 health survey: Manual and interpretation guide*. New England Medical Center, MA.

Warren, C. W., Santelli, J. S., Everett, S. A., Collins, J. L., Cassell, C., Morris, L., and Kolbe, L. J. (1998). Sexual behavior among U.S. high school students, 1990–1995. *Family Planning Perspectives* 30(4): 170–172, 200.

Watson, J. P., and Davies, T. (1997). Psychosexual problems. *British Medical Journal* 315: 239–242.

Weiss, J. N., and Mellinger, B. C. (1990). Sexual dysfunction in elderly men. *Clinics in Geriatric Medicine* 6(1): 185–196.

Wellings, K., Macdowall, W., Catchpole, M., and Goodrich, J. (1999). Seasonal variations in sexual activity and their implications for sexual health promotion. *Journal of Research in Social Medicine* 92(2): 60–64.

Whelehan, P. (2000). *Cross-cultural sexual practices: Encyclopedia of gender*. Academic Press.

Whipple, B., and Komisaruk, B. R. (1998). Beyond the G Spot: Recent research on female sexuality. *Medical Aspects of Human Sexuality* 1: 19–23.

Willke, R. J., Glick, H. A., McCarron, T. J., Erder, M. H., Althof, S. E., and Linet, O. I. (1997). Quality of life effects of alprostadil therapy for erectile dysfunction. *Journal of Urology* 157: 2124–2128.

Wise, M. and J. Watson. 2002. A new treatment for premature ejaculation: Case series for a desensitizing band. *Sexual and Relationship Therapy* 15(4): 345–50.

Wolfenberger, W. (1972). *The principle of normalization in human services*. Toronto: National Insitute of Mental Retardation.

Wood, K., Maforah, F., and Jewkes, R. (1998). "He forced me to love him": Putting violence on adolescent sexual health agendas. *Social Science and Medicine* 47(2): 233–242.

World Association for Sexology. (1989). *Book I*. Bianco, F., and Hernández-Serrano, R. Caracas.

World Association for Sexology. (1993). *Book II*. Bianco, F., and Hernández-Serrano, R. Caracas.

World Association for Sexology. (1997). Proceedings of the XII World Congress of Sexology, Valencia.

World Association for Sexology (1999). Proceedings of the XIV World Congress of Sexology, Hong Kong.

World Health Organization. (1948). *The constitution of the World Health Organization*.

World Health Organization. (1948). *Manual of the international statistical classification of diseases, injuries and causes of death* (6th rev.). Geneva: World Health Organization.

World Health Organization. (1967). *Manual of the international statistical classification of diseases, injuries and causes of death*. Based on the recommendations of the Eighth Revision Conference, 1965, and adopted by the Nineteenth World Health Assembly.

World Health Organization. (1974). *Glossary of mental health disorders and guide to their classification*. For use in conjunction with the International Classification of Diseases (8th rev.). Geneva: World Health Organization.

World Health Organization. (1975). *Education and treatment in human sexuality: The training of health professionals*. Geneva: World Health Organization.

World Health Organization. (1977). *International classification of diseases: Manual of the international statistical classification of diseases, injuries and causes of death* (9th rev.). Geneva: World Health Organization.

World Health Organization. (1978). *Mental disorders: Glossary and guide to their classification in accordance with the ninth revision of the international classification of diseases*. Geneva: World Health Organization.

World Health Organization. (1978). *International classification of diseases*. Based on the 9th revision of 1975. (Spanish presentation.)

World Health Organization. (1992a). *Guidelines for the use of androgens in men*. Session 111: Pharmacological Effects of Androgens on Non-reproductive Organs. Geneva: World Health Organization.

World Health Organization. (1992b). *The ICD-10 classification of mental and behavioral disorders: Clinical descriptions and diagnostic guidelines*. Geneva: World Health Organization.

World Health Organization. (1993). *The ICD-10 classification of mental and behavioral disorders: Diagnostic criteria for research*. Geneva: World Health Organization.

World Health Organization. (1996). *Multiaxial classification of child and adolescent psychiatric disorders*. Geneva: World Health Organization.

World Health Organization. (1997). *Multiaxial presentation of the ICD-10 for use in adult psychiatry*. Cambridge, UK: Cambridge University Press.

World Health Organizatidin. (1997). *International classification of impairments, activities and participation: A manual of dimensions of disablement and functioning*.

World Health Organization. (1999). *Report of the Executive Board Meeting*.

WHO (2002). *World Health Organization's statement on sexual health*. Geneva: World Health Organization.

World Health Organization. (In press). *International classification of functioning, disability, and health (ICF)*. Geneva: World Health Organization.

World Psychiatric Association. (2001). *Essentials of the international guidelines for diagnostic assessment*. Technical report.

Worthman, C. (1999). Faster, farther, higher: Biology and discourses on human sexuality. In Suggs, D., and Miracle, A. (eds.). *Culture, biology and sexuality* (pp. 64–75). Athens: University of Georgia Press.

Wylie, K. R. (1993). Treatment outcome of brief couple therapy in psychogenic male erectile disorders. *Arch Sexual Behav* 26(5): 527–545.

Yanase, M. (1977). A possible involvement of adrenaline in facilitation of lordosis behavior in the ovariec-tomized rat. *Endocrinology Japan* 24: 507–512.

Young, T. K., and Katz, A. (1998). Survivors of sexual abuse: Clinical, lifestyle and reproductive conse-quences. *Canadian Medical Association Journal* 159(6): 329–334.

Zierler, S., Feingold, L., Laufer, D., et al. (1991). Adult survivors of childhood sexual abuse and subse-quent risk of HIV infection. *American Journal of Public Health* 81: 572–575.

Zilbergeld, B. (1992). *The new male sexuality.* New York: Bantam.

Zucker, K. J., and Bradley, S. J. (1995). *Gender identity disorder and psychosexual problems in children and ado-lescents.* New York: Guilford.

Zucker, K. J., and Green, R. (1996). Gender identity disorders. In Lewis, M. (ed.), *Child and adolescent psy-chiatry: A comprehensive textbook* (2nd ed.) (pp. 611–622). Baltimore, MD: Lippincott Williams & Wilkins.

Zucker, K. J., et al. (1998). Gender identity disorders of childhood: Diagnostic issues. In Widiger, T. A., et al. (eds.), *DSM-IV sourcebook* (Vol. 4) (pp. 503–512). Washington, DC: American Psychiatric Association.

Index

abortion, 20, 43
adjunctive therapies, 128, 143
adolescents, 15–17, 42
adrenergic agonists, 114
adults: older, 17–19, *152*, 174–75; sexual development, 17–18
affective disorders, 78, *99*
Africa, AIDS/HIV pandemic, 15, 39
agencies, international, 21–22
aging, 18–19, *152*, 174–75
AIDS/HIV pandemic, 6, 15, 19–20, 173; official documents, 22–23; psychiatric conditions and, 39–40
alcohol, 38, 138
alpha-adrenergic antagonists, 116
alpha-blockers, 113, 117–18
Althof, S., 28
American Association for Sex Education and Therapy (AASECT), 99
anatomy and physiology, 107, 132
androgen dihydroepiandrosterone (DHEA), 13
androgens, 120
anorexia nervosa, 38, 78
anthropology, 10
antidepressant medications, 113–14
anxiety, performance and, 9, 107, 127, 130
anxiety disorders, 36–37, 78
aphrodisiacs, 4
apomorphine, 118, *119*
Aristotle, 4–5
arousal, types/styles of, 133–34
arousal disorders, 32, 57, 140–42, *156*, 164
arterial and vascular reconstruction surgery, 125
attitudes, values and insights, 177
audiovisual materials, 135
autonomy, 4, 24, 31
Avoidance of Discrimination against Women in National Strategies for the Prevention and Control of Acquired Immunodeficiency Syndrome (AIDS) (UN document), 22–23

Baltimore Longitudinal Study of Aging, 174
Bancroft, J., 9, 14
Barlow, D. H., 9
behavioral therapy, 128, 129, 130. *See also* cognitive-behavioral therapy
Beijing Declaration and Platform for Action (UN document), 23
beneficence, 12–13
benzodiazepines, 114
bibliotherapy, 107
Bieber, I., 83
Bill of Rights for Retarded Individuals (UN document), 172
biological factors, *101*
biological procedures for diagnosis, *53*
biological treatment, *150–62*; devices for men, 123–24; devices for women, 123; gender identity disorder, 168; general perspective, 111–12; surgical interventions, 124–25. *See also* pharmacological treatment
biopsychosocial approach, 13, 95, 105, 111, 149; diagnosis and, 48–49, 51. *See also* integrative approaches
birth control, 5, 6, 11–12, 13, 16–17
Bolin, A., 10
bulimia, 38
bupriopion, 113–14
buspirone, 114

children: effect on couple's sexuality, 9, 174; poverty and, 43; primary and secondary school education, 30; sexual abuse of, 40–41, *151*; sexual development, 14–15; trauma, 15–16, 99, 163
Chinese Classification (CCMD-3), *58*

223